Listening to Okudzhava

Twenty-Three Aural Comprehension Exercises in Russian

Listening to Okudzhava

Twenty-Three Aural Comprehension Exercises in Russian

Vladimir Tumanov
University of Western Ontario

Focus Publishing
R. Pullins & Company
Newburyport MA 01950

ISBN *Listening to Okudzhava with Audio CD* 0-941051-53-6
Listening to Okudzhava with Cassette Tape 0-941051-99-4

This book is published by Focus Publishing, R. Pullins & Company, Inc., PO Box 369, Newburyport MA 01950.

10 9 8 7 6 5 4 3 2

Table of Contents

Introduction

This book is intended to supplement the traditional classroom experience by improving the student's aural comprehension skills. It is meant to make the student concentrate on decoding *natural native speech*: not merely the gist of a given discourse, but its every element. The ultimate aim is to attune the ear to spoken language, to create a certain habit of understanding and to give the student the ability to compensate for the imperfections and imprecisions of articulation in real linguistic interaction. Furthermore, the student's vocabulary and grammatical range are supposed to increase as he or she is exposed to a variety of new words and expressions. This material is reinforced through guided translation exercises.

The linguistic material in this workbook consists entirely of songs by Bulat Okudzhava: one of Russia's most revered bards. His music and poetry have been chosen for a number of reasons. Okudzhava's lyrics are not very complicated, and in his recordings he articulates so well that it is almost as if he had foreign students in mind. The subject matter of the songs is varied and interesting. The songs reflect many issues of importance in Russian and Soviet society. The artistic component of the poetry is very impressive and stimulating. Finally, by learning these songs, the students will become acquainted with an important part of Russian culture: virtually everyone knows Okudzhava in Russia and in many parts of the former U.S.S.R.

Musical and poetic material has been chosen for this workbook because it offers three mnemonic aids that facilitate comprehension and the learning process: melody, rhythm and rhyme. All three constitute networks of parallelisms where various elements evoke other elements, which makes it possible to decode discourse material by association. The student may not grasp all the sounds in a given word initially, but when this word rhymes with its counterpart, it is reassessed and can be grasped on the basis of these additional cues. Such material can then be more easily remembered because it is part of a melody with a clear rhythmic structure. Together these elements constitute an associative chain which will hopefully "cling" to the student the way songs and poetry tend to "cling" to people for many years.

Song Texts and In-Class Exercises

Each song chapter consists of three parts: song text, commentary and translation exercises. The song text is divided into three sections: Version A, Version B and the complete text of the song with questions. Version A consists of the song with most of the words missing. The missing words are presented as blanks with a dash for every missing letter. All students are encouraged to use Version A during classroom exercises, but it is intended primarily for advanced learners. Version B follows the same layout as Version A, but most of the missing words are presented as partial blanks, i.e., with some of the letters given. Students using Version A may find themselves unable to decode a particular word. They can then turn to Version B, locate this word and try decoding it on the basis of the letters provided. Some students may feel more comfortable working with Version B only. In this manner both advanced and intermediate students can benefit from the exercises.

In Versions A and B each missing or incomplete word is identified grammatically in parentheses. Most of these grammatical markers are abbreviated: n.=noun; acc.=accusative; gen.=genitive; dat.=dative; instr.=instrumental; prep.=prepositional; adj.=adjective; pron.=pronoun; conj.=conjunction; adv.=adverb; v.=verb; inf.=infinitive; imperat.=imperative, pred.=predicate.

The songs are arranged in the order of difficulty, which means that for maximum benefit, this sequence ought to be observed. However, because all songs are cross-referenced in the commentaries, it is possible not to follow the song order.

Here is a possible format that can be followed or used as a partial model in the classroom.

1. Students are asked in the beginning of the semester not to examine the material in this book on their own before a given song has been covered in class: the song comprehension exercises are intended only as classwork, and **no mark is given** for in-class song transcription performance.
2. Students are asked to bring a good Russian-English dictionary to class for each song exercise.
3. Students begin each song by listening to it once without opening their books or writing anything down.
4. Students are asked to open the first page of Version A, or some students may wish to go straight to Version B. The instructor plays the song in short segments (maybe line by line), stopping each time for a short while and giving the class a chance to fill in the blanks. The blanks should be filled in with pencils for easy revision. Students use their dictionaries and ask for a given segment to be replayed as they search for the correct transcription. **N.B.** If a certain segment is going to come up again in the song, the class need not dwell on its first occurrence, i.e., students should do their best to decode it, but too much time should not be taken up by something that will be repeated.
5. After the song has been completed in the manner described above, it is once again played in short segments. Now students take turns reconstructing the Russian original and translating it into English *out loud.* The instructor tries to give away as little as possible, i.e., encourages the use of dictionaries at every stage and guides students with hints.
6. Once the song has been reconstructed and translated, students are asked to turn to the page with the complete text of the song. They follow the text as the song is played again. There is a two-volume edition of Okudzhava's songs (*Bulat Okudzhava: 65 songs.* Ed. Vladimir Frumkin. Ann Arbor: Ardis, 1980 and *Bulat Okudzhava: Songs Volume II.* Ed. Vladimir Frumkin. Ann Arbor: Ardis, 1986). Whenever the text of the recordings used as a basis for this book differs from the Frumkin edition, this is indicated in the footnotes.
7. The instructor asks the questions provided after the text. In the best scenario students will have prepared the answers to these questions before class. This means that the questions should be left for another day.
8. The song can be assigned to be memorized and performed (as a poem or as a song) by one or two students for subsequent classes.

9. Time permitting, the instructor asks students to paraphrase the song with their books closed.

Translation exercises

Exercises intended to reinforce the text are assigned to be handed in (for marks). It is *essential* to base the translations on the commentaries and songs: all material related to the songs and commentaries is in boldface type. Thus, if "look at" is to be translated, and "глядеть на" appears in a given song or commentary to that song, "смотреть на" should not be used. The marks given for these assignments should reflect this requirement. Students should pay special attention to material in parentheses, since it consists of hints, suggestions and fillers for English constructions with no Russian equivalents. Much of this material is **not for literal translation.** Students should take all footnotes into account. Most of them are used as cross-references that indicate in which song and commentary a given concept can be found.

N.B. Because constructions with "if," "when," "before," and "after" appear very frequently in the sentences to be translated, students should keep in mind that in English these conjunctions are followed by the present tense even if reference is being made to the future, e.g., "If you come, I will show you my computer." In Russian the **future** tense is required in such a situation, hence the previous example should be translated as "Если ты придёшь [not 'идёшь'], я покажу тебе свой компьютер."

Commentaries

The commentaries are meant to be concise and do not aspire to completeness, which is why students should have access to standard grammar sources for additional information. The material in each set of commentaries follows the sequence of a given song text, but sometimes this sequence is not observed if it is important to juxtapose certain concepts that are related. Each entry is introduced by the symbol •. If a related issue (but one that does not appear in the song) is raised within a given entry, it is introduced by the symbol ••.

Most verbs are given as aspect pairs with the **imperfective in first place**. The same sequence is followed in the verb conjugation provided. Most verb conjugations consist of three forms: first and second person singular and third person plural. The other forms can be reconstructed on the basis of rules learned in elementary Russian classes. If the difference between the perfective and the imperfective form of a given verb is only a prefix, the perfective conjugation is not given.

Many concepts appearing in more than one song are explained only once and then cross-referenced for all other occurrences. It is extremely important that each cross-reference be followed through, since most translations cannot be done properly otherwise.

Testing

It is suggested that after every *five* songs the instructor administer tests. These tests can consist of two parts: aural comprehension and translation. Excerpts from songs covered so far are prerecorded on a separate tape. This tape is played to the class, and the students have to transcribe what they hear and then translate it in writing. The second part consists of Russian-English and English-Russian translations based on materials covered by the songs.

Acknowledgements

I would like to express my gratitude to Dr. Alexander Tumanov, Dr. Gregory Eramian, and Dr. Larissa Klein-Tumanov for their revisions and suggestions. I am very grateful to Vladimir Frumkin, Vitaly Reyf and especially to Bulat Okudzhava Senior and Bulat Okudzhava Junior for all their assistance. I would also like to thank Ronald Pullins for his expert editing work. The students who acted as "guinea pigs" during my work on this book at the University of Western Ontario deserve to be thanked as well, especially Chris Dixon, Louise White, Anna Morin and Asta Pocius. The same goes for my students at Indiana University: Alexander Diener, Kathleen Wilde, Renne Traicova, Amy McGoldrick, Jennifer Cash and Antoaneta Velikina.

1 A (Blanks)

_ _ _(v.) _ _ _ _ _ _ _ _ _ _ _(n.) по _ _ _ _ _(n.: dat.),
_ _ _ _ _ _ _(n.) _ _ _(v.) _ _ _ _ _ _ _(adv.).
И все _ _ _ _ _ _ _(n.) в _ _ _ _ _ _ _ _ _ _ _(n.: prep.)
_ _ _ _(n.: gen. plur.) не _ _ _ _ _ _ _(v.) с неё.

_ _ _ _ _ _ _ _ _ _(n.) _ _ _ _ _ _ _ _ _ _(v.) _ _ _ _(adv.),
_ _ _ _ _ _ _(n.: acc.) он _ _ _ _ _ _ _(v.).
Но все _ _ _ _ _ _ _(n.) в _ _ _ _ _ _ _ _ _ _ _(n.: prep.)
_ _ _ _ _(adv.) _ _ _ _ _ _ _ _ _(v.) ей _ _ _ _ _(adv.).

И _ _ _ _ _ _(particle) _ _ _ _ _ _ _ _(n.)
_ _ _ _ _ _ _ _ _ _ _ _(n.:gen.) —
Он _ _ _ _ _ _ _(n.: instr.) не _ _ _ _ _ _(v.).
_ _ _ _(conj.) _ _ _ _ _ _(short-form adj.)
_ _ _ _(particle) бы _ _ _-_ _ _ _ _ _(pron.)
всё _ _ _ _ _(n.) _ _ _ _ _ _ _ _ _(v.: inf.) _ _ _ _ _ _(adv.).

1 B (Partial Blanks)

_ё_(v.) т_ _ _ _ _ _ _ _ _(n.) по у_ _ _ _(n.: dat.),
же_ _ _ _ _(n.) ш_ _(v.)[1] вп_ _ _ _ _(adv.).
И все му_ _ _ _ _(n.) в тр_ _ _ _ _ _ _ _ _(n.: prep.)
г_ _ _(n.: gen. plur.) не св_ _ _ _ _(v.) с неё.

тро_ _ _ _ _ _ _(n.) пром_ _ _ _ _(v.) м_ _ _(adv.),
жен_ _ _ _(n.: acc.) он обог_ _ _(v.).
Но все муж_ _ _ _(n.) в трол_ _ _ _ _ _ _(n.: prep.)
д_ _ _ _(adv.) с_ _ _ _ _ _ _(v.) ей вс_ _ _(adv.).

И т_ _ _ _ _(particle) вод_ _ _ _ _(n.)
тролл_ _ _ _ _ _(n.: gen.) —
Он го_ _ _ _ _(n.: instr.) не ве_ _ _ _(v.).
В_ _ _(conj.) д_ _ _ _ _(short-form adj.)
х_ _ _(particle) бы _ _ _-_ _ _ _ _ _(pron.)
всё в_ _ _ _(n.) см_ _ _ _ _ _(v.: inf.) вп_ _ _ _(adv.).

[1]Feminine form of the verb in the previous line.

Song 1. Шёл троллейбус по улице

Шёл троллейбус по улице,
женщина шла впереди.
И все мужчины в троллейбусе
глаз не сводили с неё.

Троллейбус промчался мимо,
женщину он обогнал.
Но все мужчины в троллейбусе
долго смотрели ей вслед.

И только водитель троллейбуса —
он головой не вертел.
Ведь должен хотя бы кто–нибудь
всё время смотреть вперёд.

Вопросы по тексту (ответы полными предложениями):
1) Где находились мужчины? 2) Кто привлёк их внимание? 3) Где была женщина, и что она делала? 4) Что говорит о том, что мужчины проявили очень живой интерес к женщине? 5) Почему женщина скоро исчезла из поля зрения мужчин? 6) Кто не мог последовать примеру этих мужчин? 7) Почему? 8) Можно ли истолковать последнее предложение в переносном смысле?

Комментарии к тексту песни
•идти́ || пойти́ (to go/walk [**uni**directional])
иду́, –ёшь, –у́т || пойду́, –ёшь, –у́т (шёл/шла)
••ходи́ть (to go [**multi**directional]) хожу́, хо́дишь, хо́дят
N.B. Verbs derived from "идти" and "ходи́ть" are used **a**) if it is important to stress that motion on foot is involved or **b**) if it is not important to specify how the motion is taking place. They are not used if **c**) it is important to stress that the movement involves some kind of transportation or **d**) if distances greater than the area of a city are involved (unless it is specified that long-distance walking is taking place). For **c** & **d** use verbs derived from "е́хать" and "е́здить."
Она пошла на работу. (She went to work [how is not important].)
N.B. Verbs derived from "идти" and " ходи́ть" can be applied to regularly scheduled means of (usually public) transit, e.g., trolleys.
These verbs can be used with "война, фронт, поход" regardless of the distances involved, e.g., Мы ушли на войну (We went to war).
••вот + verb of motion ||(here comes / goes)
N.B. When motion and reference to this motion are simultaneous, "идти́" or another verb of motion can mean either "to come" or "to go," e.g., Вот идёт папа (Here comes / goes dad [depending on the context]).
•verb of motion + по + dat. (to go [along some kind of surface])
Автобус шёл по проспекту. (A bus was going down the prospekt / avenue.)
Я гулял по полю. (I was strolling around the field [this is multidirectional move-

ment <u>within</u> a given area and not around its periphery].)

•впереди́ + gen. ([up] ahead, at the front, in front [indicates **location**])
Впереди ста́да шёл пастух. (A shepherd walked in front of the herd.)

•вперёд (ahead, forward, to the front [indicates **movement**])
Иди вперёд и не оглядывайся. (Walk ahead and don't look back.)

•мужчина (man [human male, as opposed to the sexless "человек"→ "person"])
N.B. This is a second declension masculine noun, i.e., declined like "мама."

•не своди́ть глаз с + gen. (not to take one's eyes off something)
сво<u>жу́</u>, св<u>о́</u>дишь, сво́дят

•мча́ться || промча́ться (to dash / race / tear) мчусь, –и́шься, –а́тся

•verb of motion + мимо + gen. (to move <u>by</u> / <u>past</u> something)
Самолёт пролетел мимо горы. (The plane flew past the mountain.)

•обгоня́ть || об<u>ог</u>на́ть (to pass [i.e., to overtake])
обгоня́ю, –ешь, –ют || обгоню́, обг<u>о́</u>нишь, обго́нят

•долго + imperf. (for a long time)
N.B. This applies to **a)** future actions, **b)** past actions not extending to the present moment and **c)** actions occuring at no particular point in time, e.g., intermittent or regular actions.
Он долго жил в Париже. (He lived in Paris for a long time.)
Он долго будет жить в Париже. (He will live in Paris for a long time.)
Каждый вечер он долго читает. (Every evening he reads for long time.)
••давно + present tense (have been doing something <u>for a long time</u>)[1]
N.B. This refers to action that began in the past and extends into the present.
Я давно здесь стою. (I have been standing here for a long time [now].)
N.B. As this example illustrates, in Russian the **present tense** is used to translate the English "have been doing / have done" construction that refers to an action extending from the past into the present.
••давно + past tense (a long time ago, long ago)

•смотреть + dat. + вслед (to follow with one's eyes [a person moving away])
Мужчины смотрели ей вслед.
(The men followed her with their eyes [as she was moving away].)
N.B. In the song this phrase implies that the woman turned the corner as the trolley overtook her, since her back must be turned to the observer for "смотреть вслед" to work.

•смотре́ть || посмотре́ть + на + acc. (to look at [directing one's gaze at])
смотрю́, см<u>о́</u>тришь, смо́трят
Мы посмотрели на собаку. (We looked at the dog.)
••смотре́ть || посмотре́ть + acc. ([examining visually] to <u>look at</u> / <u>watch</u>)
Мы смотрим фотографии/кино.
(We are <u>looking at pictures</u> / <u>watching a film</u> [detailed observation].)

•верте́ть || заверте́ть + instr./acc. ([transitive] to turn / spin / twirl)
вер<u>чу́</u>, в<u>е́</u>ртишь, ве́ртят

•ведь ("after all" or simply an untranslatable intensifier used before a statement intended to bolster a previous proposition)
Пусть он спит: ведь он устал. (Let him sleep: [after all] he is tired.)

•должен/должна + inf. (must, should, is supposed to, have to)
Ты должна [будешь/была] уйти. (You have [<u>will have</u> / <u>had</u>] to leave.)

•хоть/хотя́ + бы (at least [with "хоть" the particle "бы" may be dropped])

---

[1]Cf. "depuis" in French and "seit" in German.

•[кто/где/как/что/какой]–нибудь (some-[one/where/how/thing/kind of])

N.B. This refers to an **abstract** entity whose existence is unknown to the speaker, e.g., Если вы куда–нибудь сегодня пойдёте, не забудьте зонтик (If you go somewhere today, don't forget your umbrella). The "somewhere" is a hypothetical place: the trip may not even take place.

••[кто/где/как/что/какой]–то (some-[one/where/how/thing/kind of])

N.B. This refers to a **concrete** existing entity which is not being identified,e.g., Она с кем–то где–то гуляет (She is strolling with someone somewhere). The "someone" is a real but unidentified person whose existence is a fact, and the location of this walk is also real.

Переведите на русский язык, пользуясь песней и комментариями

1. I (can) see **someone going**[1] **through** our park and **twirling** an umbrella. Is it a **man** or a **woman**? I (can't) see this **person's head**. Oh, it's a **man**. Now he is **passing** a young **woman**. He isn't even **looking at** her. He is impolite. **After all**, he **should at least** greet her. Now it's too late: he is already **ahead of** her. But the **woman** has noticed him: she is **following him with her eyes**. And he continues **to walk** (on) **ahead**. And now he is running **down** our **street**. He is not just running: he is **tearing by** the school and toward the **trolleybus** stop. But this is an old stop, and the **trolleybus has not been going**[2] **through** our **street for a long time**. He **will have to** wait here **for a long time**! Ha-ha! Well, if he leaves,[3] I will see him leaving because **I am not taking my eyes off him**. I have lots of **time**,[4] and this is such fun! But here **comes** a streetcar. Probably now **someone** will get off[5] the streetcar. No, the **driver** doesn't stop. I have been living here **for a long time**, and I often **go** to work at this **time** of day, but I have never seen such amazing events on our **street**. Maybe **somewhere someone** has seen **something** similar, but not I. Wait a minute! In fact **a long time ago someone** (did) tell me **something** similar, but I don't remember[6] what it was. It was in **some kind of** a train station. But that's another story.

---

[1] **SEE** "слы́шать/ви́деть + как + verb" in "Я пишу исторический роман."

[2] Unidirectional or multidirectional motion?

[3] **SEE** "Песенка о Моцарте" and Introduction (under Translation Exercises: if, when, before and after).

[4] **SEE** "Молитва (Франсуа Вийона)."

[5] To get off (a bus, streetcar, train etc.) = сходи́ть||сойти́ с + gen.

[6] **SEE** "Дежурный по апрелю."

2 A (Blanks)

_ _ _ _ _ _ _ _(n.) _ _ _ _ _ _ _(v.):

_ _ _ _ _(n.: dimin.) _ _ _ _ _ _ _(v.).

Её _ _ _ _ _ _ _ _(v.), а _ _ _ _ _(n.: dimin.) _ _ _ _ _(v.).

_ _ _ _ _ _ _ _(n.) _ _ _ _ _ _ _(v.): _ _ _ _ _ _ _(n.: gen.) всё нет.

Её _ _ _ _ _ _ _ _(v.), а _ _ _ _ _(n.: dimin.) _ _ _ _ _(v.).

_ _ _ _ _ _ _ _(n.) _ _ _ _ _ _ _(v.): _ _ _(n.) _ _ _ _(v.)

к _ _ _ _ _ _(substantivized adj.: dat.).

Её _ _ _ _ _ _ _ _(v.), а _ _ _ _ _(n.: dimin.) _ _ _ _ _(v.)

_ _ _ _ _ _ _(v.) _ _ _ _ _ _ _ _(n.): _ _ _ _(adv.) _ _ _ _ _ _ _(v.).

А _ _ _ _ _(n.: dimin.) _ _ _ _ _ _ _ _ _ _(v.), а он _ _ _ _ _ _ _ _(adj.).

2 B (Partial Blanks)

Д_ _ _ч_ _(n.) _ _ _ _ _ _(v.):

_ _ _ _ _(n.: dimin.) ул_ _ _ _(v.).

Её у_ _ _ _ _ _(v.), а _ _ _ _ _(n.: dimin.) _ _ _ _ _(v.).[1]

Д_ _ _ш_ _(n.) п_ _ _ _ _(v.): же_ _ _ _(n.: gen.) всё нет.

Её ут_ _ _ _ _(v.), а ш_ _ _ _(n.: dimin.) л_ _ _ _(v.).

Жен_ _ _ _(n.) пл_ _ _ _(v.): м_ _(n.) у_ _ _(v.)

к др_ _ _ _(substantivized adj.: dat.).

Её уте_ _ _ _(v.), а ша_ _ _(n.: dimin.) ле_ _ _(v.).

Пла_ _ _(v.) ста_ _ _ _(n.): м_ _ _(adv.) по_ _ _ _(v.).

А шар_ _(n.: dimin.) ве_ _ _ _ _ _(v.), а он го_ _ _ _ _(adj.).

---

[1]Imperfective form of the verb in the second line.

Song 2. Песенка о голубом шарике

Девочка плачет: шарик улетел.
Её утешают, а шарик летит.

Девушка плачет: жениха всё нет.
Её утешают, а шарик летит.

Женщина плачет: муж ушёл к другой.
Её утешают, а шарик летит.

Плачет старуха:[1] мало пожила.
А шарик вернулся, а он голубой.

Вопросы по тексту (ответы полными предложениями):
1) Что делает девочка? 2) Почему она плачет? 3) Кто ее утешает? 4) А где в это время шарик? 5) Девочка выросла. Кто теперь плачет? 6) Почему плачет девушка? 7) Теперь она не девушка. Кто теперь плачет? 8) Почему плачет женщина? 9) Женщина состарилась. Кто теперь плачет? 10) Почему плачет старуха? 11) Что значит "а он голубой"? 12) Как вы понимаете эту песню, и какое она у вас вызывает настроение?

Комментарии к тексту песни
•девочка (girl [up to approximately 15-16 years of age])
•девушка (girl, young girl, young lady [approximately 16-30 years of age])
•женщина (woman, lady)
    N.B. Although "да́ма" does mean "lady," it is a rather formal term.
•старуха/старушка (old woman, old lady ["старуха": unflattering term])
•пла́кать || запла́кать (to cry [за-: to start crying; по–: to have a cry, to cry for a while]) пла́чу, –ешь, –ут
•лете́ть || улете́ть (to fly → **uni**directional [у-: "to fly away"])
    лечу́, лети́шь, летя́т
    Я лечу́ домой. (I am flying home [no mention of a return trip].)
    ••лета́ть (to fly [**multi**directional]) лета́ю, –ешь, –ют
    Я часто лета́ю в Москву. (I often fly to Moscow [and return every time].)
•утеша́ть || уте́шить (to console)
    утеша́ю, –ешь, –ют || уте́шу, –ишь, –ат
    N.B. "Её утешают" is literally "they are consoling her," which is an indefinite personal construction with an implicit "они." Such constructions are best translated into English by the **passive** voice: "She is being consoled."

[1] "Старушка" in the Frumkin edition.

•а (and, whereas, in the meantime)
N.B. Both "а" and "и" mean "and," but "а" joins two unlike elements and can also be translated as "whereas," e.g., Она работает, а он отлынивает. (She is working, and / whereas he is slacking off). The conjunction "и," on the other hand, joins two similar elements, e.g., Я гуляю, и ты гуляешь.
•всё (still [often followed by "ещё" for emphasis], everything)
Миша всё [ещё] играет? (Is Misha still playing?)
•gen. + нет (something is absent / not there)
N.B. This construction is used when the absent person/thing can be reasonably expected to be there, e.g., a person in his/her own house.
Их нет / не было / не будет на работе.
(They aren't / weren't / won't be at work.)
•уходи́ть || уйти́ (to leave [**SEE** "Песенка о Моцарте"])
•друга́я/о́й (other [when not modifying a noun: another one, another person, something else, someone else])
•уйти + от + gen. + к + dat. (to leave someone for someone else)
Он ушёл от неё к другой.
(He left her for someone else [another woman].)
N.B. SEE "к + dat." and "у + gen." in "Старый пиджак."
•мало + gen./verb (little, few, not much, not enough)
У него мало денег, так как он мало зарабатывает.
(He doesn't have much money, since he earns little.)
••много + gen./verb (much, many, a lot, a great deal [**SEE** "сколько" in "Ещё раз о дураках"])
•жить || пожи́ть (to live [по–: "to live for a while" or a general perfective form; вы́-: to survive]) живу́, –ёшь, –у́т
N.B. "Прожить + time unit [acc.]" means to live for a certain amount of time.
Мы прожили в Каире две недели. (We lived in Cairo for two weeks.)
Они не выжили во время эпидемии. (They didn't survive the epidemic.)
Мы поживём в Риме пока не надоест, и переедем в Брест.
(We'll live in Rome until we get sick of it, and then we'll move to Brest.)
•возвраща́ть[ся] || верну́ть[ся] (to return [with –ся: intransitive])
возвраща́ю[сь], –ешь[ся], –ют[ся] || верну́[сь], –ёшь[ся], –у́т[ся]
Когда ты вернёшься [назад], ты вернёшь мне очки.
(When you return, you will bring back/return my glasses ["назад": optional].)
••возвраща́ться || верну́ться + к + dat. (to return / come back to someone [cf. "уйти от + gen. + к + dat." above])

Переведите на русский язык, пользуясь песней и комментариями

1. "Why are you **crying,** (little) **girl**?" "I am not a (little) **girl**: I am a **young lady** already."

2. The **woman** who[1] makes **balloons still lives** in this **blue** house, but today **she is not** (at) home.

3. The **old lady** said to her **husband**: "I am **leaving** now. Don't forget about your little granddaughter in the other room. If the **girl** (starts) **crying**, I hope that you will **console** her."

---

[1]**SEE** "тот + кто/который" in "Я вновь повстречался с надеждой."

4. One day[1] a **woman** that I know told me the following: "Although I **have lived** with my **husband** for a long time (now),[2] tomorrow I will **leave** him for **someone else**." But I answered: "I think that you will **live** with the **other** (one) (for a while) **and**[3] then you will **come back to your husband**." I was wrong: she is **still living** with the **other** (man).

5. The lovesick youth often **visited** a **young girl**, who **lived** nearby, **whereas** she never **came to see him**.[4]

6. Katia **cried** all day yesterday because her **fiancé** is **flying**[5] to Paris today. Soon he **will fly away**. He often **flies** there, and Katia's parents have to **console** her every time.

7. He has read **little**, and he buys **few** books, **whereas** she reads **a lot and** spends **a great deal of** money on books.

8. Yesterday, when the (little) **girl** (began to) **cry**, her mother **consoled** her.[6] But today, when her mother **was not** home, she **had a** (good) **cry and** then ceased to **cry** (by) herself.[7]

---

[1]**SEE** "Ещё раз о дураках."

[2]**SEE** "Шёл троллейбус по улице."

[3]Living with one man and going back to one's husband are two **unlike** elements.

[4]To visit / come to see someone: **SEE** "к + dat." in "Старый пиджак."

[5]The firm intention to do something soon is often indicated by the present tense.

[6]She succeeded in consoling her. Verbal aspect?

[7]**SEE** "Чёрный кот."

3 A (Blanks)

_ _ _ _ _ _ _(substantivized adj.) _ _ _ _ _(n.: gen.)
на Смоленской _ _ _ _ _(v.)
_ _ _ _ _ _ _(substantivized adj.) _ _ _ _ _(n.: gen.)
у Никитских не _ _ _ _(v.).
_ _ _ _ _ _ _(substantivized adj.) _ _ _ _ _(n.: gen.)
по Петровке _ _ _ _(v.) _ _ _ _ _ _ _ _ _ _(adv.)...
_ _ _ _ _ _ _(substantivized adj.: dat.) _ _ _ _ _ _ _ _ _ _ _(v.) _ _ _ _ _(n.).

О _ _ _ _ _ _ _(adj.) _ _ _ _ _ _(adj.) _ _ _ _ _(n.),
где не _ _ _ _ _ _ _(adj. short form) _ _ _ _ _(n.) и _ _ _ _ _(n.),
где все — _ _ _ _ _ _ _(substantivized adj.):
_ _ _ _(conj.) _ _ _ _ _ _ _ _ _(n.: gen.) нет у _ _ _ _ _(n.: gen.)!

_ _ _ _ _(particle) _ _ _ _ _(n.) никогда ваш не _ _ _ _ _ _ _ _ _(v.).
_ _ _ _ _ _ _(v.) только эти _ _ _ _ _ _(n.)!..
_ _ _ _ _ _(adv.) _ _ _ _(n.) и _ _ _ _ _(n.)
к _ _ _ _ _ _(proper n.: dat.) _ _ _ _ _ _ _ _ _ _ _(v.) _ _ _ _ _(n.).

_ _ _ _ _ _ _(substantivized adj.) _ _ _ _ _(n.: gen.)
на Волхонке _ _ _ _ _(v.).
_ _ _ _ _ _ _(substantivized adj.) _ _ _ _ _(n.: gen.)
на Неглинной не _ _ _ _(v.).
_ _ _ _ _ _ _(substantivized adj.) _ _ _ _ _(n.: gen.)
по Арбату _ _ _ _(v.) _ _ _ _ _ _ _ _ _ _(adv.)...
_ _ _ _ _ _ _(substantivized adj.: dat.) _ _ _ _ _ _ _ _ _ _ _(v.)_ _ _ _ _ (n.).

3 B (Partial Blanks)

_ _ _ _ _ _ _(substantivized adj.) _ _ _ _ _(n.: gen.)
на Смоленской _ _ _ _ _(v.).

_ _ _ _ _ _ _(substantivized adj.) _ _ _ _ _(n.: gen.)
у Никитских не с_ _ _(v.).
_ _ _ _ _ _ _(substantivized adj.) _ _ _ _ _(n.: gen.)
по Петровке и_ _ _(v.) неи_ _ _ _ _ _(adv.)...
_ _ _ _ _ _ _(substantivized adj.: dat.) по_ _ _ _ _ _ _ _(v.) с_ _ _ _(n.).

О вел_ _ _ _(adj.) веч_ _ _(adj.) ар_ _ _(n.),
где не вл_ _т_ _(adj. short form) с_ _ _ _(n.) и ру_ _ _(n.),
где все — ря_ _ _ _ _(substantivized adj.):
в_ _ _(conj.) мар_ _ _ _ _(n.: gen.) нет у _ _ _ _ _(n.: gen.)!

П_ _ _ _(particle) по_ _ _(n.) никогда ваш не ко_ _ _ _ _ _(v.).
приз_ _ _(v.) только эти вой_ _ _(n.)!..
Сквозь з_ _ _(n.) и вь_ _ _(n.)
к М_ _ _ _ _(proper n.: dat.) подс_ _ _ _ _ _(v.) ве_ _ _(n.).

_ _ _ _ _ _ _(substantivized adj.) л_ _ _ _(n.: gen.)
на Волхонке ст_ _ _(v.),
Ч_ _ _ _ _ _(substantivized adj.) лю_ _ _(n.: gen.)
на Неглинной не сп_ _(v.).
Ча_ _ _ _ _(substantivized adj.) люб_ _(n.: gen.)
по Арбату ид_ _ (v.) неизм_ _ _ _(adv.)...
Час_ _ _ _(substantivized adj.: dat.) пола_ _ _ _ _ _(v.) см_ _ _(n.).

Song 3. Часовые любви

Часовые любви на Смоленской стоят.
Часовые любви у Никитских не спят.
Часовые любви по Петровке идут неизменно...
Часовым полагается смена.

О великая вечная армия,
где не властны слова и рубли,
где все — рядовые:
ведь маршалов нет у любви!

Пусть поход никогда ваш не кончится.
Признаю только эти войска!..
Сквозь зимы и вьюги к Москве подступает весна.

Часовые любви на Волхонке стоят.
Часовые любви на Неглинной не спят.
Часовые любви по Арбату идут неизменно...
Часовым полагается смена...

Вопросы по тексту (ответы полными предложениями):
1) Кто стоит на Смоленской площади и в других точках Москвы? 2) Что и почему полагается часовым любви? 3) Чем их армия отличается от обыкновенной армии? 4) Как поэт относится к армии любви? 5) С каким временем года связан “поход” этих “войск”? 6) Почему поэт использует армейскую и военную тематику для развёрнутой метафоры, на которой основана эта песня?

Комментарии к тексту песни
•часовой (sentry, sentinel)
•рядовой (private, soldier [in the rank of private])
•Смоленская (a square in Moscow [the word “площадь” is implied])
•Никитские (a passage in Moscow called “Никитские ворота”)
•Петровка, Волхонка, Неглинная, Арбат (Moscow street names)
•стоя́ть || постоя́ть (to stand) → стою́, стои́шь, стоя́т
N.B. Do not confuse with “сто́ить” (to cost [сто́ю, сто́ишь, сто́ят])
•спать || уснуть (to sleep, [усну́ть: to fall asleep; поспа́ть: to sleep for a while])
сплю, спишь, спят || усну́, –ёшь, –у́т
•идти́ || пойти́ (to go/come/walk [**SEE** “Шёл троллейбус по улице”])
•неизме́нно (without fail, always [неизме́нный/ая: unchanging])
•dat. + полага́ться (to be entitled to something)
Мне полагается/полагался отпуск. (I am/was entitled to a vacation.)
•смена (shift; relief person / team)
Им полагалась смена. (They were entitled to be relieved.)

Я работаю во вторую смену. (I work in the second shift.)

•не властен/на + inf. (powerless to do something)

Я не [был] властен изменить судьбу.

(I am [was] powerless to change fate.)

••не властен/властна + над + instr. (powerless over)

Политика не властна над любовью. (Politics is powerless over love.)

•у + possessor [gen.] + нет + gen. (someone doesn't have something)

у + possessor [gen.] + есть + nomin. (someone has something [**SEE** "Молитва (Франсуа Вийона)"])

•пусть + present tense / future perf. (may / let something happen)

Пусть Миша по/играет на улице. (Let Misha play outside.)

Пусть их любовь никогда не кончится. (May their love never end.)

•похóд (hiking trip [поход с палаткой / на байдарке], military campaign, war, military expedition)

••пойти в поход на + acc. (to go to war against...)

••быть в походе (to be on a hike / at a war / in a military expedition)

•ни[interrog. word] + не (no one, nothing, never, in no way/manner, nowhere [**SEE** "Примета"])

•кончáть[ся] || [о]кóнчить[ся] (to end/finish/run out [-ся→ third pers.: intrans.])

кончáю, –ешь, –ет[ся], –ют[ся] || [о]кóнчу, –ишь, –ит[ся], –ат[ся]

Я [о]кончил смену. Смена кончилась. (о-: optional)

(I finished my shift. The shift is / was finished.)

Вода никогда не кончается. (Water never runs out.)

•признавáть || признáть (to recognize [aspect change: via stress change])

признаю́, признаёшь, признаю́т || признáю, признáешь, признáют

N.B. This is "to recognize" in the sense of "to accept" or "to admit."

Китай не признаёт правительство Тайваня.

(China does not recognize the government of Taiwan.)

••узнавáть || узнáть (to recognize [the identity of], to find out [a fact])

Вы так постарели, что я вас не узнал.

(You have aged so much that I did not recognize you.)

Я вчера узнал о её смерти. (Yesterday I found out about her death.)

N.B. To account for the relationships within the aspect triplets "знать || узнáть || узнавáть" and "знать || признáть || признавáть," **SEE** "лить || проли́ть" in "Простите пехоте."

•войско/армия (army [войско: more archaic; plur. "войска": armed forces])

•сквозь + acc. (through)

•подступáть || подступи́ть (to approach [**SEE** "Ночной разговор"])

Переведите на русский язык, пользуясь песней и комментариями

1. The **private approached** the enemy[1] **marshall** and said: "I will **never recognize**[2] your rank. You are **powerless** to force me to talk, and you are **powerless over** all the prisoners that you hold."

2. When this **private** was a **sentry**, even an officer was **powerless over** him.

3. Every day **without fail** we go to the park and feed the pigeons. We buy

---

[1]An adjectival suffix is required here to turn the noun into an adjective.

[2]Indicate stress.

the bread crumbs on (the) **Arbat** (street). The crumbs **cost**[1] very little.

4. **No one** is **entitled** to **love** (noun). (You) have to earn it. **May this never** change.

5. The **army** did not **recognize**[2] its **great marshall** without his medals.

6. **May** you **never find out**[3] what real **love** (is). A person in love doesn't eat, doesn't **sleep** and just withers away.

7. The **sentries stood** (for) so long that they **fell asleep** and did not **finish** their **shift**.

8. "I am so tired: I've been **standing** here for a long time,[4] and I am **entitled** to a rest," said the **sentry**, "fortunately here **comes** my **relief** (person)."

9. If the **words** (of) the **great** leader are **eternal**, why have I already forgotten them?

10. The **army**[5] was **approaching** the enemy capital in **spring** after a long **winter** and a hard **campaign**. Its patience **was running out**.

11. The salesman looked **through** the **rouble** and said: "It is a fake."

12. Our **hike ended** when our food **ran out**. **We didn't have** a choice: we **ended the hike.**

13. **Let** the **sentry stand** in the **storm**: I don't care! I am **finishing** an interesting book, and I can't **relieve**[6] him.

14. "**Do you have** (any) **roubles**?" "I **don't have** (any) **roubles**: **only** dollars. My roubles **have run out**. They always **run out** very quickly."

---

[1]Indicate stress.

[2]Here it is a question of identity, i.e., they mistook him for someone else.

[3]Future perfective. Indicate stress.

[4]**SEE** "Шёл троллейбус по улице."

[5]Do not use the same word as in number 5.

[6]This verb has the same root as the corresponding noun in the song.

4 A (Blanks)

_ _ _ _ _ _ _ _ _(n.)-_ _ _ _ _ _ _ _ _ _ _ _(n.),
как _ _ _ _ _ _(adv.) ты _ _ _ _ _(v.)!
_ _ _ _ _ _ _ _ _(n.)-_ _ _ _ _ _ _ _ _ _ _ _(n.),
куда меня _ _ _ _ _ _(v.)?

_ _ _ _ _(v.) _ _ _-_ _ _(adv.) — _ _ _ _ _ _ _(n.)
за _ _ _ _(numeral) _ _ _ _ _(n.: gen.).
Ну как _ _ _ _ _(v.: inf.) до _ _ _ _(n.: gen.),
когда _ _ _ _ _ _ _ _(n.) _ _ _ _(v.)?

_ _ _ _ _ _(n.) есть _ _ _ _ _ _ _(n.).
_ _ _ _ _ _(n.) есть _ _ _ _ _ _ _(adv.).
_ _ _ _ _ _ _ _(v.) б только _ _ _ _(n: gen.) на все мои _ _ _ _(n.).

_ _ _ _ _ _ _ _ _(n.) за _ _ _ _ _ _ _(n.) — она ведь
тоже _ _ _ _(n.)...
_ _ _ _ _ _ _ _(v.) бы _ _ _ _ _ _ _(n.: gen.),
когда под _ _ _ _ _(n.) _ _ _ _(v.).

_ _ _ _ _ _(n.) есть _ _ _ _ _ _ _(n.).

4 B (Partial Blanks)

Ша_ _ _ _ _ _(n.)-ша_ _ _ _ _ _ _ _(n.),
как сл_ _ _ _(adv.) ты п_ _ _ _(v.)!
шар_ _ _ _ _(n.)-шар_ _ _ _ _ _ _(n.),
куда меня зо_ _ _ _(v.)?

Ша_ _ _(v.) е_ _-е_ _(adv.) — вер_ _ _(n.)
за п_ _ _(numeral) _ _ _ _ _(n.: gen.).
Ну как д_ _ _ _(v.: inf.) до ц_ _ _(n.: gen.),
когда бо_ _ _ _ _(n.) ж_ _ _(v.)?

_ _ _ _ _ _(n.) есть _ _ _ _ _ _(n.).
Р_ _ _ _ _(n.) есть вс_ _ _ _(adv.).
Х_ _ _ _ _ _(v.) б только п_ _ _(n: gen.) на все мои г_ _ _(n.).

Расп_ _ _ _(n.) за ош_ _ _ _(n.) — она ведь
тоже т_ _ _(n.)...
Хв_ _ _ _ _(v.) бы ул_ _ _ _(n.: gen.),
когда под р_б_ _(n.) б_ _ _(v.).

Ра_ _ _ _(n.) есть раб_ _ _(n.)...

Song 4. Песенка старого шарманщика

(Посвящается Е.Евтушенко)[1]

Шарманка–шарлатанка, как сладко ты поёшь!
Шарманка–шарлатанка, куда меня зовёшь?

Шагаю еле–еле — вершок за пять минут.
Ну как дойти до цели, когда ботинки жмут?

Работа есть работа. Работа есть всегда.
Хватило б(ы) только пота на все мои года.

Расплата за ошибки — она ведь тоже труд...
Хватило бы улыбки, когда под рёбра бьют.

Работа есть работа...

Вопросы по тексту (ответы полными предложениями):
1) К кому обращается шарманщик? 2) Приятно ли звучит его шарманка? 3) С какой скоростью двигается шарманщик? 4) Что мешает шарманщику дойти до цели? 5) Что значит "когда ботинки жмут" и "когда под рёбра бьют" [см. сноску]? 6) В чём нет нехватки у шарманщика? 7) Как себя надо вести когда бьют под рёбра? 8) Почему песня кончается повторением с многоточием?

Комментарии к тексту песни

•петь || спеть (to sing) пою́, –ёшь, –ю́т

••пить || вы́пить (to drink) пью, пьёшь, пьют || вы́пью, –ешь, –ют

•где/куда (where [**SEE** "Он, наконец, явился в дом"])

•зва́ть || позва́ть (to call [**not** by phone]/invite/summon) зову́, –ёшь, –ут

••звони́ть || позвони́ть + dat. (to call [on the telephone], to phone)
Позвони ему и позови его в гости. (Call him up and invite him over.)

••называ́ться (to be called [not used with people])
называ́юсь, –ешься, –ются
Этот город называется Рим. (This city is called Rome.)

•шага́ть || шагну́ть (imperf.: to march / walk; perf.: to take a step)
шага́ю –ешь, –ют || шагну́, –ёшь, –у́т

•е́ле (barely, hardly, scarcely [repetition for more emphasis])
Он еле–еле говорит по–японски. (He can barely speak Japanese.)

•verb. + за + time unit [acc.] (to do something in... [to take a given amount of time to do something])
Я кончил работу за час. (I finished the job in an hour [it took me an hour].)

••verb + че́рез + time unit [acc.] (to do something in... [after the end of a given time period])

---

[1]Считалось, что в 60–е годы советский поэт, Евгений Евтушенко, шел "против течения" и говорил правду, за что у него иногда бывали неприятности.

Я к вам приеду через час. (I'll be at your place in an hour.)

•как дойти до цели (how do you reach your goal
[**SEE** "interrog. word + dat. + inf." in "Ещё раз о дураках"])

•до–[verb] + до + gen. (to reach / go up to / go as far as / make it to / finish)
Мы не доехали до Москвы — кончилось горючее.
(We did not make it to / reach Moscow because we ran out of fuel.)
Я дописал роман до конца. (I wrote the novel to the end.)

•dat. + жать (to be tight [footwear])
Мне жмёт ботинок. (My boot is too tight [lit.: squeezes me].)
••жать || сжать (to squeeze) жму, –ёшь, –ут || сожму́, –ёшь, –у́т

•есть (is)
N.B. This form is used in proverb-like expression of the type x is x, i.e., "you cannot change the nature of..." or "that is the way things are with..."
Собака есть собака, и математике её не научишь.
(A dog is a dog, and you can't teach it math.)

•хвата́ет || хва́тит (to be / have enough [**SEE** "Песенка о старом короле"])

•если + б[ы] + past tense form (if only ["если" can be used or omitted])
Хватило б[ы] только / если бы только хватило пота.
(If only one had enough sweat [here sweat is a metaphor for endurance].)
Был бы я / если бы я был молодым! (If only I were young!)

•расплата за + acc. (atonement / retribution for)

•работа (work) труд (labor)

•бить || поби́ть (to beat / hit / strike / vanquish) бью, бьёшь, бьют

•ведь (after all [**SEE** "Шёл троллейбус по улице"])

Переведите на русский язык, пользуясь песней и комментариями

1. The **old organ-grinder's work** brought so little money that sometimes he **did not have enough** money for food. Every day he **walked**[1] through[2] towns and villages where he **sang** and **called** the public, but no one[3] listened. One day[4] he was so exhausted that he **barely made it to** the local cheap hotel with his old (street) **organ**.

2. The workers **never had enough** food, and now too **there is not enough** food in their houses. I think that **they will have enough** bread for a week: no more. So don't expect (any) **smiles** from them. Their life consists of **sweat** and hard **labor**.

3. Science **is** science: it is hard **labor** with no easy solutions. Its **goal** is knowledge, and it does not tolerate **charlatans**.

4. "Do you like[5] these **shoes**?" "No, they are so **tight** (on) **me** that I cover[6]

---

[1]Do not use a verb derived from "идти" or "ходить."

[2]**SEE** "verb of motion + по + dat." in "Шёл троллейбус по улице."

[3]**SEE** "Примета."

[4]**SEE** "Ещё раз о дураках."

[5]**SEE** "Ещё раз о дураках."

[6]A verb of motion with the prefix про–.

only three kilometers **in** (an) hour. At this speed I will be home **in** four hours."

5. My child **squeezed** a berry, and its **sweet** juice squirted on my fresh painting: all my **work** was ruined!

6. Whom will you **phone**? **After all**, you know no one[1] in this city.

7. The **retribution** for your treason is not far.

8. **How am I supposed to march**[2] in the parade with no **shoes**?

9. When the clerk **calls** you, you will **take a step** forward and stop.

10. Why does Georgii **beat** his dog? **If only** people treated dogs kindly. But **how does**[3] (one) force people not to **beat** their animals?

11. "How did you break a **rib**?" "I fell." "How did you fall?" "I (had) **drunk** a bottle of vodka. I know that I **drink** too much."

12. He always made **mistakes** when he **sang** the national anthem.

---

[1]**SEE** "Примета."

[2]**SEE** "как дойти до цели" above.

[3]**SEE** previous note.

5 A (Blanks)

_ _ _ _(conj.) _ _ _ _ _(n.) в _ _ _ _ _ _(n.: prep.),
_ _ _ _(n.), стало быть, к _ _ _ _ _(n.: dat).
А _ _ _ _(conj.) _ _ _ _(v.: inf.) ему _ _ _ _ _ _ _(v.: inf.),
_ _ _ _(conj.) _ _ _ _(v.: inf.) ему _ _ _ _ _ _ _(v.: inf.),
_ _ _ _ _ _(conjunctive adv.), всем на _ _ _ _ _(n.) идти(ть).

Чтобы не было _ _ _ _ _(n.: gen.),
надо _ _ _ _ _ _(n.: acc.) _ _ _ _ _(v.: inf.).
Чтобы _ _ _ _ _ _(n.: acc.) _ _ _ _ _(v.: inf.),
Чтобы _ _ _ _ _ _(n.: acc.) _ _ _ _ _(v.: inf.),
надо _ _ _ _ _(n.) _ _ _ _ _ _ _ _(v.: inf.).

А как _ _ _ _ _ _(v.) _ _ _ _ _ _ _ _(v.: inf.),
всем _ _ _ _ _ _ _ _ _ _(v.) _ _ _ _ _ _ _ _(v.: inf.).
Ну а как _ _ _ _ _ _ _ _(n.) _ _ _ _ _ _(v.),
ну а как _ _ _ _ _ _ _ _(n.) _ _ _ _ _ _(v.),
_ _ _ _(n.) _ _ _ _ _ _ _(n.: acc., dimin.) _ _ _ _ _ _(v.).

Ей не _ _ _ _ _(pred. adv.) _ _ _ _ _ _ (pron.).
Ей _ _ _ _ _ _ _(v.: inf.) бы _ _ _ _(particle) в кого:
_ _ _ _(particle) в _ _ _ _ _ _(substantivized adj.)
_ _ _ _(particle) в сво(е)го,
_ _ _ _(particle) бы — всех до _ _ _ _ _ _(cardinal numeral)...
Во(т) и боле(е) _ _ _ _ _ _(pron.).

Во(т) и боле(е) _ _ _ _ _ _(pron.).
Во(т) и боле(е) _ _ _ _ _ _(pron.),
во(т) и боле(е) _ _ _ _ _ _(pron.),
_ _ _ _ _(preposition) _ _ _ _ _ _(n.: gen.) того.
_ _ _ _ _ _ _ _ _ _ _(n.: inf.) нéкому в него.

5 B (Partial Blanks)

_ _ _ _(conj.) _ _ _ _ _(n.)[1] в вы_ _ _ _(n.: prep.),
д_ _ _(n.), стало быть, к в_ _ _ _(n.:dat).[2]
А е_ _ _(conj.) _ _ _ _(v.: inf.) ему к_ _ _ _ _ _(v.: inf.),
ес_ _(conj.) д_ _ _(v.: inf.) ему кр_ _ _ _ _(v.: inf.),
зн_ _ _ _(conjunctive adv.), всем на фр_ _ _(n.) идти(ть).[3]

Чтобы не было во_ _ _(n.: gen.),
надо _ _ _ _ _ _(n.: acc.) _ _ _ _ _(v.: inf.).
Чтобы в_ _ _ _ _(n.: acc.) _ _ _ _ _(v.: inf.),
Чтобы вó_ _ _ _(n.: acc.) у_ _ _ _(v.: inf.),
надо р_ _ь_(n.) за_ _ _ _ _ _(v.: inf.).

А как ст_ _ _ _(v.) зар_ _ _ _ _(v.: inf.),[4]
всем зах_ _ _ _ _ _(v.) _ _ _ _ _ _ _ _(v.: inf).
Ну а как с_ _ _ _ _ _ _(n.)[5] п_ _ _ _ _(v.),
ну а как ст_ _ _ _ _ _(n.) по_ _ _ _(v.),
п_ _ _(n.) ды_ _ _ _ _(n.: acc., dimin.) на_ _ _ _(v.).

Ей не ж_ _ _ _(pred. adv.) _ _ _ _ _ _ (pron.).
Ей по_ _ _ _ _(v.: inf.) бы _ _ _ _(particle) в кого:
_ _ _ _(particle) в чу_ _ _ _(substantivized adj.)
х_ _ _(particle) в сво(е)го,[6]
л_ _ _(particle) бы — всех до _ _ _ _ _ _(cardinal numeral)...[7]
Во(т)[8] и боле(е)[9] _ _ _ _ _ _(pron.).

Во(т) и боле(е) н_ _ _ _ _(pron.).
Во(т) и боле(е) ни_ _ _ _(pron.),
во(т) и боле(е) ник_ _ _(pron.),
кр_ _ _(prep.) вóр_ _ _(n.: gen.) того.
стр_ _ _ _ _ _ _(n.: inf.)[10] нéкому в него.

[1]Carefully observe the location of stress in this noun in order not to confuse it with a very similar and yet different word. Hint: this noun is masculine.

[2]The first noun in this line + к + dat. constitutes an idiomatic construction.

[3]This last consonant is indicative of colloquial speech and is used here for rhyme.

[4]This is the imperfective form of the last word (verb) in the previous stanza.

[5]This noun is derived from the last word (verb) in the previous line.

[6]The missing vowel is indicative of colloquial speech and is omitted for rhythm.

[7]"Все(х) до _ _ _ _ _ _" is an idiomatic construction.

[8]The missing consonant is indicative of colloquial speech and is omitted for rhyme.

[9]The missing vowel is indicative of colloquial speech and is omitted for rhythm.

[10]The singer deliberately pronounces this verb with the wrong stress, which is also indicative of colloquial usage.

Song 5. Примета

Если вóрон в вышине,
дело, стало быть, к войне.
А если дать ему кружить,
если дать ему кружить,
значит, всем на фронт идти(ть).

Чтобы не было войны,
надо вóрона убить.
Чтобы вóрона убить,
чтобы вóрона убить,
надо ружья зарядить.

А как станем заряжать,
всем захочется стрелять.
Ну а как стрельба пойдёт,
ну а как стрельба пойдёт,
пуля дырочку найдёт.

Ей не жалко никого.
Ей попасть бы хоть в кого:
хоть в чужого, хоть в сво(е)го,
лишь бы — всех до одного...
Во(т), и боле(е) ничего,

Во(т), и боле(е) ничего,
во(т), и боле(е) никого,
во(т), и боле(е) никого,
кроме вóрона того.
Стрéльнуть нéкому в него.

Вопросы по тексту (ответы полными предложениями):
1) О какой примете идёт речь в этой песне, и что она означает? 2) Почему поэт выбрал именно эту птицу как образ войны? 3) Что будет, если вóрону дать кружить? 4) Как можно предотвратить войну? 5) Какой парадокс заключается в этой "войне" с войной? 6) В чём заключается абсурдный ужас войны? 7) Как в этой песне выражается мысль, что война неотвратима?

Комментарии к тексту песни
•дело + к + dat. (it looks like [something is about to happen])
Дело [идёт] к войне. (It looks like war [is going start { "идёт": optional}].)
•стало быть / значит (that means, so, then, must)
Если студенты не занимаются, стало быть им неинтересно. (If students don't study, they must not be interested.)
•давáть || дать + dat. + inf. (to let / allow)
даю́, даёшь, даю́т || дам, дашь, даст, дади́м, дади́те, даду́т
Не давай ребенку есть червей. (Do not let the child eat worms.)
•кружи́ть || покружи́ть (to circle [intransitive])
кружу́, кру́жишь, кру́жат
Ворóна долго кружила вокруг трупа.
(The crow circled around the corpse for a long time.)
•dat. + inf. imperf. (one must [**SEE** "О Володе Высоцком"])
Всем идти на фронт. (Everyone must go the front.)
•идти́ || пойти́ (to go/come/walk [**SEE** "Шёл троллейбус по улице"])
•чтобы + past tense form / inf. ([in order] to, so that)

N.B. If "чтобы" introduces a subordinate clause whose subject is different from that of the main clause, the verb after "чтобы" assumes a **past tense** form, e.g., Я зарядил твоё ружьё, чтобы ты убил вóрона (I loaded your gun, so that you would kill the raven). If "чтобы" is not followed by a (new) subject, the verb after it is in the **infinitive**, e.g., Я зарядил ружьё, чтобы убить вóрона (I loaded my gun [in order] to kill the raven).

•чтобы не было + gen. ([in order] to avoid, so that there is no, so that there would / will not be, in order for something not to exist / be)
Чтобы не было стрельбы, надо выбросить все пули.
(To avoid / so that there will be no shooting, we should discard all bullets.)

•dat. + надо/нужно + inf. (it is necessary to, one needs / has to, one should)
Надо [было/будет] поститься. (It is [was/will be] necessary to fast.)
Мне надо [было/будет] помыться. (I have [had /will have] to wash up.)
••dat. + нýжен/нужнá + nom. (one needs something)
Мне нужна машина. (I need a car.)
N.B. "Нýжен/нужнá" agrees in gender and number with the needed thing.
••dat. + нýжно/надо + gen. (one needs some [with non-countable entities])
Мне нужно воды. (I need some water [нужно/надо: invariable].)

•dat. + бы + inf./noun (one ought to, one would like to ["надо" is implied])
Вам [надо] бы к врачу сходить. (You should see a doctor.)
Цветы полить бы. (I'd like to water the flowers ["мне": optional].)
Мне бы поспать. (I would like to take a nap ["мне": optional].)
N.B. "Бы" cannot be the first element in the sentence.

•убивáть || убúть (to kill, to murder) убивáю, –ешь, –ют || убьó, –ёшь, –ют

•заряжáть || зарядúть (to load [a gun], to charge [a battery])
заряжáю, –ешь, –ют || заряжý, зарядúшь, зарядят

•стать [perf. only] + imperf. inf. (to begin) стáну, –ешь, –ут (стал)
После бомбёжки у Пети стали дрожать руки.
(After the bombing raid Petia's hands began to tremble.)

•dat. + хотéться || захотéться + inf. (to feel like) хóчется (хотелось)
Миле вдруг очень захотелось пострелять.
(Mila suddenly felt like doing some shooting [felt a strong urge to shoot].)
N.B. "Really" in "I really [don't] feel like" is rendered by "очень."

•как [только] (when, as soon as ["только" may be omitted])
Как [только] Баграт пришёл домой, солнце село за горой.
(As soon as Bagrat came home, the sun set behind the mountain.)

•идтú || пойтú (to take place / occur / go on) идёт || пойдёт (шёл/шла)
Война шла семь лет. (The war went on for seven years.)

•находúть || найтú (to find)
нахожý, нахóдишь, нахóдят || найдý, –ёшь, –ýт

•dat. + жалко + acc. (to feel sorry / compassion for)
Коле было жалко мёртвую птичку. (Kolia felt sorry for the dead birdie.)
••dat. + жалко + gen. (to be stingy/sparing with, to be reluctant to spend/give up something, to regret having lost something [with abstract concepts])
Коле было жалко денег, он не пошёл к врачу и умер.
(Kolia didn't want to spend the money, so he didn't go to a doctor and died.)

•попадáть || попáсть + в + acc. (to hit [a target])
попадáю, –ешь, –ют || попадý, –ёшь, –ут
Снаряд / снайпер попал в стену. (The shell / sniper hit a wall.)

•хоть + interrog. word (anything, anyone etc.)
Это удивит хоть кого. (That will surprise anyone.)

•хоть... хоть (either... or, both... and)

Наш пёс всё ест: хоть фрукты, хоть овощи.

(Our dog eats everything: both fruit and vegetables.)

•чужой/ая (strange, not one's own, someone else's, foreign [when not modifying a noun: stranger, unknown person, not one of "us"])

•свой/своя (one's own, not strange [when not modifying a noun: one of us, one of our own, known person, not a stranger; **SEE** "Бумажный солдат"])

•dat. + лишь бы + inf. (just as long as [someone gets to do something])

Им лишь бы поесть, а что — неважно.

(Just as long as they get to eat something: it doesn't matter what.)

••лишь бы + past tense form (just as long as [something happens / is present])

Лишь бы водка была, а закуска найдётся.

(Just as long as there is some vodka: the hors d'œuvres are not a problem.)

•все до одного/одной + noun [plur.] (every single [without a noun: every single one/person])

•все до одного стуенты ушли домой (Every single student went home.)

все до одного ушли домой (Every single one/person went home.)

•ни[interrog. word] + не (no one, nothing, never, in no way / manner, nowhere)

Я никогда не был в Албании и ничего не знаю о ней.

(I've never been to Albania and know nothing / don't know anything about it.)

Мы никак не пытались им помочь.

(We did not try to help them in any manner / way.)

N.B. If a preposition is required, "ни[interrog. word]" splits:
"ни + preposition + interrog. word. + не."

Я ни с кем не здороваюсь. (I don't say "hello" to anyone [to no one].)

N.B. "Ничто"→ nomin.; "ничего"→ acc. (cf. Albania example above).

••dat. + нé[interrog. word] + inf. (to have nothing / nowhere / no one to...; there is nothing / nowhere / no one to...)

N.B. If a preposition is required, "нé[interrog. word]" splits:
"нé + preposition + interrog. word."

Мне нé во что верить. (I have nothing to believe in.)

Было нéчего кушать. (There was nothing to eat.)

Ей [было/будет] нéгде жить. (She has [had/will have] nowhere to live.)

N.B. The acc. case of "nothing" is "нéчего" (cf. "eating" example above).

N.B. Compare the use of "нé[interrog. word]" and "ни[interrog. word]" (note the stress): Ей нéкуда бежать (She has nowhere to run) v. Она никуда не бежит (She isn't running anywhere).

•нéкому + inf. (there is no one to do something / the ....ing)

В вóрона некому [было/будет] стрельнýть.

(There is [was/will be] no one to take a shot at the raven.)

Нéкому [было] стирать. (There is [was] no one to do the washing.)

N.B. "Нéкому" in this construction acts as a **logical subject** (the person [not] doing the shooting / washing) whereas in the "dat. + нé[interrog. word] + inf." formula "нéкому" acts as an **object**, e.g., Мне нéкому показать эту картину (I have no one to show this picture to).

•более/больше + ни[interrog. word] + не + verb (no one else, nothing else / more, no more, anymore, no longer, nowhere else)

Я больше ничего не хочу. (I want nothing / don't want anything else.)

Мы больше нигде не бываем. (We don't go anywhere else.)

Она больше не плавает. (She doesn't swim anymore.)

N.B. "Больше" is more common than "более" in this construction.

•стрелять || стрельнýть + из ружья/пистолета + в + acc. (to shoot / fire a gun at...

[with –н–: to take a shot at...])
стреля́ю, –ешь, –ют || стрельну́, –ёшь, –у́т
••застрели́ть (perf. of "стреля́ть" [to shoot dead])
застрелю́, застре́лишь, застре́лят
Она стреляла в него из пистолета, но не застрелила.
(She shot at him with a pistol but did not kill him.)
•кроме + gen. (apart from, besides)
•примета (omen)

Переведите на русский язык, пользуясь песней и комментариями

1. Nadia doesn't care **at what** she **shoots** (her) **rifle**: **just as long as she** (gets) to **shoot**. She **will shoot either at** a duck, **or at** a **raven, or at** a log. **Just as long as** (there) **are bullets**. I myself don't like **shooting**.[1]

2. **Up above**, the clouds were dark, and I thought: "**It looks like** rain. I **would like to find** an umbrella now." Therefore, I **went** home **so that** the rain (would) not drench me.

3. Not everyone **kills** at **war**: only those who[2] are at the **front**. **Just as long as we don't go** to the **front**. If we **go** to the **front**, we will **kill** someone:[3] maybe even **one of our own**.

4. "Why are these **ravens**[4] **circling up above**," thought Gerasim and **took a shot at** one of them, and then he **shot** (dead) **every single one so that they** (would) not **circle** over his house.

5. You are a saint: **you feel compassion** (for) **everyone**! I don't know **anyone else** like you. **No one** behaves as you (do).

6. I know that **I will have to** reread this translation, but **I don't want to spend** the time.

7. "If you did not translate the last sentence, **that means** you did not understand it." "Unfortunately **there is no one** to explain it to me. **Apart from** me **no one** knows Russian here." "**You should** use a dictionary."

8. If you do not **load** your **rifle**, you will not **shoot**, and if you do not **shoot**, you will not **hit anyone**, and if you do not **hit anyone**, you will not **kill anyone**. **That means, in order (for) violence not to exist we need** to throw away all **rifles** and other weapons.

9. **I feel like** dancing and **nothing more**, but my mother **does not let** me dance **anymore**! And I have **no one** to complain (to).

10. **Apart from** Aliona, **there was no one** to sew up the (little) **hole** in the

---

[1]Use a verbal noun here.
[2]**SEE** "тот + кто/который" in "Я вновь повстречался с надеждой."
[3]**SEE** "Шёл троллейбус по улице."
[4]Indicate stress.

tablecloth.

11. **War** has finished,[1] and now all the soldiers **should** go home. They will not **kill anymore**.

12. **In order to avoid war**, we **should** think **less** about bad **omens** and **more** about reality.

13. "**Never** talk to **strangers**." "But this man is not a **stranger**: he is **one of us**!"

14. **As soon as** the musician **found** his trumpet, he **began** to play. He played for his dog because **no one else** was listening.

15. The **shooting went on** for a long time.[2] But then it **began** to subside. Almost **every single** (person) **was shot dead**[3] and finally **there was no one** (left) **to do the shooting** and **the killing** and **there was no one** (left) to **kill**.

16. I will go **anywhere**, **just as long as** there is spinach there.

17. **So that there will be no** famine, **it is necessary** to cultivate all the fields and **every single** peasant, **except for** the sick, **should** work if they can **find** the tools. **Apart from** the peasants, **there is no one to** save us.

18. These plants don't grow **anywhere else**, and **no one else** knows about them, but since I am alone, **I have no one with whom** to share my discovery.

19. **I had no one from whom** to borrow money because **no one felt like** lending me (any) money.

---

[1]**SEE** "Часовые любви."

[2]**SEE** "Шёл троллейбус по улице."

[3]This should be an indefinite personal construction with an implicit "они" subject: lit.→ "almost every single one (they) shot dead."

6 A (Blanks)

Ах, какие _ _ _ _ _ _ _ _ _ _ _ _ _(adj.) _ _ _ _(n.)!
Только мама моя в _ _ _ _ _ _(n.: prep.)
и _ _ _ _ _ _ _(n.: prep.):
« Что же ты _ _ _ _ _ _ _(v.), мой _ _ _ _ _ _ _(n.: dimin.),
_ _ _ _ _ _ _ _ _(adj.), _ _ _ _ _ _ _ _ _(adj.)?
Что же ты _ _ _ _ _ _ _(v.), мой _ _ _ _ _ _ _(n.: dimin.),
_ _ _ _ _ _ _ _ _(adj.), _ _ _ _ _ _ _ _ _(adj.)?»

«Из _ _ _ _ _(n.: gen.) в _ _ _ _ _(n.) _ _ _ _ _ _(n.: gen.)
_ _ _ _(n.) _ _ _ _ _(v.)[1] я.
Стали _ _ _ _ _ _(n.) и _ _ _ _ _ _ _(adj.: comparative)
и _ _ _ _ _ _(adj.: comparative).
Мама, мама, это я _ _ _ _ _ _(v.).
Я _ _ _ _ _ _ _ _ _(substantivized adj.) по _ _ _ _ _ _(n.: dat.).
Мама, мама, это я _ _ _ _ _ _(v.).
Я _ _ _ _ _ _ _ _ _(substantivized adj.) по _ _ _ _ _ _(n.: dat.)» ...

«Мой _ _ _ _ _ _ _(n.: dimin.), _ _ _ _ _ _ _ _ _ _(v.) всё, что было.
Стали _ _ _ _ _ _ _ _ _ _(adj.: instr.) _ _ _ _ _(n.) твои,
_ _ _ _ _ _ _ _(n.: dimin.).
Может быть, она тебя _ _ _ _ _ _(v.) —
_ _ _ _ _(v. inf.) не _ _ _ _ _(v.),
_ _ _ _ _(v.: inf.) не _ _ _ _ _(v.)?
Может быть, она тебя _ _ _ _ _ _(v.) —
_ _ _ _ _(v.: inf.) не _ _ _ _ _(v.),
_ _ _ _ _(v.: inf.) не _ _ _ _ _(v.)?»

«Из _ _ _ _ _(n.: gen.) в _ _ _ _ _(n.) _ _ _ _ _ _(n.: gen.)
_ _ _ _(n.) _ _ _ _ _(v.) я.
Стали _ _ _ _ _ _(n.) и _ _ _ _ _ _ _(adj.: comparative)
и _ _ _ _ _(adj.: comparative).
Что ты, мама, _ _ _ _ _ _(adv.) я _ _ _ _ _ _(v.).
Я _ _ _ _ _ _ _ _ _(substantivized adj.) по _ _ _ _ _ _(n.: dat.).
Мама, мама, это я _ _ _ _ _ _(v.).
Я _ _ _ _ _ _ _ _ _(substantivized adj.) по _ _ _ _ _ _(n.: dat.)» .

---

[1]The last two words constitute an idiomatic construction.

6 B (Partial Blanks)

Ах, какие уди_ _ _ _л_ _ _ _(adj.) н_ _ _(n.)!
Только мама моя в г_ _ _ _ _(n.: prep.)
и тре_ _ _ _(n.: prep.):
«Что же ты г_ _ _ _ _ _(v.), мой _ _ _ _ _ _ _(n.: dimin.),
_ _ _ _ _ _ _ _(adj.), о_ _ _ _ _ _ _(adj.)?
Что же ты гу_ _ _ _ _(v.), мой с_ _ _ _ _ _(n.: dimin.),
од_ _ _ _ _ _(adj.), оди_ _ _ _ _(adj.)?»

«Из _ _ _ _ _(n.: gen.) в _ _ _ _ _(n.) _ _ _ _ _ _(n.: gen.)
_ _ _ _(n.) д_ _ _ _(v.)[1] я.
Стали з_ _ _ _ _(n.) и к_ _ _ _ _ _(adj.: comparative)
и д_ _ _ _ _(adj.: comparative).
Мама, мама, это я _ _ _ _ _ _(v.).
Я _ _ _ _ _ _ _ _(substantivized adj.) по _ _ _ _ _ _(n.: dat.).
Мама, мама, это я _ _ _ _ _ _(v.).
Я _ _ _ _ _ _ _ _(substantivized adj.) по _ _ _ _ _ _(n.: dat.)» ...

«Мой сы_ _ _ _ _(n.: dimin.), всп_ _ _ _ _ _(v.) всё, что было.
Стали гр_ _т_ _ _ _(adj.: instr.) г_ _ _ _(n.) твои,
сы_ _ _ек(n.: dimin.).
Может быть, она тебя з_ _ _ _ _(v.) —
_ _ _ _ _(v.: inf.) не _ _ _ _ _(v.),
_ _ _ _ _(v.: inf.) не _ _ _ _ _(v.)?
Может быть, она тебя за_ _ _ _(v.) —
з_ _ _ _(v.: inf.) не х_ _ _ _(v.),
зн_ _ _(v.: inf.) не хо_ _ _(v.)? »

«Из к_ _ _ _(n.: gen.) в ко_ _ _(n.) а_ _ _ _ _(n.: gen.)
п_ _ _(n.) де_ _ _(v.) я.
Стали зв_ _ _ _(n.) и кр_ _ _ _ _(adj.: comparative)
и до_ _ _ _(adj.: comp.).
Что ты, мама, пр_ _ _ _(adv.) я _ _ _ _ _ _(v.).
Я д_ _ _ _ _ _ _(substantivized adj.) по ап_ _ _ _(n.: dat.).
Мама, мама, это я де_ _ _ _(v.).
Я деж_ _ _ _ _(substantivized adj.)[2] по апр_ _ _(n.: dat.)» .

[1]The last two words constitute an idiomatic construction.
[2]This adjective has the same root as the verb preceding it.

Song 6. Дежурный по апрелю

Ах, какие удивительные ночи!
Только мама моя в грусти и тревоге:
«Что же ты гуляешь, мой сыночек, одинокий, одинокий?
Что же ты гуляешь, мой сыночек, одинокий, одинокий?»

«Из конца в конец апреля путь держу я.
Стали звёзды и крупнее и добрее.
Мама, мама, это я дежурю. Я дежурный по апрелю.
Мама, мама, это я дежурю. Я дежурный по апрелю»...

«Мой сыночек, вспоминаю всё, что было.
Стали грустными глаза твои, сыночек.
Может быть, она тебя забыла — знать не хочет,
  знать не хочет?
Может быть, она тебя забыла — знать не хочет,
  знать не хочет?»

«Из конца в конец апреля путь держу я.
Стали звёзды и крупнее и добрее.
Что ты, мама, просто я дежурю. Я дежурный по апрелю.
Мама, мама, это я дежурю. Я дежурный по апрелю».

Вопросы по тексту (ответы полными предложениями):
1) В какой форме написана эта песня — как монолог, описание и т.д.? 2) Кто с кем разговаривает? 3) В каком настроении мама героя? 4) Почему? 5) Почему герой одинок? 6) Что он имеет в виду, когда называет себя дежурным по апрелю? 7) Какие главные темы этой песни?

Комментарии к тексту песни
•какой/какая (which [one], what a, what, [**SEE** "Ещё раз о дураках"])
•удивительный (amazing, surprising, wonderful)
•ночь (night) ночью (at night [вчера ночью: last night])
  N.B. In North America "night" can refer to any time from sunset to dawn, but in Russian "ночь" is the time of sleep (from around midnight). "Вечер" is from about sunset to bedtime (evening [ве́чером = in the evening]).
•что же (why)
•гуля́ть || погуля́ть (to stroll/walk [always in the "stroll" sense])
  гуля́ю, –ешь, –ют
  SEE "verb of motion + по + dat." in "Шёл троллейбус по улице."
  Мы гуляем по улице. (We are walking/strolling down/along the street.)
  N.B. In colloquial Russian this verb also has the sense of "partying."
  N.B. Verbs derived from "идти" and "ходить" do not have the "stroll" connotation

(**SEE** "Шёл троллейбус по улице").

•оди́нокий/ая (alone, lonely, without a family)

•из конца в конец + gen. (from one end of something to another)

Крыса мечется из конца в конец длинной клетки.

(The rat is dashing from one end of its long cage to another.)

•держа́ть путь (to be headed somewhere) держу́, де́ржишь, де́ржат

Держи путь на восток! (Head east!)

•станови́ться || стать + instr. (to become [often with instrumental])

становлю́сь, стано́вишься, стано́вятся || ста́ну, –ешь, –ут

Соня, ты станешь художницей! (Sonia, you will become a painter!)

•дежу́рить || подежу́рить + по + dat. (to be on duty) дежу́рю, –ишь, –ят

Кто дежурит по заводу? (Who is on duty at the factory?)

•дежу́рный/ая ([a person] on duty)

Сегодня я дежурный по этажу. (Today I am on duty on our floor.)

•вспомина́ть || вспо́мнить (to remember / recall)

вспомина́ю, –ешь, –ют || вспо́мню, –ишь, –ят

N.B. This verb has to do with recalling information that is forgotten or no longer fresh in memory. The imperf. means **a**)to refresh one's memory on more than one occasion or **b**)to be in the process of trying to reconstruct something forgotten. The perf. means to recall something once at a particular point in time.

Он часто вспоминал Машу. (He often remembered Masha.)

Он долго вспоминал фамилию Лады, но так и не вспомнил.

(He tried to remember [retrieve from memory] Lada's last name but failed.)

••по́мнить (to remember [to keep a recollection fresh]) по́мню, –ишь, –ят

Я помню вашу книгу. (I remember your book [hold in memory].)

N.B. To account for the relationships within the aspect triplet "по́мнить || вспо́мнить || вспомина́ть" **SEE** "лить || проли́ть" in "Простите пехоте."

•забыва́ть || забы́ть (to forget) забыва́ю, –ешь, –ют || забу́ду, –ешь, –ут

•не хотеть + знать + acc. (not to want to have anything to do with someone)

Боря Мишу знать не хочет.

(Boria wants to have nothing to do with Misha.)

•знать || узна́ть (to know [у–: to find out, to recognize) зна́ю, –ешь, –ют

•хоте́ть || захоте́ть (to want) хочу́, хо́чешь, хо́чет, хоти́м, хоти́те, хотя́т

•что́ ты / вы? (expression of disagreement or disbelief: "are you kidding?")

"Ты дру́жишь с ним? " "Что́ ты?! Он знать меня не хочет."

("Are you friends with him?" "Are you kidding?! He wants to have nothing to do with me.")

Переведите на русский язык, пользуясь песней и комментариями

1. **At night**[1] my neighbor's **son walks**[2] along[3] our corridor: **from one end** of the corridor **to the other**. (It's) as if[4] he (were) **on duty** there. **Last night**, when I asked him where **he** (was) **heading**,[5] he **did not want** to tell me. He **does not want to have anything to do with** his neighbors even

---

[1]Assume that this refers to a time past midnight.

[2]Not strolling.

[3]**SEE** "verb of motion + по + dat." in "Шёл троллейбус по улице."

[4]**SEE** "как будто" in "Чёрный кот."

[5]Present tense.

though we are all **kind** people. I think that he is a **sad** and **lonely** boy.

2. Ania was **lonely** because she was arrogant, but now she is **becoming kinder** and **kinder**. **Maybe** when she **becomes** really **kind**, she will not be **lonely** anymore.[1]

3. I feel a **wonderful anxiety** when, after supper, I **stroll** along our street in **April** and look at the **large stars** in the **night**[2] sky.

4. "**Were you on duty** at the palace **last night** at 12:30?" "**Are you kidding**!? I was sleeping at home. Don't you **remember**[3] that I am (a person) **on duty only in the evening**."

5. **Night** is a time when **sadness**, **anxiety** and **loneliness** are especially noticeable.

6. "He is a **wonderful son**: every year he **remembers**[4] his **mother's** birthday in **April**." "Yes, but **why**[5] did he not **remember** it in **April** of last year?" "**Maybe** he **forgot** it because he was **simply** too busy."

7. I **remember**[6] what you said to me fifty years ago but I **have forgotten** what you said **last night**.[7] I always **forget** such things. I can't even **recall** now what time I am going to be **on duty tonight**. **What an amazing** thing the human memory (is)!

8. The ship was **heading** towards the North[8] **Star**.

---

[1]**SEE** "Примета."

[2]This is an adjective with the suffix –н–.

[3]In other words, isn't this information fresh in your memory?

[4]In other words, he recalls something of which he is not constantly aware.

[5]Not "почему, зачем, для чего, отчего."

[6]I hold in my memory: not just at a particular point in time but always.

[7]People normally talk **before** bedtime.

[8]Lit.: polar.

7 A (Blanks)

Он, _ _ _ _ _ _ _(adv.), _ _ _ _ _ _(v.) в _ _ _(n.),
где она _ _ _(numeral) _ _ _(n.: gen.) _ _ _ _ _ _ _(v.) о нём,
куда он _ _ _(pron.) _ _ _(numeral) _ _ _(n.: gen.) _ _ _ _ _ _(v.),
_ _ _ _(conj.) она так _ _ _ _ _ _(v.), и он _ _ _ _ _(v.)

_ _ _ _ _ _ _(v.), что это _ _ _ _ _ _(n.) была.
_ _ _ _ _ _ _ _(v.: imperat.), _ _ _ _(conj.) это её _ _ _ _(n.).
Но, _ _ _ _ _ _(v.), _ _ _ _(conj.) _ _ _ _(n.: acc.)
к себе _ _ _ _ _ _ _(v.: imperat.),
_ _ _ _ _(particle) _ _ _ _ _(pred. adv.) _ _ _ _ _ _(v.: inf.)
_ _ _-_ _ _ _ _ _(pron.) в _ _ _ _ _(n.: prep.)?

И _ _ _ _ _ _ _(adj.) _ _ _ _ _(n.) в _ _ _ _(n.) _ _ _ _ _ _(v.),
и она _ _ _ _ _ _ _(v.), и он _ _ _ _ _ _(v.).
И он _ _ _ _ _ _ _ _ _ _(v.), чтобы _ _ _ _(v.: inf.),
и она не _ _ _ _ _ _ _(v.) к его _ _ _ _ _(n.: dat.).

Я _ _ _ _ _ _ _(v.), что это _ _ _ _ _ _(n.) была.
_ _ _ _ _ _ _ _(v.: imperat.), _ _ _ _(conj.) это её _ _ _ _(n.).
Но, _ _ _ _ _ _(v.), _ _ _ _(conj.) _ _ _ _(n.: acc.)
к себе _ _ _ _ _ _ _(v.: imperat.),
_ _ _ _ _(particle) _ _ _ _ _(pred. adv.) _ _ _ _ _ _(v.: inf.)
_ _ _-_ _ _ _ _ _(pron.) в _ _ _ _ _(n.: prep.)?

7 B (Partial Blanks)

Он, на_ _ _ _ _(adv.), я_ _ _ _ _(v.) в д_ _(n.),
где она _ _ _(numeral) _ _ _(n.: gen.) меч_ _ _ _(v.) о нём,
куда он с_ _(pron.) с_ _(numeral) л_ _(n.: gen.) сп_ _ _ _(v.),
_ _ _ _(conj.) она так р_ _ _ _ _(v.), и он ре_ _ _(v.)

К_ _ _ _ _ _(v.), что это _ _ _ _вь(n.) была.
по_ _ _ _ _ _(v.: imperat.), _ _ _ь(conj.) это её _ _ _ _(n.).
Но, з_ _ _ _ _(v.), _ _ _ _(conj.) _ _ _ _(n.: acc.)
к себе пр_ _ _ _ _(v.: imperat.),
р_ _ _ _(particle) м_ _ _ _(pred. adv.) п_ _ _ _ _(v.: inf.)
_ _ _—н_ _ _ _ь(pron.) в л_ _ _ _(n.: prep.)?

И _ _зд_ _ _(adj.) д_ _ _ _(n.) в о_ _ _(n.) ст_ _ _ _(v.),
и она м_ _ _ _ _ _(v.), и он мо_ _ _ _(v.).
И он пове_ _ _ _ _ _(v.), чтобы у_ _ _(v.: inf.),
и она не при_ _ _ _(v.) к его г_ _ _ _(n.: dat.).

Я кл_ _ _ _ _(v.), что это л_ _ _вь(n.) была.
посм_ _ _ _(v.: imperat.), в_ _ь(conj.) это её д_ _ _(n.).
Но, зн_ _ _ _(v.), х_ _ _(conj.) Б_ _ _(n.: acc.)
к себе при_ _ _ _(v.: imperat.),
ра_ _ _(particle) мо_ _ _(pred. adv.) по_ _ _ _(v.: inf.)
ч_ _–ни_ _ _ь(pron.) в лю_ _ _(n.: prep.)?

Song 7. Он, наконец, явился в дом

Он, наконец, явился[1] в дом,
где она сто лет мечтала[2] о нём,
куда он сам сто лет спешил,
ведь она так решила, и он решил.

Клянусь, что это любовь была.
Посмотри, ведь это её дела.
Но, знаешь, хоть Бога к себе призови,
разве можно понять что-нибудь в любви?

И поздний дождь в окно стучал,
и она молчала, и он молчал.
И он повернулся, чтобы уйти,
и она не припала к его груди.

Я клянусь, что это любовь была.
Посмотри, ведь это её дела.
Но, знаешь, хоть Бога к себе призови,
разве можно понять что-нибудь в любви?

Вопросы по тексту (ответы полными предложениями):
1) Какая главная тема в этой песне? 2) Кто главные герои песни? 3) Где и как они встретились? 4) Долго ли они были в разлуке? 5) Какая была погода при их встрече? 6) В какое время суток они встретились? 7) Опишите их "разговор". 8) Чем кончился их разговор? 9) Чего она не сделала, когда он уходил? 10) Как поэт объясняет эту ситуацию? 11) Что остаётся необъяснимым в этом "объяснении"?

Комментарии к тексту песни
•явля́ться || яви́ться (to show up / arrive)
 являю́сь, –ешься, –ются || явлю́сь, я́вишься, я́вятся
•verb + time unit [acc.] (to do something **for** a time unit [**SEE** "ненадо́лго/недо́лго" in "О Володе Высоцком"])
 Она сто лет мечтала о нём. (She dreamed of him **for** a hundred years.)
•мечта́ть || помечта́ть + о + prep. (to dream of [not dreaming during sleep])
 мечта́ю, –ешь, –ют (noun: мечта)
 Все мечтают о счастье. (Everyone dreams of happiness.)
 ••dat. + сни́ться || присни́ться + nom./что ([in one's sleep] to dream of /that)
 сню́сь, –и́шься –я́тся (noun: сон)
 Мне вчера приснился дед. (I dreamt of my grandfather last night.)
•сам/а́/о́/са́ми (myself, yourself, herself etc. [**SEE** "Чёрный кот"])
•спеши́ть || поспеши́ть (to hurry [куда: movement]) спешу́, –и́шь, –а́т
•где (where [location]) куда (where [destination])

---

[1]"Вернулся" in the Frumkin edition.

[2]"Вздыхала" in the Frumkin edition.

Куда он идёт? Где он работает?
(Where is he going? Where does he work?)

•ведь (after all [**SEE** “Шёл троллейбус по улице”])

•так (thus, so, this way [такой→ such, so; **SEE** “Старый пиджак”])

•реша́ть || реши́ть (to <u>decide</u> / <u>[re]solve</u> [a problem, a riddle])
решáю, –ешь, –ют || решу́, –и́шь, –áт

•кля́сться || покля́сться (to swear [that something is true])
кляну́сь, –ёшься, –у́тся (кля́лся/клялáсь)

•смотре́ть || посмотре́ть (to look [**SEE** “Шёл троллейбус по улице”])

•дело (affair, matter, the thing that one does)
У меня много дел. (I have many things to do.)

•знать || узнáть (to know [у–: to find out, to recognize) знáю, –ешь, –ют

•хоть + imperat. (even if)
Хоть бегай, хоть прыгай — никогда не похудеешь. Ешь меньше!
(Even if you run, even if you jump: you’ll never lose weight. Eat less!)

•призывáть || призвáть (to summon/call [archaic and/or elevated style])
призывáю, –ешь, –ют || призову́, –ёшь, –у́т
N.B. In the song “призвать к себе Бога” means to invoke God’s help (lit.: to call God), but a more typical meaning is to summon/call someone to one’s side or to one’s person (something a person in power might do).
N.B. To account for the relationships within the aspect triplet “звать || призвáть || призывáть” **SEE** “лить || проли́ть” in “Простите пехоте.”

•разве (“really” or an untranslatable intensifier in questions)
Разве ты умеешь плавать?
(Can you [really] swim? **or** I didn’t know you could swim)

•dat. + мóжно + infinitive (one <u>can</u> / <u>may</u> / <u>is allowed to</u>, it is possible to)
Здесь можно курить? (<u>Can</u> / <u>may</u> one [is one allowed to] smoke here?)
Ей можно [идти] домой? (<u>Can</u> / <u>may</u> she [is she allowed to] go home?)
Им можно [было/будет] есть. (They are [<u>were</u> / <u>will be</u>] allowed to eat.)
На земле можно дышать, а на луне нет.
(<u>It is possible to</u> / <u>you can</u> breathe on earth but not on the moon.)

•понимáть || поня́ть (to understand / comprehend / grasp)
понимáю, –ешь, –ют || пойму́, –ёшь, –у́т

•[кто/где/как/что/какой]–нибудь (some-[one/where/how/thing/kind of]; **SEE** “Шёл троллейбус по улице”)

•поздний/яя (late, tardy)
N.B. “Поздний” is an adjective, while “поздно” is an adverb, although both are translated into English as “late.”

•стучáть || постучáть + в + acc. (to knock on something) стучу́, –и́шь, –áт
Глеб постучал в окно. (Gleb knocked on the window.)

•молчáть || замолчáть (to be silent, [<u>за</u>–: to stop talking]) молчу́, –и́шь, –áт

•поворáчивать[ся] || поверну́ть[ся] (to turn [-<u>ся</u>: intransitive])
поворáчиваю[сь], –ешь[ся], –ют[ся] || поверну́[сь], –ёшь[ся], –у́т[ся]
Я попытался повернуть ключ в скважине, но он не повернулся. (I tried to turn the key in the keyhole, but it did not turn.)

•чтобы (in order to, so that [**SEE** “Примета”])

•уходи́ть || уйти́ (to leave [**SEE** “Песенка о Моцарте”])

•припадáть || припáсть + к + dat. (to press oneself against [often: грудь])
припадáю, –ешь, –ют || припаду́, –ёшь, –у́т (припáл)
N.B. This action is often indicative of strong devotion.

Переведите на русский язык, пользуясь песней и комментариями

1. The nurse **turns** (over) the weak patients **so that** they don't exert themselves, but the others **turn** (over) (by) **themselves**: they **are allowed to turn over** without (any) help.

2. I **know** that the children who[1] **will show up** tomorrow **understand** how important (it is) to **be silent** during the performance.

3. First **someone knocked** on the door, and then **something** creaked outside the **window**. The queen **decided** that at this **late** hour she **could**[2] forget about bravery, and she **summoned** the guards **to her person**. When they **finally showed up**, they found nothing, but she **swore** that she (had) heard **someone**. When she **finally stopped talking**, the guards **looked** out of the **window** and saw only **rain**. The queen **understood** their **silence** and exclaimed: "**Does rain really knock** on bedroom doors?! **After all**, I am not crazy!" Then one guard **left in order to** bring a **hundred** men to the queen's bedroom. Satisfied, she fell asleep and **dreamt** of monsters under the **rain**.

4. A grieving mother **pressed herself against** the tombstone on her son's grave.

5. When smart children hear or see **something**[3] strange **late** at night, they always **turn** (around) and **leave** immediately.

6. The dying count **decided** to **summon** his sons to **his side in order to** tell them about his will, but when they came, (it) was too **late**: their father was already **silent** because God (had) **summoned** his soul before[4] his heirs (had) **shown up**. And so they **turned** (around) and **left**.

7. You **dream of love**, but when it **finally** comes, you might regret it.

8. (It is) **possible** to **say** that **love** is blind, but **even if** (you) close (your) eyes, **even if** (you) plug (your) ears, **can** (one) **really** ignore every single fault in the character of (one's) beloved?

9. "I don't **understand** why you have tattooed a rose on your **chest**." "It's a symbol of **love**."

10. If we **hurry**, we will **solve** our problem **somehow**.

11. Managers **decide** which[5] **matters** are important, and which (ones) are not.

12. A mathematician has only one **thing to do**:[6] he **solves** math problems. A good mathematician never **hurries**. **After all**, only **this way** (is it) **possible** to achieve **something** in math.

13. "**Where** were you **hurrying** last night?" "Home" "And **where** do you live?"

---

[1]**SEE** "тот + кто/который" in "Я вновь повстречался с надеждой."

[2]Present tense. Here "could" has the sense of "is allowed to [by circumstances]."

[3]This is a hypothetical scenario.

[4]Before / after + verb = перед тем / после того + как + verb.

[5]**SEE** "Ещё раз о дураках."

[6]Thing to do = one word.

8 A (Blanks)

_ _ _ _ _(n.: instr.) _ _ _ _ _(adv.)
всё _ _ _ _ _ _ _ _ _ _ _(participle),
и _ _ _ _ _ _(n.) как на _ _ _(n.: prep.)...
Ваше _ _ _ _ _ _ _ _ _ _ _(n.), _ _ _ _ _ _ _ _(n.),
да _ _ _ _ _ _ _(particle) ко мне?

_ _ _ _ _ _ _(adj.) здесь _ _ _ _ _ _ _ _ _ _ _ _ _ _(n.),
с _ _ _ _ _(n.: gen.) _ _ _ _ _ _ _ _(v.) _ _ _ _(n.).
_ _ _ _ _ _ _(n.), ваше _ _ _ _ _ _ _ _ _ _ _(n.),
как вы _ _ _ _ _ _ _ _ _(v.) _ _ _ _(adv.)?

Ах, ваш _ _ _ _ _ _(n.) — как _ _ _ _ _ _ _ _ _(n.).
_ _ _ _ _(adv.) и _ _ _ _ _ _(adv.) _ _ _ _ _ _(v.: inf.)...
Ну, _ _ _ _ _ _ _ _(v.: imperat.), пожалуйста.
Что ж на _ _ _ _ _ _(n.: prep.) _ _ _ _ _ _(v.: inf.)?

Кто вы такая? _ _ _ _ _ _(adv.) вы?
Ах, я _ _ _ _ _ _ _(adj.) _ _ _ _ _ _ _(n.)...
_ _ _ _ _ _(adv.) вы _ _ _ _ _(n.) _ _ _ _ _ _ _ _ _ _ _(v.),
_ _ _ _ _(n.: acc.), _ _ _ _ _(n.) и _ _ _(n.).

8 B (Partial Blanks)

Ть_ _ _(n.: instr.) з_ _ _ _(adv.)
всё зана_ _ _ _ _ _(participle),
и т_ _ _ _ _(n.) как на д_ _(n.: prep.)...
Ваше ве_ _ _ _ _ _ _ _(n.), ж_ _ _ _ _ _(n.),
да неу_ _ _ _(particle) ко мне?

Ту_ _л_ _(adj.) здесь эл_ _ _р_ _ _ _ _ _ _(n.),
с к_ _ _ _(n.: gen.) со_ _ _ _ _(v.) в_ _ _(n.).
Же_ _ _ _ _(n.), ваше вел_ _ _ _ _ _ _(n.),
как вы р_ _ _ _ _ _ _(v.) с_ _ _(adv.)?

Ах, ваш пр_ _ _ _(n.) — как пож_ _ _ _ _(n.).
ды_ _ _(adv.) и тр_ _ _ _(adv.) д_ _ _ _ _(v.: inf.)...
Ну, зах_ _ _ _ _(v.: imperat.), пожалуйста.
Что ж на п_ _ _ _ _(n.: prep.) с_ _ _ _ _(v.: inf.)?

Кто вы такая? От_ _ _ _(adv.) вы?
Ах, я см_ _ _ _ _(adj.) че_ _ _ _ _(n.)...
Пр_ _ _ _(adv.) вы д_ _ _ь(n.) переп_ _ _ _ _(v.),
ул_ _ _(n.: acc.), г_ _ _ _(n.) и в_ _(n.).

Song 8. Ваше величество, женщина

Тьмою здесь всё занавешено,
и тишина как на дне...
Ваше величество, женщина,
да неужели ко мне?

Тусклое здесь электричество,
с крыши сочится вода.
Женщина, ваше величество,
как вы решились сюда?

Ах, ваш приход — как пожарище.
Дымно и трудно дышать...
Ну, заходите, пожалуйста.
Что ж на пороге стоять?

Кто вы такая? Откуда вы?
Ах, я смешной человек...
Просто вы дверь перепутали,
улицу, город и век.

<u>Вопросы по тексту (ответы полными предложениями)</u>:
1) Какое освещение в жилище поэта? 2) Шумно ли у него? 3) С чем сравнивается тишина и почему? 4) Откуда влага капает в жилище поэта? 5) К кому обращается поэт? 6) Как он обращается к женщине, и что это говорит об отношении поэта к ней? 7) Почему поэт удивлён, что женщина пришла к нему? 8) Как он воспринимает ее приход? 9) Оказывает ли поэт гостеприимство незнакомке? 10) Что он хочет узнать о ней? 11) Почему поэта постигает разочарование? 12) Кто эта женщина? 13) Как вы относитесь к рыцарской идее, что женщину следует боготворить и перед ней надо преклоняться?

<u>Комментарии к тексту песни</u>:
•тьма/темнота (darkness, the dark)
  N.B. "Темнота" is a neutral term, while "тьма" has an emotional coloring and is often used figuratively, e.g., to mean "ignorance."
•занаве́шен/а (veiled, curtained [full-form participle: занавешенный/ая])
  ••занаве́шивать || занаве́сить (to veil, to draw a curtain over something)
  занаве́шиваю, –ешь, –ют || занаве́<u>щ</u>у, занаве́сишь, занаве́сят
  Операционный стол был занавешен. Его занавесил хирург.
  (The operating table was curtained off. A surgeon had drawn the curtain over it.)
•дно (bottom [of a body of water or of a vessel, e.g., glass, bowl etc.])

•реша́ться || реши́ться (to bring oneself / dare / get up the courage to...)
решáюсь, –ешься, –ются || решýсь, –и́шься, –áтся
Как вы решились [пойти] на войну?
(How did you get up the courage to go to war?)
N.B. If motion is involved, the verb of motion is often left out.
•к + dat. / у + gen. (to / at someone's place [**SEE** "Старый пиджак"])
•неужели (really [intensifier in questions: sometimes indicates disbelief])
Неужели вы миллионер?! (Are you really a millionaire?!)
•сюда/здесь (here [сюда: with motion; здесь: with location])
•электричество (electricity [general electric power], lighting)
•сочи́ться || просочи́ться (to trickle / ooze) сочýсь, –и́шься, –áтся
Вода сочится с потолка. (Water is trickling from the ceiling.)
•с + gen. (from [a surface: cf. "на + acc./prep."])
На навесе была вода. Вода просочилась **с** навеса в дом.
(There was some water on the lean-to. It trickled from the lean-to into the house.)
••из + gen. (from / out of [an enclosed space: cf. "в + acc./prep."])
Он сидел в самолёте. Он выпал из самолёта.
(He was sitting in a plane. He fell out of the plane)
•пожа́рище (the site of a fire [destructive fire: cf. "пожар" below])
••пожа́р (fire [not general combustion but fire that causes damage.])
••огонь (fire [general combustion: any kind of burning])
••костёр (bonfire, campfire)
•дымно (smoky, full of smoke [дым = smoke])
Здесь очень дымно. (There is a lot of smoke here [it's smoky here].)
•дыша́ть || подыша́ть (to breathe) дышý, ды́шишь, ды́шат
•заходи́ть || зайти́ (to come in / drop by)
захожý, захóдишь, захóдят || зайдý, –ёшь, –ýт
•что ж[е] + inf. (what is the point of doing something)
Что ж[е] читать без очков? (What's the point of reading without glasses?)
N.B. This phrase can mean "what" as an indicator of surprise in questions, e.g., Что ж(е) вы всё забыли!? (What, have you forgotten everything?!)
•порóг (threshold, doorway [на пороге: in the doorway])
•стоя́ть || постоя́ть (to stand [**SEE** "Часовые любви"]
•так (thus, so, this way [такой→ such, so; **SEE** "Старый пиджак"])
•человек (person, man [in the sense of "person." i.e., sexless])
Она — хороший человек. (She is a nice person.)
•пýтать || перепýтать + acc. (to mistake, to get wrong, to get confused)
пýтаю, –ешь, –ют
Я опоздал в кино, потому что я перепутал время сеанса.
(I was late for the film because I had gotten the show time wrong.)
Я часто путаю близнецов. (I often get twins confused.)
••пýтать || запýтать + acc. (to confuse [by misleading or confounding])
Не путайте меня. (Don't confuse me.)

Переведите на русский язык, пользуясь песней и комментариями

1. One day[1] we will **get up the courage** to **drop by**[2] **her place** if she doesn't **drop by here** first.

---

[1] **SEE** "Ещё раз о дураках."
[2] "Dropping by" involves movement to her place.

2. You are **such** a **funny person**: **what is the point of** sewing if the **lighting here** is **so dim**? You will **get** all your fabrics **confused**.
3. Because the juice had **trickled so** quickly **out of** the bottle, only a little bit remained on the **bottom**.
4. Kolia is **so funny**: he always (gets) telephone numbers **wrong**.
5. Because **the curtains were drawn on all the windows**[1] on our **street**, (it) was **difficult** to determine who (was) home.
6. (It) was **smoky** and **difficult to breathe** in Rome because of the **fire**,[2] but in the **darkness** the Romans (could) hear Nero's fiddle.
7. **From** the **roof** I saw a **woman** who[3] was **standing** in the **doorway** of her apartment, but I did not **get up the courage** to wave to her.
8. Who discovered **electricity**? A man or a **woman**? In which[4] **century**?
9. "(Does) **your majesty really** want to abdicate now, and do you **really** want to do it **here** — in this **city**?!" "Yes, I have come **here** today for that (purpose). I (could) not **bring myself** (to do it) for a long time,[5] but now I have **gotten up the courage** (to do it)."
10. "**Come in**." "Oh, sorry, I've **got the wrong door**."
11. **Who is he**? **Where is he from** and why is he **standing** in the **doorway** and not **coming in**?
12. The **woman drew the curtains** on the window and closed all the **doors**.
13. When she was **at her parents' place**, Mila took a log **from** the table, and threw it in the **fire**. Then she took a book **from** her purse and began to read it in the **quiet** of the evening.
14. Only a crazy **person will get up the courage** to dive **to** the very **bottom** of the lake.
15 When predators hunt, they **breathe** very **quietly**. Only in this **quiet** can they catch their prey.
16. The prisoner **confused** his interrogators by his contradictory answers.

---

[1]Lit.: the windows were curtained (off).
[2]This fire is the result of arson.
[3]**SEE** "тот + кто/который" in "Я вновь повстречался с надеждой."
[4]**SEE** "Ещё раз о дураках."
[5]**SEE** "Шёл троллейбус по улице."

9 A (Blanks)

Со _ _ _ _ _(n.: gen.) — _ _ _ _ _ _ _ _(n.) _ _ _ _ _ _ _ _ _ _(adj.)
под _ _ _ _ _ _ _ _ _ _(n.: instr.) _ _ _ _ _ _(adj.) _ _ _(n.).
В том _ _ _ _ _ _ _ _ _(n.: prep.), как в _ _ _ _ _ _ _ _ _(n.),
_ _ _ _ _ _ _ _ _ _(v.) _ _ _ _ _ _(adj.) _ _ _(n.).

Он в _ _ _(n.) _ _ _ _ _ _ _ _(n.: acc.) _ _ _ _ _ _(v.).
_ _ _ _ _ _ _ _(n.) ему как _ _ _(n.).
Все _ _ _ _(n.) _ _ _ _(v.) и _ _ _ _ _ _(v.).
Этот _ _ _ _ _ _(adj.) _ _ _(n.) _ _ _ _ _ _(v.).

Он _ _ _ _ _(adv.) _ _ _ _ _(n.: gen.) не _ _ _ _ _(v.) —
_ _ _ _ _ _ _ _ _ _ _(v.) в _ _ _(n.),
_ _ _ _ _(v.) нас на _ _ _ _ _ _ _ _(adj.) _ _ _ _ _(n.: prep.),
на _ _ _ _ _ _ _ _(n: prep., dimin.) _ _ _ _ _ _ _ _(n.: gen.).

Он и _ _ _ _ _(n.: gen.) не _ _ _ _ _ _ _ _ _(v.) —
_ _ _ _ _ _(adv.) _ _ _(v.) и _ _ _ _ _ _(adv.) _ _ _ _(v.).
_ _ _ _ _ _ _ _(adj.) _ _ _(n.) _ _ _ _ _ _ _ _(n.) _ _ _ _ _ _(v.) —
как по _ _ _ _ _(n.: dat.) _ _ _ _ _ _ _ _ _ _(v.).

Он не _ _ _ _ _ _ _(v.), не _ _ _ _ _ _(v.).
_ _ _ _ _ _(adj.) _ _ _ _(n.) его _ _ _ _ _(v.).
_ _ _ _ _ _(substantivized adj.) сам ему _ _ _ _ _ _ _(v.)
и спасибо _ _ _ _ _ _ _(v.).

Оттого–то, знать, не _ _ _ _ _(adj.: short form)
_ _ _(n.), в _ _ _ _ _ _ _ _ (relative adj.: prep.) мы _ _ _ _ _(v.).
Надо б(ы) _ _ _ _ _ _ _ _(n.: acc., dimin.) _ _ _ _ _ _ _ _ _(v.: inf.) —
_ _ _ _ _(n.: gen.) всё не[1]_ _ _ _ _ _ _ _(v.).

[1]Всё не = idiomatic construction.

9 B (Partial Blanks)

Со дв_ _ _(n.: gen.) — по_ _ _ _ _(n.) из_ _ _т_ _ _(adj.)
под н_ _в_ _ _ _ _(n.: instr.) _ _ _ _ _ _(adj.) _ _ _(n.).
В том подъ_ _ _ _(n.: prep.), как в пом_ _ _ь_(n.),
прож_ _ _ _ _(v.) ч_ _ _ _ _(adj.) _ _ _(n.).

Он в _ _ _(n.) ус_ _ _ _ _(n.: acc.) пр_ _ _ _(v.).
Т_ _н_ _ _(n.) ему как щ_ _(n.).
Все _ _ _ _(n.) п_ _ _(v.) и пл_ _ _ _(v.).
Этот чё_ _ _ _(adj.) к_ _(n.) мо_ _ _ _(v.).

Он д_ _ _ _(adv.) м_ _ _ _(n.: gen.) не л_ _ _ _(v.) —
усм_ _ _ _ _ _ _(v.) в у_ _(n.),
ло_ _ _(v.) нас на ч_ _т_ _ _(adj.) сл_ _ _(n.: prep.),
на ку_ _ _ _ _(n: prep., dimin.) кол_ _ _ _(n.: gen.).

Он и з_ _ _ _(n.: gen.) не про_ _ _ _ _(v.) —
т_ _ _ _ _(adv.) е_ _(v.) и т_ _ь_ _(adv.) пь_ _(v.).
Гр_ _ _ _ _(adj.) п_ _(n.) ког_ _ _ _(n.) тр_ _ _ _(v.) —
Как по го_ _ _(n.: dat.) пос_ _ _ _ _ _(v.).

Он не тр_ _ _ _ _(v.), не пр_ _ _ _(v.).
Жё_ _ _ _(adj.) г_ _ _(n.) его го_ _ _(v.).
К_ _ _ _ _(substantivized adj.) сам ему вы_ _ _ _ _(v.)
и спасибо го_ _ _ _ _(v.).

Оттого–то, знать, не ве_ _ _(adj.: short form)
д_ _(n.), в ко_ _ _ _ _ (relative adj.: prep.) мы ж_ _ _ _(v.).
Надо б(ы) ла_ _ _ _ _ _(n.: acc., dimin.) по_ _ _ _ _ _(v.: inf.) —
де_ _ _(n.: gen.) всё не[1] со_ _ _ _ _(v.).

---

[1]Всё не = idiomatic construction.

Song 9. Чёрный кот

Со двора — подъезд известный
под названием чёрный ход.
В том подъезде, как в поместье,
проживает чёрный кот.

Он в усы усмешку прячет.
Темнота ему как щит.
Все коты поют и плачут.
Этот чёрный кот молчит.

Он давно мышей не ловит —
усмехается в усы,
ловит нас на честном слове,
на кусочке колбасы.

Он и звука не проронит —
только ест и только пьёт.
Грязный пол когтями тронет —
как по горлу поскребёт.

Он не требует, не просит.
Жёлтый глаз его горит.
Каждый сам ему выносит
и спасибо говорит.[1]

Оттого–то, знать, не весел
дом, в котором мы живём.
Надо б(ы) лампочку повесить —
денег всё не соберём.

Вопросы по тексту (ответы полными предложениями):
1) О ком эта песня? 2) Где живёт чёрный кот? 3) С чем сравнивается жилище кота? 4) Как кот себя чувствует в темноте? 5) Чем он отличается от других котов? 6) Какую кошачью работу больше не выполняет кот? 7) Чем он занимается вместо этой работы? 8) Просит ли кот еду? 9) Как жильцы дома ведут себя с этим котом? 10) Что странно в поведении жильцов? 11) Что делает кот, когда ему приносят еду? 12) Как жильцы воспринимают присутствие кота у себя в доме? 13) Почему не весел их дом? 14) Чего нет в подъезде их дома? 15) Почему? 16) Если это аллегория, то что она означает, т.е., кто этот кот с усами и что это за такой невесёлый дом?

---

[1] Stanzas 4 and 5 appear in reverse order in the Frumkin edition.

Комментарии к тексту песни:
•двор (courtyard, court [physical court or royal court, but not a court for trials])
•подъезд (building entrance, driveway)
N.B. Russian apartment buildings often enclose a courtyard and are accessed through several entrances (подъезды) that lead into this courtyard.
•под названием (entitled, named [with reference to **inanimate** nouns only; название: title, name]
Павленко написал роман под названием « Счастье».
(Pavlenko wrote a novel called / entitled *Happiness.*)
Роман называется «Счастье». (The novel is called / entitled *Happiness.*)
Как называется его роман? (What is his novel called?)
•чёрный ход (back door)
•как (like / as) Темнота́ ему как щит. (Darkness is like a shield to him.)
•как будто (as if ["будто" is left out in the song])
Когда кот пол когтя́ми трогает, он как будто по го́рлу скребёт.
(When the tomcat touches the floor with his claws, it is as if he were scratching your throat.)
N.B. In the song the future tense (тро́нет, поскребёт) denotes **habitual** action: the cat always does this.
•прожива́ть (to reside) прожива́ю, –ешь, –ют
•пря́тать[ся] || спря́тать[ся] (to hide [-ся: to hide oneself])
пря́чу[сь], пря́чешь[ся], пря́чут[ся]
Перед налётом я спрятал деньги, а потом спрятался в подвале.
(Before the raid I hid the money, and then I hid in the basement.)
•тьма/темнота (darkness, the dark [**SEE** "Ваше величество, женщина"])
•петь || спеть (to sing [**SEE** "Песенка старого шарманщика"])
•пла́кать || запла́кать (to cry [**SEE** "Песенка о голубом шарике"])
•молча́ть || замолча́ть (to be silent, [за–: to stop talking]) молчу́, –и́шь, –а́т
•давно (for a long time, long ago [**SEE** "Шёл троллейбус по улице"])
•лови́ть || пойма́ть (to catch)
ловлю́, ло́вишь, ло́вят || пойма́ю, –ешь, –ют
•лови́ть || пойма́ть на [честном] слове (to use someone's own words / promises against that person)
Он нас ловит на слове. (He uses our own words / promises against us.)
N.B. "Лови́ть || пойма́ть на кусочке колбасы" in the song means to trap someone with a piece of lunch meat (as bait), i.e., it's a pun.
•усмеха́ться || усмехну́ться (to smirk)
усмеха́юсь, –ешься, –ются || усмехну́сь, –ёшься, –у́тся
•колбаса (lunch meat, cold cuts [the translation "sausage" may be misleading])
•тре́бовать || потре́бовать + у + gen. + acc./partitive gen. (to demand)
тре́бую, –ешь, –ют
Он потребовал у меня паспорт. (He demanded [my] passport from me.)
•проси́ть || попроси́ть + у + gen. + acc./partitive gen. (to ask someone for...)
прошу́, про́сишь, про́сят
Он попросил у меня мяч/бумаги. (He asked me for a ball/some paper.)
••проси́ть || попроси́ть + acc. + inf. (to ask someone to...)
Он попросил меня дать ему отдохнуть. (He asked me to let him rest.)
••спра́шивать || спроси́ть + acc. (to ask someone [for information])
спра́шиваю, –ешь, –ют || спрошу́, спро́сишь, спро́сят
Мы спросили его, сколько ему лет. (We asked him how old he was.)
••задава́ть || зада́ть + dat. + вопрос (to ask someone a question)

задаю́, –ёшь, –ют ||
задáм, задáшь, задáст, зададúм, зададúте, зададýт
Я ей зáдал вопрос. (I asked her a question.)
•горéть || сгорéть (to burn [intransitive; с–: to burn down])
горю́, –и́шь, –я́т
Дом сгорел. (The house burned down.)
••жечь || сжечь + acc. (to burn [transitive; с–: to burn something down/completely; под–: to set fire to something; за– to ignite, to light, to turn on {electricity or an electric light}])
жгу, жжёшь, жжёт, жжём, жжёте, жгут ||
сожгý, сожжёшь, сожгýт etc. / подожгý etc.
(поджёг/подожгла, сжёг/сожгла)
Она сожгла / подожгла дом. (She burned the house down / set fire to it.)
•каждый (every, each [when not modifying a noun: everyone, all])
•выноси́ть || вы́нести (to take out)
выношý, выно́сишь, выно́сят || вы́несу, –ешь, –ут
Я вынес собаке миску супа. (I took a bowl of soup out to the dog.)
•сам/á/ó/сáми ([by] oneself, without being asked, on one's own initiative)
Кáждый сам котý выно́сит.
(Everyone takes [food] out to the cat without being asked/forced.)
Они сами не пришли, но прислали своих детей.
(They did not come themselves, but sent their children.)
Петя завязал шнурки сам. (Petia tied his shoelaces [all] by himself)
•говори́ть || сказáть (to speak / talk / tell [perf.: to say / tell one thing])
говорю́, –и́шь, –я́т || скажý, скáжешь, скáжут
•не пророни́ть ни звýка / ни сло́ва (not to utter a sound / word)
не пророню́, не проро́нишь, не проро́нят [perf. only]
•есть || съесть (to eat) ем, ешь, ест, еди́м, еди́те, едя́т
•тро́гать || тро́нуть (to touch) тро́гаю, –ешь, –ют || тро́ну, –ешь, –ут
•скрести́ || поскрести́ (to scratch with something hard [claws])
скребý, –ёшь, –ýт (скрёб/скреблá)
•оттого–то (that is why)
•знать (apparently, probably, I guess, something must be the case)
Знать он врёт. (I guess he is / he must be lying.)
•вéсел/веселá (jolly, joyful, in a good mood [**SEE** "Старый король"])
•жить || пожи́ть (to live [**SEE** "Песенка о голубом шарике"])
•надо + б[ы] + inf. (one should [**SEE** "dat. + бы + inf./noun" in "Примета")
•вéшать || повéсить (to hang something / someone)
вéшаю, –ешь, –ют || повéшу, повéсишь, повéсят
••висéть || повисéть (to hang [intransitive]) вишý, виси́шь, вися́т
Он повесил ленту на шесте, но она повисела недолго и улетела.
(He hung a ribbon on a pole, but it didn't hang there long before it flew off.)
•лáмпочка (light bulb [лáмпа = lamp])
•повесить лампочку (to put in / screw in / install a lightbulb)
•собирáть || собрáть (to collect / gather)
собирáю, –ешь, –ют || соберý, –ёшь, –ýт
•всё (still [often used with "ещё"], everything)
Он всё [ещё] не сделал работу. (He still hasn't finished the job.)
•всё не + future perf. (cannot manage to / get around to do something)

Мы всё не соберём денег на лампочку.
(We just can't manage to collect enough money to buy a new light bulb)
Мы всё не поедем к ней. (We just can't get around to visiting her.)

Переведите на русский язык, пользуясь песней и комментариями

1. Okudzhava wrote a **famous** song **called "Black Cat**." This is not a **jolly** song.

2. The tomcat **did not utter a sound** when the vet **touched** him. Then the vet **smirked** and **asked** the cat's owner: "(Has) your cat (been) **eating** rotten **lunch meat for a long time**?"

3. The junk dealer always **demands** a lot of **money from** his customers for his old **lamps** even though he sells them without **light bulbs**.

4. I (just) **can't get around to taking** (some) food (out to) the **cat**. **I guess that is why** it is **still catching mice** at night and **scratching** the door when we **eat**.

5. The owner of the **estate** said to his guest: "You may **live** here as long as you want." The guest was (as) sly **as** a fox. He **used the host's own words against him** and said: "Fine, I will **live** here until you **ask** me to leave."[1]

6. When my son washed the **dirty yellow floor on his own initiative**, I **said**: **"Thank you**."

7. **I guess** this singer always **drinks** vodka before[2] he **sings**: **that is why** his songs are so **jolly**. But after his concerts he **won't utter a sound** and **just drinks** and **drinks**.

8. The **cat** thinks that it **has eaten** all the **lunch meat**, but I **have hidden a piece** for another day. It **still** doesn't know that.

9. The child (began to) **cry** because it was afraid of the **dark**. Later he **asked** me to **install a light bulb** in our (building) **entrance**.

10. "I have always **hanged**, I always **hang** and I will always **hang** all criminals. When I **gather** a big enough group, I **will hang** them **all**," said the **jolly** judge, and my **throat** constricted... "He will **probably hang** me too," I thought and **touched** my **throat**.

11. Yesterday the acrobat **hung** on the trapeze **for a long time**. He **hangs** there very often, and he is afraid every time. **That is why** he closes (his) **eyes**. But he **hides** his fear in order[3] not to ruin the **joyful** atmosphere of the circus.

12. The cat **caught a mouse** in the **yard, touched** its **throat** (with its) **claws**, but did not **eat** it.

---

[1]**SEE** "Песенка о Моцарте."
[2]Before / after + verb = перед тем / после того + как + verb.
[3]**SEE** "Примета."

13. The **back entrance** of the **estate** was in the **courtyard**. I am **saying** "was" because the whole **estate burned down** yesterday. The east wall is **still burning**.

14. The police have **gathered** all the books in the dissident's house and **burned** them. Now they are **asking** his neighbors various **questions** about him.

15. The baker **stopped talking** and **kept silence for a long time**. Then he **asked** me **a question**.

16. (We) **should collect** (some) **money** for the man with the **black moustache** who **lives** in the **dirty building** across the street. He is very poor and **eats** only **black** bread and cheap **cold cuts**. He can't **live** like that **for a long time**.

17. **Everyone**, or at least **every** historian, knows that **shields** became obsolete when gunpowder was invented.

18. The woman who **collects** rare stamps has **resided** in this **house for a long time**.

19. There are five **entrances** in our **building**.

20. If someone[1] **sets fire** to this **building**, it **will burn down**.

---

[1]**SEE** "Шёл троллейбус по улице."

10 A (Blanks)

_ _ _ _(numeral) _ _ _ _ _ _(n.) на _ _ _ _ _(n.: prep.) _ _ _(v.),
_ _ _ _ _ _ _ _ _(adj.) и _ _ _ _ _ _ _ _ _(adj.),
Но он _ _ _ _ _ _ _ _ _(n.: instr.) _ _ _ _ _ _ _ _(adj.) был —
_ _ _ _(conj.) был _ _ _ _ _ _(n.) _ _ _ _ _ _ _ _ _(adj.).

Он _ _ _ _ _ _ _ _ _ _ _(v.: inf.) _ _ _(n.) _ _ _ _ _(v.),
чтоб(ы) был _ _ _ _ _ _ _ _ _ _ _(adj.: instr.)
_ _ _ _ _ _(substantivized adj.),
а сам на _ _ _ _ _ _ _ _(n.: prep., dimin.) _ _ _ _ _(v.) —
_ _ _ _(conj.) был _ _ _ _ _ _(n.) _ _ _ _ _ _ _ _ _(adj.).

Он был бы _ _ _(short-form adj.) —
в _ _ _ _ _(n.) и в _ _ _(n.),
за вас _ _ _ _ _ _ _ _ _ _(v.: inf.) _ _ _ _ _ _(adv.),
но _ _ _ _ _ _ _ _ _ _ _(v.) вы над ним:
_ _ _ _(conj.) был _ _ _ _ _ _(n.) _ _ _ _ _ _ _ _ _(adj.).

Не _ _ _ _ _ _ _ _ _(v.) вы ему
своих _ _ _ _ _ _ _ _ _(n.: gen.) _ _ _ _ _ _(adj.).
А почему? А потому,
что был _ _ _ _ _ _(n.) _ _ _ _ _ _ _ _ _(adj.).

А он, _ _ _ _ _ _(n.: acc.) свою _ _ _ _ _(verbal adv.),
не _ _ _ _ _(adj.) _ _ _ _ _(n.: gen.) _ _ _ _ _ _(v.)
и всё _ _ _ _ _ _(v.): « _ _ _ _(n.)! _ _ _ _(n.)!»,
_ _ _ _ _(verbal adv.), что он _ _ _ _ _ _ _ _ _(adj.).

В _ _ _ _ _(n.)? Ну, что ж, _ _ _(v.: imperat.)! _ _ _ _ _(v.)?
И он _ _ _ _ _ _(v.) _ _ _ _ _ _ _ _(adv.).
И там _ _ _ _ _ _(v.) он ни за _ _ _ _(n.) —
_ _ _ _(conj.) был _ _ _ _ _ _(n.) _ _ _ _ _ _ _ _ _(adj.).

10 B (Partial Blanks)

О_ _ _(numeral) _ _ _ _ _ _(n.) на с_ _ _ _(n.: prep.) _ _ _(v.),
кр_ _ _ _ _ _(adj.) и отв_ _ _ _ _(adj.),
но он иг_ _ _ _ _ _(n.: instr.) де_ _ _ _ _(adj.) был —
_ _ _ _(conj.) был _ _ _ _ _ _(n.) _ _ _ _ _ _ _ _ _(adj.).

Он перед_ _ _ _ _(v.: inf.) м_ _(n.) х_ _ _ _(v.),
чтоб(ы) был сч_ _т_ _ _ _ _(adj.)
к_ _ _ _ _(substantivized adj.),
а сам на ни_ _ _ _ _(n.: prep., dimin.) в_ _ _ _(v.) —
_ _ _ _(conj.) был _ _ _ _ _ _(n.) _ _ _ _ _ _ _ _ _(adj.).

Он был бы р_ _(short-form adj.) —
в _ _ _ _ _(n.) и в д_ _(n.),
за вас пог_ _ _ _ _ _(v.: inf.) д_ _ _ _ _(adv.),
Но пот_ _ _ _ _ _ _(v.) вы над ним:
_ _ _ь(conj.) был _ _ _ _ _ _(n.) _ _ _ _ _ _ _ _ _(adj.).

Не дов_ _ _ _ _(v.) вы ему
своих се_ _ _ _ _ _(n.: gen.) ва_ _ _ _(adj.).
А почему? А потому,
что был с_ _ _ _ _(n.) б_ _ _ _ _ _ _(adj.).

А он, с_ _ь_ _(n.: acc.) свою кл_ _ _(verbal adv.),
не т_ _ _ _(adj.) ж_ _н_(n.: gen.) жа_ _ _ _(v.)
и всё пр_ _ _ _(v.): « _ _ _ _(n.)! _г_ _(n.)!»,
за_ _ _(verbal adv.), что он бу_ _ _ _ _ _(adj.).

В о_ _ _ _(n.)? Ну, что ж, _ _ _(v.: imperat.)! и_ _ _ь(v.)?
И он ша_ _ _ _(v.) од_ _ _ _ _(adv.).
И там сг_ _ _ _(v.) он ни за г_ _ _(n.) —
в_ _ь(conj.) был со_ _ _ _(n.) бум_ _ _ _ _(adj.).

Song 10. Бумажный солдат

Один солдат на свете жил,
красивый и отважный,
но он игрушкой детской был —
ведь был солдат бумажный.

Он переделать мир хотел,
чтоб(ы) был счастливым каждый,
а сам на ниточке висел[1]—
ведь был солдат бумажный.

Он был бы рад — в огонь и в дым,
за вас погибнуть дважды,
но потешались вы над ним —
ведь был солдат бумажный.

Не доверяли вы ему
своих секретов важных.
А почему? А потому,
что был солдат бумажный.

А он, судьбу свою кляня,
не тихой жизни жаждал
и всё просил: «Огня! огня!»
забыв, что он бумажный.

В огонь? Ну, что ж, иди! Идёшь?
И он шагнул однажды.
И там сгорел[2] он ни за грош —
ведь был солдат бумажный.

Вопросы по тексту (ответы полными предложениями):
1) Был ли солдат привлекателен и смел? 2) Из чего был сделан солдат? 3) Что хотел сделать солдат? 4) Зачем он хотел переделать мир? 5) Почему он не мог переделать мир? 6) Что он был готов сделать? 7) Для кого он был готов это сделать? 8) Как обращались с солдатом? 9) Что ему не доверяли? 10) На каком основании? 11) О какой жизни мечтал солдат? 12) Чего просил солдат и почему это было опасно особенно для него? 13) Какой безумный шаг сделал солдат? 14) Какую категорию людей символизирует этот солдат?

---

[1]Variant: "но над кроваткой всё висел."
[2]"Погиб" in the Frumkin edition.

Комментарии к тексту песни

•солдат (soldier, private [irregular genitive plural: много солдат])

•один (a, a certain, alone, one, nothing but, no one but, only)

Я знаю одно дешёвое кафе. (I know a [certain] cheap café.)

•свет (light, world) мир (world)

N.B. Usage nuances: переделать мир, страны мира, весь мир/свет, на свете (in the world).

••мир (peace)

Они за мир во всём мире. (They stand for world peace.)

•жить || пожи́ть (to live [**SEE** "Песенка о голубом шарике"])

•ведь (after all [**SEE** "Шёл троллейбус по улице"])

•де́лать || переде́лать (to do / make [пере–: to change / redo])

де́лаю, –ешь, –ют

Я переделаю это упражнение. (I will redo this exercise.)

••сде́лать (to do [non-specific perfective counterpart of "де́лать"])

•чтобы (so that, to, in order to [**SEE** "Примета"])

•каждый (every, each [when not modifying a noun: everyone, all])

•сам/а́/о́/са́ми (myself, yourself, herself etc. [**SEE** "Чёрный кот"])

•висе́ть || повисе́ть (to hang [**SEE** "Чёрный кот")

•past tense form + бы (would, would have)

Он был бы рад [броситься] в огонь и в дым.

(He would have been glad to jump in the fire and smoke.)

•рад/а/ы + что/inf. (glad that / to)

N.B. Used as a predicate regarding gladness about something specific.

Она ра́да, что вы пришли. (She is glad that you have come.)

Сергей был рад вам помочь. (Sergei was glad to help you.)

•счастливый (happy, lucky)

N.B. The short-form "счастлив" can replace "рад" (above), but it indicates a much greater intensity of happiness (being thrilled). Without "что/inf." it indicates a state of happiness in a specific happiness-generating context, e.g. "Она с ним / здесь счастлива. (She is happy with him / here [the happiness-generating context is "с ним / здесь"]).

The full form "счастливый" can mean "happy" outside a specific happiness-generating context, e.g., Он очень счастливый человек (He is a very happy person), or it can mean "lucky/fortunate."

•огонь (fire [**SEE** "Ваше величество, женщина"])

•погиба́ть || поги́бнуть (to perish, to die [not of natural causes], to be killed)

погиба́ю, –ешь, –ют || поги́бну, –ешь, –ут (perf.: поги́б/поги́бла)

••умира́ть || умере́ть (to die [a non-violent death: of natural causes])

умира́ю, –ешь, –ют || умру́, умрёшь, умру́т (perf.: у́мер/умерла́)

N.B. Unless there are concrete reasons for using "погиба́ть || погибну́ть," the normal translation of "to die" is "умира́ть || умере́ть."

•потеша́ться || потёшиться + над + instr. (to make fun of, to mock)

потеша́юсь, –ешься, –ются || потёшусь, –ишься, –атся

•доверя́ть || дове́рить (to trust) доверя́ю, –ешь, –ют || дове́рю, –ишь, –ят

Мы ему дове́рили свои деньги. (We trusted him with our money.)

•судьба (fate, life, life story)

•свой (my, your, his, her, its, our, their [**SEE** "Примета"])

N.B. "Свой" can replace "мой, твой" etc. In the third person "свой" is mandatory if the possessor and the possessed thing appear in the same clause, and the possessor is the subject; otherwise "его, её, их" have to be used.

Я взял мои/свои деньги. (I took my money [no difference in meaning].)
Он потратил свои деньги, и теперь его деньги потрачены.
(He spent his [own] money, and now his money is spent [in the second clause there is no possessor-subject.])
Он взял его деньги. (He took his [not his own] money.)
N.B. In impersonal constructions with "logical" subjects "свой" is also used:
Ему нужно повидаться со своим сыном (He has to see his [own] son).

•кляня́ (cursing [verbal adverb])
••клясть || прокля́сть (to curse) кляну́, –ёшь, –у́т
Осенью я всегда кляну погоду. (In the fall I always curse the weather.)
Он проклял свою судьбу. (He cursed his fate.)

•жа́ждать + gen./infin. (to thirst / yearn for) жа́жду, –ешь, –ут
N.B. This is used with abstract concepts.
Она жаждала славы. (She yearned for glory.)

•проси́ть || попроси́ть (to ask [**SEE** "Чёрный кот"])
•забы́в (having forgotten [from "забы́ть": **SEE** "Дежурный по апрелю"])
•идти́ || пойти́ (to go / come / walk [**SEE** "Шёл троллейбус по улице"])
•шага́ть || шагну́ть (to march/step [**SEE** "Песенка старого шарманщика"])
•однажды/когда–нибудь (one day [**SEE** "Ещё раз о дураках"])
•горе́ть || сгоре́ть (to burn [**SEE** "Чёрный кот"])
•ни за грош ([to perish/die] in vain, for nothing)

Переведите на русский язык, пользуясь песней и комментариями

1. Even though **everyone** thinks that he[1] will **change** the **world**, we are all **toys** of **fate**, and our **life hangs on a thread**. We know that **one day** we **will all die**.

2. **One day** all these **brave soldiers** will **perish for nothing** in some (kind of)[2] war, and we will **forget** them. **After all**, at war **everyone dies** in a way[3] **in vain**.

3. Only **handsome** and **happy soldiers** will **march** around[4] the city **so that** our **brave** army does not frighten the population.

4. Why is Mila **cursing her happy life** in the countryside? **After all**, she **lives** so well! She **herself** told me that she is so **happy** there, and I was **glad** to hear it.

5. Even if we **live** twenty more years together, I will never **trust** him (with) anything:[5] even my **paper toys**.

6. We are **thrilled** that you have finally bought **paper** and **thread**. Now you can[6] **make children's toys** (by) **yourself**.

7. The whole[7] **world** knows that **fire** creates **smoke**.

---

[1]"Everyone" is masculine unless it refers to women only.
[2]**SEE** "Шёл троллейбус по улице."
[3]In a way = в каком–то смысле.
[4]**SEE** "verb of motion + по + dat." in "Шёл троллейбус по улице."
[5]**SEE** "ни[interrog. word]" in "Примета."
[6]**SEE** "О Володе Высоцком."
[7]**SEE** "Песенка о старом короле."

8. "**Why** do you **make fun of** our **soldiers**? Every day they **die for you** in battle." "Do you think that I **ask them** to **die for me**?"

9. I knew **a** (certain) man whose house (had) **burned down twice**. Afterwards he **asked me for** a fire extinguisher and **hung** it by **his** door. This fire extinguisher **hung** there for a long time.[1] It is probably still **hanging** there even though this man **died** last year.

10. She **thirsts** to find out[2] all **his important secrets**, and when he **forgets** to keep his mouth shut, he **trusts** her (with) information that she should not know.

11. **Everyone** knows that all living creatures and plants **die** in **fire**.

12. **Having forgotten** all its troubles, the dog **died quietly** in (its) sleep.

13. "**Private** Lutsenko, **step** forward. Have you **redone** all the work that you had **done** so poorly." "Yes." "Good. Now you **will go** to your regiment."

14. "Where in the **world** is there **quiet life** and **peace**?" "Why are you **asking** such funny **questions**?"

15. All day (long) the father **cursed his** son because the boy (had) **burnt** all of **his** father's **important papers**. Now he will never **trust his** son (with) the key to the office.

16. If you **hang** this **paper** doll over a **fire**, it will **burn** (up).

17. **One day a** (certain) **soldier went** to a sewing shop and **asked** the salesman for **thread**. Then he **asked** him how much the **thread** costs.[3]

18. According to the Old Testament, God **cursed** Cain.

19. Blessed are those who **thirst** for righteousness.

20. I gave her **her** books. She loves **her** books.

---

[1]**SEE** "Шёл троллейбус по улице."
[2]**SEE** "Часовые любви."
[3]**SEE** "Часовые любви."

11 A (Blanks)

_ _ _ _ _ _ _ _(n.: dimin.) _ _ _ _ _(v.),
_ _ _ _ _ _(n.) _ _ _ _ _ _(v.).
_ _ _ _ _ _(adv.) ж так _ _ _ _ _ _(n.) _ _ _ _ _ _ _ _(v.)?
Там за _ _ _ _ _ _ _ _ _(n.: instr.),
_ _ _ _ _ _ _(adj.: short form) собóю,[1]
п_ _ _(n.) _ _ _ _ _(n.: gen.)[2] _ _ _ _ _(v.)
_ _ _ _ _(preposition) _ _ _ _ _ _(n.: instr.).

_ _ _ _ _ _ _(n.) _ _ _ _ _ _ _ _ _(v.),
_ _ _ _ _(n.) _ _ _ _ _ _ _ _ _ _ _ _(v.),
кто кому _ _ _ _ _ _ _ _ _ _(v.) _ _ _ _ _ _(v.).
_ _ _ _ _ _ _(n.) _ _ _ _ _ _ _ _ _(v.),
_ _ _ _ _(n.) _ _ _ _ _ _ _ _ _ _ _ _(v.).
кто кому _ _ _ _ _ _ _ _ _ _(v.) _ _ _ _ _ _(v.).

Но _ _ _ _ _ _ _ _ _(n.) _ _ _ _ _ _ _(adj.),
на _ _ _ _ _ _(adj.) _ _ _ _ _ _(n.: prep.),
_ _ _ _ _ _ _(v.): « Да что ж вы всё _ _ _ _ _ _(v.)?
_ _ _ _ _(n.) были в _ _ _ _ _(n.: acc.);
_ _ _ _ _(adv.)[3] _ _ _ _ _ _ _ _ _ _ _(n.),
с _ _ _ _ _ _ _ _(n.: gen.) — _ _ _ _ _(n.) и нет _ _ _ _ _ _ _ _(n.: gen.).
А на _ _ _ _(n.: prep.) _ _ _ _ _(n.: gen.)
_ _ _ _ _ _(n.) _ _ _ _ _ _(v.) _ _ _ _ _(adv.).
_ _ _ _ _(v.)[4] не _ _ _ _ _ _ _ _ _(v.), _ _ _ _ _(v.: inf.) не буду.
А на _ _ _ _(n.: prep.) _ _ _ _ _(n.: gen.)[5]
_ _ _ _ _ _(n.) _ _ _ _ _ _(v.) _ _ _ _ _(adv.).
_ _ _ _ _(v.) не _ _ _ _ _ _ _ _ _(v.), _ _ _ _ _(v.: inf.) не буду».

(continued)

[1] The last two words constitute an idomatic construction. The instrumental ending –оюis archaic/poetic. The standard ending is –ой.
[2] This masculine noun has an irregular genitive plural.
[3] Archaic.
[4] Here this verb implies the word "быть."
[5] The last two words constitute an archaic/poetic idiomatic construction.

_ _ _ _ _ _ _ _(n.) не _ _ _ _ _ _(v.),
в _ _ _ _ _ _ _ _(n.: dimin.) _ _ _ _ _ _ _ _(v.).
_ _ _ _ _ _ _ _ _ _(adv.) , что _ _ _ _ _ _ _ _(adv.)
_ _ _ _ _ _ _ _ _ _ _ _(v.).
Вы, мол, _ _ _ _ _ _ _ _ _(v.: imperat.),
если вам _ _ _ _ _ _(n.),[6]
да[7] не _ _ _ _ _ _ _ _ _ _ _(v.: imperat.) из _ _ _ _ _ _ _(n.: gen.).

_ _ _ _ _ _ _ _ _ _(n.: dimin.) _ _ _ _ _ _(v.),
_ _ _ _ _ _ _(n.) _ _ _ _ _ _ _(v.).
_ _ _ _ _ _ _(adv.) ж так _ _ _ _ _ _ _(n.) _ _ _ _ _ _ _ _ _ _(v.)?
_ _ _ _ _ _ _ _ _ _(n.: dimin.) _ _ _ _ _ _(v.),
_ _ _ _ _ _ _(n.) _ _ _ _ _ _ _(v.).
_ _ _ _ _ _ _(adv.) ж так _ _ _ _ _ _ _(n.) _ _ _ _ _ _ _ _ _ _(v.)?

---

[6]"Вам _ _ _ _ _(n.)" constitutes an idiomatic construction.
[7]Here "да" = "но."

11 B (Partial Blanks)

С_ _ _ _ _ _ _(n.: dimin.) _ _ _ _ _(v.),
_ _ _ _ _ _(n.) _ _ _ _ _ _(v.).
_ _ _ _ _ _(adv.) ж так _ _ _ _ _ _(n.) _ _ _ _ _ _ _ _ _(v.)?
Там за пов_ _ _ _ _ _(n.: instr.),
нед_ _ _ _(adj.: short form) собóю,[1]
п_ _ _(n.) гу_ _ _(n.: gen.)[2] с_ _ _ _(v.)
п_ _ _ _(preposition) то_ _ _ _(n.: instr.).

Б_ _ _ _ _ _(n.) к_ _ _ _ _ _ _(v.),
_ _ _ _ _(n.) пре_ _ _ _ _ _ _ _ _(v.),
кто кому до_ _ _ _ _ _ _ _(v.) р_ _ _ _ _(v.).
Ба_ _ _ _ _(n.) кр_ _ _ _ _ _ _(v.),
т_ _ _ _(n.) предвк_ _ _ _ _(v.),
кто кому дост_ _ _ _ _ _(v.) ре_ _ _ _(v.).

Но пол_ _ _ _ _ _(n.) гл_ _ _ _ _(adj.),
на гн_ _ _ _(adj.) ко_ _ _ _(n.: prep.),
г_ _ _ _ _ _(v.): « Да что ж вы всё за_ _ _ _(v.)?
т_ _ц_(n.) были в ср_ _ _(n.: acc.);
ны_ _ _(adv.)[3] воск_ _ _ _ _ _ _(n.),
с чет_ _ _ _ _(n.: gen.) — во_ _ _(n.) и нет спа_ _ _ _ _(n.: gen.).
А на _ _ _ _(n.: prep.) б_ _ _ _(n.: gen.)
с_ _ _ _ _(n.) г_ _ _ _ _(v.) _ _ _ _ _(adv.).
М_ _ _ _(v.)[4] не ве_ _ _ _ _ _(v.), в_ _ _ _(v.: inf.) не буду.
А на п_ _ _(n.: prep.) бр_ _ _(n.: gen.)[5]
см_ _ _ _(n.) гу_ _ _ _(v.) в_ _ _ _(adv.).
Мо_ _ _(v.) не верн_ _ _ _(v.), вр_ _ _(v.: inf.) не буду».

(continued)

[1]The last two words constitute an idiomatic construction. The instrumental ending –ою is archaic/poetic. The standard ending is –ой.
[2]This masculine noun has an irregular genitive plural.
[3]Archaic.
[4]Here this verb implies the word “быть.”
[5]The last two words constitute an archaic/poetic idiomatic construction.

Бар_ _ _ _(n.) не в_ _ _ _(v.),
в ку_ _ _ _ _(n.: dimin.) см_ _ _ _ _(v.).
Нев_ _ _ _ _(adv.), что впр_ _ _ _(adv.)
расс_ _ _ _ _ _(v.).
Вы, мол, пово_ _ _ _(v.: imperat.),
если вам ох_ _ _(n.),[6]
да[7] не опо_ _ _ _ _ _(v.: imperat.) из по_ _ _ _(n.: gen.).

Со_ _ _ _ _ _(n.: dimin.) с_ _ _ _(v.),
м_ _ _ _ _(n.) и_ _ _ _ _(v.).
О_ _ _ _ _(adv.) ж так с_ _ _ _ _(n.) за_ _ _ _ _ _(v.)?
Сол_ _ _ _ _(n.: dimin.) си_ _ _(v.),
му_ _ _ _(n.) иг_ _ _ _(v.).
От_ _ _ _(adv.) ж так с_ _д_ _(n.) зам_ _ _ _ _(v.)?

[6]“Вам _ _ _ _ _(n.)” constitutes an idiomatic construction.
[7]Here “да” = “но.”

Song 11. Солнышко сияет

Солнышко сияет, музыка играет.
Отчего ж так сердце замирает?
Там за поворотом, недурён собою,
полк гусар стоит перед толпою.

Барышни краснеют, танцы предвкушают,
кто кому достанется решают.
Барышни краснеют, танцы предвкушают,
кто кому достанется решают.

Но полковник главный,
на гнедой кобыле,
говорит: «Да что ж вы всё забыли?
Танцы были в среду;
нынче воскресенье, с четверга — война
и нет спасения. А на поле брани
смерть гуляет всюду. Может не вернёмся,
врать не буду. А на поле брани
смерть гуляет всюду. Может не вернёмся, врать не буду».

Барышни не верят, в кулачки смеются.
Невдомёк, что вправду расстаются.
Вы, мол, повоюйте,[1]
если вам охота,
да не опоздайте из похода.

Солнышко сияет,
музыка играет.
Отчего ж так сердце замирает?
Солнышко сияет,
музыка играет.
Отчего ж так сердце замирает?

Вопросы по тексту (ответы полными предложениями):
1) В какую эпоху происходит действие? 2) Какая стоит погода? 3) Что говорит о праздничной атмосфере в этой сцене? 4) Почему собралась толпа? 5) Почему девушки краснеют? 6) Где они собираются встретиться с офицерами? 7) Как они относятся к этой встрече? 8) Что они обсуждают? 9) Кто начальник полка? 10) Какая у него лошадь? 11) О чём полковник напоминает молодым людям? 12) Почему полковник допускает, что полк не вернётся с войны? 13) Как девушки реагируют на слова полковника? 14) Как они рассматривают военный поход? 15) О чём девушки просят офицеров? 16) Ответьте на вопрос, заданный в конце песни? 17) Какой основной контраст в тоне и содержании этой песни? 18) Какой эффект создаётся, благодаря совмещению темы войны и дней недели?

Комментарии к тексту песни
•сия́ть || засия́ть (to shine / beam): сия́ю, –ешь, –ют
•игра́ть || заигра́ть (to play [**SEE** "Песенка о Моцарте"])
•отчего (why, for what reason])
  ••заче́м (why, what for [for what purpose; cf. для чего])
•так (thus, so, this way [такой→ such, so; **SEE** "Старый пиджак"])
•замира́ть || замере́ть (to become still, stop moving, to "freeze")

[1]"Погуляйте" in the Frumkin edition.

замира́ю, –ешь, –ют || замру́, –ёшь, –у́т (perf.: за́мер/за́мерла)
•за поворотом (around the bend)
•недурён/недурна́ (pretty good, not bad [full-form adj.: недурной/ая])
•недурной/ая собой (attractive, good-looking)
•стоя́ть || постоя́ть (to stand [**SEE** "Часовые любви"])
•перед (before, in front of [**SEE** "Батальное полотно"])
•барышня (young lady: archaic [cf. барин/барыня: gentleman/woman])
•красне́ть || покрасне́ть (to blush) красне́ю, –ешь, –ют
•танцы (dance [a party with dancing], dancing)
У нас в школе были танцы. (There was a dance at our school.)
••танец (dance [a particular kind of dance, e.g., the polka, the tango])
•танцева́ть || потанцева́ть (to dance)
танцу́ю, –ешь, –ют +сс.
•предвкуша́ть (to look forward to, to anticipate with pleasure)
предвкуша́ю, –ешь, –ют
•dat. + доста́ться || достава́ться + acc. (to get / receive [when things are divided up/ sold]) достаётся –ю́тся || доста́нется, –утся
Мне досталась конфета. (I got a candy [when candy was divided up].)
N.B. With negative-> gen. and neuter verb: Мне не доста́ло́сь конфе́ты.
•реша́ть || реши́ть (to decide/ [re]solve [**SEE** "Он, наконец, явился в дом"])
•главный/ая (main, head, chief, primary, principal, key [when not modifying a noun: the boss, the head person etc.])
•гнедой (bay [about horses: reddish-brown horse with a black tail and mane])
•говори́ть || сказа́ть (to speak / talk / tell [**SEE** "Чёрный кот"])
•что ж[е] (what!? [**SEE** "Ваше величество, женщина"])
•забыва́ть || забы́ть (to forget) забыва́ю, –ешь, –ют || забу́ду, –ешь, –ут
•с + point in time [gen.] ([starting] from / as of a point in time)
Клуб закрыт с полудня. (The club is closed from noon.)
•воскресенье (Sunday [cf. воскресение: resurrection])
•от + gen. + dat. + нет спасения (there is no escape from, to be doomed)
От гриппа в этом году никому нет / не было / не будет спасения.
(This year there is / was / will be no escape from the flu for anyone.)
У нас предателям нет спасения. (In our country traitors are doomed.)
N.B. "Спасение" means literally "salvation."
•поле брани (field of honor [battlefield: poetic/archaic])
•гуля́ть || погуля́ть (to be all over [the place], to be everywhere)
гуля́ю, –ешь, –ют
N.B. This verb normally means "to stroll," but it can be used figuratively with such nouns as "смерть" or "ветер" to convey the idea of omnipresence or movement in different directions, e.g., Ветер гуляет по полю (The wind is blowing all over the field).
•может [быть] (maybe, possibly [without "быть": colloquial])
•возвраща́ть[ся] || верну́ть[ся] (**SEE** "Песенка о голубом шарике")
•врать || навра́ть (to lie, to deceive [colloquial]) вру, врёшь, врут
•ве́рить || пове́рить + dat. (to believe someone): ве́рю, –ишь, –ят
Я вам не верю. (I don't believe you.)
••ве́рить || пове́рить + в + acc. (to believe in something)
Она верит в дружбу. (She believes in friendship.)
••ве́рить || пове́рить + что (to believe that...)
Мы верим, что он вернётся. (We believe that he'll be back.)
•смея́ться || засмея́ться (to laugh [за–: to burst out laughing; по-: to have a laugh])

смею́сь, –ёшься, –ю́тся

•dat. + невдомёк (it doesn't occur to someone that...)

Ребёнку [было/будет] невдомёк, что в мире есть страдание.

(It does [did/will] not occur to the child that there is suffering in the world.)

•вправду (for real, indeed, truly, really)

•расстава́ться || расста́ться + с + instr. (to part [with someone])

расстаю́сь, –ёшься, –ю́тся || расста́нусь, расста́нешься, расста́нутся

Собака нехотя рассталась с костью.

(The dog parted with its bone unwillingly.)

•мол (to say [colloquial word used to introduce paraphrased speech], as if to say)

Она, мол, ничего не знает и ничего не видела.

(She says that she does not know and has not seen anything.)

Она на меня посмотрела, мол: хватит хулиганить!

(She looked at me, as if to say: stop fooling around!)

•воева́ть || повоева́ть (to fight [military conflict]) вою́ю, –ешь, –ют

•dat. + охота + infinitive (to feel like doing something)

Мне [была] охота [пойти] в кино. (I feel [felt] like going to the movies.)

•опа́здывать || опозда́ть + на/в + acc. (to be late for)

опа́здываю, –ешь, –ют || опозда́ю, –ешь, –ют

N.B. The past perfective means **a)** "someone is late" with reference to the present moment and **b)** "someone was late." The present tense of this verb conveys generally occuring lateness.

"Я опоздал?" "Да ты опоздал. Ты всегда опаздываешь."

("Am I late?" "Yes, you are late. You are always late.")

N.B. This verb answers the question "куда/откуда" [not "где"].

•похо́д (hiking trip, war, military expedition [**SEE** "Часовые любви"])

Переведите на русский язык, пользуясь песней и комментариями

1. The **colonel's** face was **beaming** because he heard **music**: an orchestra was **playing before** the **crowd**.

2. **Around** the **bend** we saw a **regiment** that was **returning** from the **field of honor**.

3. The **young ladies** naively **believed** that the **hussars** (would) **return** on **Wednesday** or **Thursday**, and they were getting ready for the **dance** and **looking forward to** the **music**. They wanted to try (out) a new **dance** in order to[1] impress the **regiment**.

4. "I **feel like** going to the **dance** on **Wednesday**." "You **forget** that **as of Sunday** there will be no more **dancing**." "Oh, pity! On **Thursday**, because I **was late for** the **dance**, **I did not get** a ticket. Therefore, I **stood before** the door and looked in but did not **dance**."

5. "Why did this **young lady blush**?" "Because the **colonel** from the **hussar**[2] **regiment**, you know, the **good looking** (one), this **colonel** has conquered

---

[1]**SEE** "Примета."

[2]The suffix –ск– is required here to turn this noun into an adjective.

[3]Lit.: to make a proposal to her.

her **heart**, and she knows that he has **decided** to propose to her.[3] I did not **believe** her when she **told** me. I thought she (was) **lying**,[1] but he **really** will propose to her. **Maybe** he will do it today. **It doesn't even occur to her** that although he rides[2] a **bay mare** and has **fought** in many **wars**, he is a **liar** and a coward on the **field of honor**. One of his **hussars told** me that his **regiment** is afraid to go on **a military expedition** with him, and everyone **laughs** at him. Of course he has **told** her how he **fought** in dangerous places where **death was everywhere** and how, when his bullets ran out,[3] he attacked the enemy with his **fists**. I think that **she doesn't feel like** admitting[4] the truth, and she is listening only to (her) **heart**. She loves him so much that she will never **part** with him. Yesterday, when he **was late** and did not **return** when he (had) promised, she waited (for) him all night and **froze** at every sound. **There is no escape** for anyone **from** Cupid's arrows, and probably **there will be no escape from** them for us. **For what reason** this is so, I don't know. I know that I **will not solve** this problem.

6. **For what purpose** do countries **everywhere fight** for a place under the **sun**?

7. "Where is the bus stop?" "**Around the bend.** But you **are late**: the bus has gone (away). Here people **are often late** for the bus, because the stop is so far away."

8. I **believe** you when you **say** that you **believe** in God and that after **death** we all **return** to Him.

9. The **mare** came up to its trough, **as if to say**: feed me!

---

[1]Present tense.
[2]**SEE** "Ночной разговор."
[3]**SEE** "Часовые любви."
[4]**SEE** "Часовые любви."

12 A (Blanks)

_ _ _ _ _ _ _(n.). _ _ _ _ _ _ _(n.). _ _ _ _ _ _(n.: gen.) _ _ _ _ _(n.)
_ _ _ _ _ _ _(adj.). _ _ _ _ _ _ _(adj.) _ _ _ _ _ _ _(n.).
На _ _ _ _ _ _ _ _(adj.) _ _ _ _ _ _(n.: prep.) _ _ _ _(v.)
_ _ _ _ _ _ _ _ _(n.) в _ _ _ _ _ _ _(adj.) _ _ _ _ _ _ _(n.: prep.).
_ _ _ _ _(adj.) _ _ _ _ _ _(n.) с _ _ _ _ _ _(adj.) _ _ _ _ _ _ _(n.: instr.),
с _ _ _ _ _ _(n.: instr.) _ _ _ _ _ _ _(adj.).
_ _ _ _ _ _ _(adj.) _ _ _ _ _ _(n.). _ _ _ _ _ _(n.) за _ _ _ _ _ _(n.: instr.),
как _ _ _ _ _(preposition) _ _ _ _ _ _(n.: instr.).

_ _ _ _ _(adv.) за _ _ _ _ _ _ _ _ _ _ _(n.: instr.) _ _ _ _(v.)
_ _ _ _ _ _ _ _(n.), _ _ _ _ _ _ _ _(n.) _ _ _ _ _(n.: gen.):
_ _ _ _ _ _(n.: instr.) _ _ _ _ _(participle), _ _ _ _ _ _ _(n.: instr.)
_ _ _ _ _ _ _(participle), только не _ _ _ _ _(participle).
_ _ _ _ _ _(adv.) — _ _ _ _ _ _ _ _(n.),
_ _ _ _ _ _ _-_ _ _ _ _ _ _ _ _(n.):
_ _ _ _ _ _(v.) _ _ _ _ _ _ _(n.).
Все они _ _ _ _ _ _ _ _(n.), все они _ _ _ _ _ _ _(n.),
все они _ _ _ _ _(n.).

Всё _ _ _ _ _ _(adj.: comparative) _ _ _ _ _(n.) _ _ _ _ _ _ _(adj.)
_ _ _ _ _ _ _ _ _ _(n.: gen.), _ _ _ _ _ _(n.) _ _ _ _ _(adj.).
Только _ _ _ _ _(n.) _ _ _ _ _ _(adj.),
_ _ _ _ _ _(n.: gen.) _ _ _ _ _(n.)
_ _ _ _ _ _ _(adj.) да[1] _ _ _ _ _ _ _(n.) _ _ _ _(adj.).
Всё _ _ _ _ _ _(adj.: comparative) _ _ _ _ _(n.) _ _ _ _ _(n.: gen.)
и _ _ _ _(n.: gen.), _ _ _ _ _ _(n.: gen.) и _ _ _ _ _(n.: gen.).
Где–то под _ _ _ _ _ _(n.: instr.) да над _ _ _ _ _ _ _ _(n.: instr.) —
_ _ _ _(particle) _ _ _ _ _(n.) и _ _ _ _(n.),
_ _ _ _(particle) _ _ _ _ _(n.) и _ _ _ _(n.),
_ _ _ _(particle) _ _ _ _ _(n.) и _ _ _ _(n.)...

[1]Here “да” = “и.”

12 B (Partial Blanks)

Сум_ _ _ _(n.). При_ _ _ _(n.). Фл_ _ _ _(n.: gen.) г_ _ _ _(n.)
не_ _ _ _ _(adj.). П_ _д_ _ _(adj.) ка_ _ _и_(n.).
На пер_ _ _ _ _(adj.) ло_ _ _ _(n.: prep.) _ _ _ _(v.)
им_ _ _ _ _ _ _(n.) в го_ _ _ _ _(adj.) каф_ _ _ _(n.: prep.).
Б_ _ _ _(adj.) ко_ _ _ _(n.) с ка_ _ _ _(adj.) гл_ _ _ _ _(n.: instr.),
с чё_ _ _ _(n.: instr.) во_ _ _ _ _(adj.).[1]
Кр_ _ _ _ _(adj.) по_ _ _ _(n.). Кр_ _ _ _(n.) за сп_ _ _ _(n.: instr.),
как п_ _ _ _(preposition) во_ _ _ _(n.: instr.).

Вс_ _ _(adv.) за импе_ _ _ _ _ _ _(n.: instr.) е_ _ _(v.)
ге_ _ _ _ _ _(n.), ген_ _ _ _ _(n.) св_ _ _(n.: gen.):
сл_ _ _ _(n.: instr.) ув_ _ _(participle), шр_ _ _ _ _(n.: instr.)
пок_ _ _ _(participle), только не уб_ _ _(participle).
Сл_ _ _ _(adv.) — дуэ_ _ _ _ _(n.),
фли_ _ _ _–адъ_ _ _ _ _ _(n.):
бл_ _ _ _(v.) эпо_ _ _ _(n.).
Все они кра_ _ _ _ _(n.), все они тал_ _ _ _(n.),
все они п_ _ _ _(n.).

Всё с_ _ _ _ _(adj.: comparative) зв_ _ _(n.) пр_ _ _ _ _(adj.)
клав_ _ _ _ _ _(n.: gen.), го_ _ _ _(n.) бы_ _ _(adj.).
Только т_ _ _ _(n.) ме_ _ _ _(adj.),
фле_ _ _(n.: gen.) го_ _ _(n.)
нер_ _ _ _(adj.) да[2] над_ _ _ _(n.) з_ _ _(adj.).
Всё сл_ _ _ _(adj.: comparative) за_ _ _(n.) оч_ _ _(n.: gen.)
и д_ _ _(n.: gen.), мо_ _ _ _(n.: gen.) и хл_ _ _(n.: gen.).
Где–то под но_ _ _ _(n.: instr.) да над го_ _ _ _ _ _(n.: instr.) —
_ _ _ _(particle) _ _ _ _ _(n.) и _ _ _ _(n.),
_ _ _ _(particle) з_ _ _ _(n.) и _ _ _ _(n.),
л_ _ _(particle) зе_ _ _(n.) и н_ _ _(n.)...

---

[1]Attention should be paid to the stress here: this is not a bird.
[2]Here "да" = "и."

Song 12. Батальное полотно

Сумерки. Природа. Флейты голос нервный. Позднее катание.
На передней лошади едет император в голубом кафтане.
Белая кобыла с карими глазами, с чёлкой воронóю.
Красная попона. Крылья за спиною, как перед войною.

Вслед за императором едут генералы, генералы свиты,
славою увиты, шрамами покрыты, только не убиты.
Следом — дуэлянты, флигель–адъютанты: блещут эполеты.
Все они красавцы, все они таланты, все они поэты.

Всё слабее звуки прежних клавесинов, голоса былые.
Только топот[1] мерный, флейты голос нервный да надежды злые.
Всё слабее запах очага и дыма, молока и хлеба.
Где–то под ногами да над головами — лишь земля и небо,
лишь земля и небо, лишь земля и небо...

Вопросы по тексту (ответы полными предложениями):
1) Какой вид искусства напоминает эта песня? 2) Можно ли сказать, что действие происходит в современную эпоху? Объясните свой ответ 3) В какое время суток движется эта кавалькада? 4) Какие звуки упоминаются в этом описании? 5) Кто находится во главе кавалькады? 6) Как он одет? 7) Опишите его лошадь. 8) Из кого состоит свита императора? 9) Какие детали говорят о боевом стаже генералов? 10) Что общего у членов свиты? 11) По каким признакам мы понимаем, что кавалькада удаляется? 12) Всё ли благополучно в этом обществе? 13) Какое настроение создаёт эта песня–картина?

Комментарии к тексту песни
- катание (horseback riding and any other kind of pleasure riding)
- éхать || поéхать (to go/drive/ride [**SEE** “Ночной разговор”])
- кáрий (dark-brown [with reference to eye color])
- чёлка (forelock [on the forehead of a horse], bangs [on a human head])
- воронóй/áя (black [with reference to horses])

  N.B. Do not confuse with “ворóна” (crow) and “вóрон” (raven).

  N.B. The ending -ою in the instrumental is archaic/poetic.
- перед + instr. (before [with reference to space or time], in front of)

  Перед едой надо помыться. (Before eating we should wash up.)

  Перед нами был лес. (Before us stood a forest.)
- verb of motion + вслед за / следом за + instr. (to follow, to go behind)

  Я шёл вслед за / следом за коровой. (I was following a cow.)

  N.B. After “следом,” the “за + instr.” combination may be dropped if it is already clear who is being followed, e.g., “Он вышел. Следом вышла его дочь.” (He went out. His daughter followed [him].)

---

[1]“Цокот” in the Frumkin edition.

•уви́т/а славой (crowned with glory [full-form participle: увитый/ая])
Генералы были увиты славой. (The generals were crowned with glory.)
•покрыт/а + instr. (covered with / in [full-form participle: покрытый/ая])
Его руки были покрыты шрамами.
(His hands were covered with scars).
••покрыва́ть || покры́ть (to cover [to be all over])
покрыва́ю, –ешь, –ют || покро́ю, –ешь, –ют
Шрамы покрывали его руки. (Scars covered his arms.)
•убит/а (killed, murdered [full-form participle: убитый/ая])
••убива́ть || уби́ть (to kill/murder)
убива́ю, –ешь, –ют || убью́, –ёшь, –ю́т
•блесте́ть || блесну́ть (to shine/sparkle)
блещу́, блести́шь/бле́щешь, блестя́т/бле́щут || блесну́, –ёшь, –у́т
•всё + adj. [comparative] (to keep getting/become increasingly ADJECTIVEer)
Запах молока [был/будет] всё слабее и слабее.
(The smell of milk keeps [kept/will keep] getting weaker.)
•былой (bygone [elevated style]) прежний (former, past [adj.])
•мерный (regular [evenly paced action], rhythmic, measured)
•топот (tread [sound of feet / hooves hitting the ground])
•[кто/где/как/что/какой]–нибудь (some-[one/where/how/thing/kind of]; **SEE** "Шёл троллейбус по улице")
•лишь (only, nothing but [more emphatic than "только"])

Переведите на русский язык, пользуясь песней и комментариями

1. The old **general** has[1] such a **weak** voice, and I think that it **keeps getting weaker and weaker** as he ages.

2. The emperor loved[2] (horseback) **riding** in **nature**, especially in the **twilight**. His whole **retinue followed** him on these **late** promenades: from the court **poets** to the **generals**. Their swords **glittered** under the evening **sky**, and the **regular tread** of their **horses** was accompanied by the **sounds** of **flutes** and drums. One day,[3] **somewhere** in the woods a very **nervous mare** was frightened by a strange **sound**. The **emperor's aide-de-camp** was **riding** this **horse** far from the others, and when the **mare** jerked, he fell and was almost **killed** by the fall. The horse lost its **blue horse-cloth**, and the **aide-de-camp** was **white** from fright. His **back** was all dirty, his **caftan** was **covered** with dust and he had lost one of his **epaulets**. He saw that the **mare's front leg** (was) broken. Then he heard the **tread** of other **horses**: **someone** was **riding** toward him. He hoped that **someone** (would) help him, but his **hope** was in vain.[4] On the **front horse** he saw one of his worst enemies: the famous **dueller** Naryshkin. He was a **good-looking man**[5]

---

[1]**SEE** "у + possessor [gen.]" in "Молитва (Франсуа Вийона)."
[2]**SEE** "Ещё раз о дураках."
[3]**SEE** "Ещё раз о дураках."
[4]**SEE** "Я вновь повстречался с надеждой."
[5]Good-looking man = one word.

but a very **malicious** person. He had a real **talent** (for) insulting[1] his friends. He stroked the **black forelock** of his **horse** and said to the **aide-de-camp**: "Now you will return **crowned with glory**, and you will show all your **scars** to the ladies."

3. "Did Pegasus have [dark] **brown eyes**?" "Who was Pegasus?" "It was a **horse** with **wings**. In **bygone** times he flew[2] **above** the **earth**, and the **regular sound** of his **wings** was often heard in the **sky over** Greece."

4. **Before** (horseback) **riding**, I advise you to drink (some) **milk**, eat (some) **bread** and relax **in front of** the **hearth**, otherwise you will get tired very quickly. And since you are a **weak** rider, I **will ride** my pony **behind** you.

5. When I hear the **harpsichord**, I think of the **regular sound** of a **horse's** hooves. I (can) even sense the **smell** of horses. It's **like** a hallucination.

6. My **former house** is **somewhere** in this neighborhood.

7. The **smell** of **smoke** reminds me of **war**, **nervous horses** and **killed** soldiers.

---

[1]Infinitive.

[2]**SEE** "Песенка о голубом шарике."

13 A (Blanks)

_ _ _ _ _ _ _ _ _(v.: imperat.) _ _ _ _ _ _(n.: dat.),
что так _ _ _ _ _ _ _ _ _ _(adj.: short form) бывает она.
_ _ _ _ _ _(adv.) мы _ _ _ _ _ _(v.),
когда над _ _ _ _ _ _(n.: instr.) _ _ _ _ _ _(v.) _ _ _ _ _(n.).
И _ _ _ _ _(n.: instr.) _ _ _ _ _ _ _ _ _(adj.)
по _ _ _ _ _ _ _ _ _ _(n.: dat. dimin.) _ _ _ _ _ _(adj.) —
_ _ _ _ _ _ _ _ _(n.: gen.) нет...
_ _ _ _(particle) _ _ _ _ _(adj.) _ _ _ _ _(n.),
как _ _ _ _ _(adj.) _ _ _ _ _ _(n.), _ _ _ _ _ _(v.)
тебе _ _ _ _ _ (adv.).
_ _ _ _(particle) _ _ _ _ _(adj.) _ _ _ _ _ (n.),
как _ _ _ _ _ (adj.) _ _ _ _ _ _(n.), _ _ _ _ _ _(v.)
тебе _ _ _ _ _(adv.).

Не _ _ _ _ _ _ (v.: imperat.) _ _ _ _ _ _ (n.: dat.),
когда _ _ _ _ _ _ _ _ _(adj.) _ _ _ _ _(n.) она _ _ _ _(v).
Не _ _ _ _ _ _(v.: imperat.) _ _ _ _ _ _(n.: dat.),
когда она _ _ _ _ _ _(adj.) _ _ _ _ _(n.) _ _ _ _(v.).
Не _ _ _ _ _ _(v.: imperat.), не _ _ _ _ _ _(v.: imperat.),
когда по _ _ _ _ _(n.: dat.)
_ _ _ _ _ _ _ _ _(v.) _ _ _ _ _ _ _(n.):
у _ _ _ _ _(n.: gen.) со _ _ _ _ _ _ _(n.: instr.)
ещё не _ _ _ _ _ _ _ _ _(participle) _ _ _ _ _(n.) свои.
у _ _ _ _ _(n.: gen.) со _ _ _ _ _ _ _(n.: instr.)
ещё не _ _ _ _ _ _ _ _ _(participle) _ _ _ _ _(n.) свои.

Нас _ _ _ _ _(n.) _ _ _ _ _(v.):
_ _ _ _(v.: imperat.) по–_ _ _ _ _ _ _ _ _ _ _ _(adv.),
дверь _ _ _ _ _ _ (verbal adv.)...
_ _ _ _ _ _ _(n.) _ _ _ _ _ _ _(n.),
а всё же _ _ _ _ _ _ _ _ _ _(adj.: short form)
_ _ _ _ _ _ _ _ _ _(n.) твоя.
_ _ _ _ _ _(adv.) ты в _ _ _ _ _ _ (n.: prep.), и только _ _ _ _(numeral)
_ _ _ _ _ _ _ _ _(v.) от _ _ _(n.: gen.):
Чего ж мы _ _ _ _ _ _ (v.),
когда над _ _ _ _ _ _ (n.: instr.) _ _ _ _ _ _ _ (v.) _ _ _ _ _(n.)?
Куда ж мы _ _ _ _ _ _(v.),
когда над _ _ _ _ _ _ (n.: instr.) _ _ _ _ _ _ _ (v.) _ _ _ _ _(n.)?

13 B (Partial Blanks)

Про_ _ _ _ _(v.: imperat.) _ _ _ _ _ _(n.: dat.),
что так нера_ _ _ _ _(adj.: short form) бывает она.
В_ _ _ _ _(adv.) мы _ _ _ _ _ _(v.),
когда над _ _ _ _ _ _(n.: instr.) _ _ _ _ _ _(v.) _ _ _ _ _(n.).
И ш_ _ _ _(n.: instr.) неве_ _ _ _(adj.)
по лест_ _ _ _ _(n.: dat. dimin.) ша_ _ _ _(adj.) —
спа_ _ _ _ _(n.: gen.) нет...
_ _ _ _(particle) _ _ _ _ _(adj.) ве_ _ _(n.),
как _ _ _ _ _(adj.) сё_ _ _ _(n.), гл_ _ _ _(v.)
тебе вс_ _ _(adv.).
Л_ _ _(particle) б_ _ _ _(adj.) вер_ _(n.),
как бе_ _ _(adj.) сёс_ _ _(n.), гля_ _ _(v.)
тебе всл_ _(adv.).

Не _ _ _ _ _ _ (v.: imperat.) по_ _ _ _(n.: dat.),
когда затя_ _ _ _(adj.) до_ _ _(n.) она ль_ _(v).
Не _ _ _ _ _ _(v.: imperat.) пе_ _ _ _(n.: dat.),
когда она бр_ _ _ _(adj.) п_ _ _ _(n.) п_ _ _(v.).
Не в_ _ _ _ _(v.: imperat.), не ве_ _ _ _(v.: imperat.),
когда по са_ _ _(n.: dat.)
закр_ _ _ _(v.) сол_ _ _ _(n.):
у ж_ _ _ _(n.: gen.) со с_ _ _ _ _ _(n.: instr.)
ещё не ок_ _ _ _ _ _(participle) с_ _ _ _(n.) свои.
у жи_ _ _(n.: gen.) со см_ _ _ _ _(n.: inst.)
ещё не ок_ _ч_ _ _(participle) сч_ _ _(n.) свои.

Нас вр_ _ _(n.) уч_ _ _(v.):
Ж_ _ _(v. imperat.) по–при_ _ _ _ _ _ _ _(adv.),
дверь отв_ _ _(verbal adv.)...
Тов_ _ _ _(n.) муж_ _ _ _(n.),
а всё же зам_ _ _ _ _ _(adj.: short form)
долж_ _ _ _ _(n.) твоя.
Вс_ _ _ _(adv.) ты в пох_ _ _(n.), и только о_ _ _(numeral)
отр_ _ _ _ _(v.) от с_ _(n: gen.):
Чего ж мы у_ _ _ _ _(v.),
когда над зе_ _ _ _(n.: instr.) бу_ _ _ _(v.) в_ _ _ _(n.)?
Куда ж мы ух_ _ _ _(v.),
когда над зем_ _ _(n.: instr.) буш_ _ _(v.) ве_ _ _(n.)?

Song 13. Простите пехоте

Простите пехоте,
что так неразумна бывает она.
Всегда мы уходим,
когда над землёю бушует весна.
И шагом неверным
по лестничке шаткой — спасения нет...
Лишь белые вербы,
как белые сёстры, глядят тебе вслед.
Лишь белые вербы,
как белые сёстры, глядят тебе вслед.

Не верьте погоде,
когда затяжные[1] дожди она льёт.
Не верьте пехоте,
когда она бравые песни поёт.
Не верьте, не верьте,
когда по садам закричат соловьи:
у жизни со смертью
ещё не окончены счёты свои.
У жизни со смертью
ещё не окончены счёты свои.

Нас время учило:
живи по–привальному, дверь отворя...
Товарищ мужчина, а всё же заманчива должность твоя.
Всегда ты в походе, и только одно отрывает от сна:
чего ж мы уходим, когда над землёю бушует весна?
Куда ж мы уходим, когда над землёю бушует весна?

Вопросы по тексту (ответы полными предложениями):
1) Какая главная тема этой песни? 2) О чём поэт просит слушателя? 3) В чём заключается неразумность пехоты? 4) Кто/что провожает пехоту? 5) Почему не следует верить погоде? 6) Почему нельзя верить бравым песням пехоты? 7) Чьё пение так же обманчиво, как песни пехоты и погода? 8) Почему? 9) Как следует жить солдатам и почему? 10) Чем хороша роль мужчин? 11) Но что странно в этой роли? 12) Что означает фраза о счётах, которые сводят жизнь и смерть? 13) Чем отличаются два вопроса, заданные в конце песни?

Комментарии к тексту песни
•проща́ть || прости́ть + dat. + что/acc. (to forgive someone something)
проща́ю, –ешь, –ют || прощу́, прости́шь, простя́т

[1]"Проливные" in the Frumkin edition.

Я ему простил, что он потерял мою собаку.
(I forgave him for losing my dog.)
Он мне простил вчерашнюю обиду. (He forgave me yesterday's offense.)
••прощáть || простúть + acc. (to forgive someone)
Она его простила. (She forgave him.)
•так (thus, so, this way [такой→ such, so; **SEE** "Старый пиджак"])
•неразýмен/неразýмна (unreasonable, irrational, silly [full-form adj.: неразýмный/ая])
•бывáть (to be/happen/visit) бывáю, –ешь, –ют
N.B. This verb indicates **occasional** "being," events and visits.
Это бывает весной. (This happens in spring.)
Она бывает в Туле. (She sometimes visits Tula.)
В молодости я бывала наразумна. (In my youth I was at times silly.)
•уходúть || уйтú (to leave, to go off [**SEE** "Песенка о Моцарте"])
•бушевáть || забушевáть (to rage) бушýю, –ешь, –ют
На море бушевал шторм. (A storm was raging at sea.)
•шаг (step [foot movement], stride)
•невéрный (shaky / uncertain [movement], incorrect)
•шаткий (shaky [object])
Шаткая лестница [лестничка - diminutive]. (Shaky ladder/stairs.)
•нет спасения (there is no escape, to be doomed [**SEE** "Солнышко сияет"])
•лишь (only, nothing but [more emphatic than "только"])
•глядéть || взглянýть + на + acc. (to peer / look at)
гляжý, глядúшь, глядя́т || взглянý, взгля́нешь, взгля́нут
•глядеть + dat. + вслед (to follow with one's eyes [**SEE** "Шёл троллейбус по улице"])
•вéрить || повéрить (**SEE** "Солнышко сияет")
•затяжной/ая (prolonged [excessively])
•лить || полúть (to pour [по–: to water; про–: to spill) лью, льёшь, льют
Они лили слёзы (They were crying [lit. "pouring tears"])
Лить воду. (To pour water.) **N.B.** Лил дождь. (It was raining.)
N.B. To make "пролить" imperfective we cannot remove про– from it, since that would change "spill" into "pour." A **derived imperfective** is needed in such a situation, and it is created by the addition of one of three suffixes: ива/ыва, ва or а/я. Hence "пролить" becomes "проливать:" проливáю, –ешь, –ют.
•бравый (gallant, manly)
•петь || спеть (to sing [**SEE** "Песенка старого шарманщика"])
•по + dat. [plur.] (throughout [places])
По лесам распускались листики.
(Leaves were opening up throughout the forests.)
•кричáть || закричáть (to shout/yell/scream) кричý, –úшь, –áт
•счёты (accounts / scores [settled for past wrongs])
У Пети с тобой свои счёты. (Petia has accounts to settle with you.)
••сводúть || свестú счёты + с + instr. (to settle accounts / scores)
свожý, свóдишь, свóдят || сведý, –ёшь, –ýт
Он свёл счёты с врагами. (He settled his scores with his enemies.)
•свой (my, your, his, her, its, our, their [**SEE** "Бумажный солдат"])
•окончен/а (finished) Работа окончена. (The work is done/finished.)
••кончáть[ся] || [о]кóнчить[ся] (to end [**SEE** "Часовые любви"])
•учúть || научúть (to teach [**SEE** "Ещё раз о дураках"])
•жить || пожúть (**SEE** "Песенка о голубом шарике")
•по–привальному (on the go [привал: a rest-stop made during a hiking trip])

•отворя́ (having opened [door/window])

••отворя́ть || отвори́ть (to open [door/window])
отворя́ю, –ешь, –ют || отворю́, –и́шь, –я́т

•всё же (still, nevertheless)

•зама́нчив/а (tempting, enticing [full-form adj.: заманчивый/ая])

•должность (job, position [in a job])

•похо́д (hiking trip, war, military expedition [**SEE** "Часовые любви"])

•acc. + отрыва́ть || оторва́ть + от + gen. (to prevent from)
отрыва́ю, –ешь, –ют || оторву́, –ёшь, –ут
Неприятная мысль меня отрывает от сна.
(An unpleasant thought keeps preventing me from sleeping.)

•чего же (why then [colloquial])

•где/куда (where [**SEE** "Он, наконец, явился в дом"])

Переведите на русский язык, пользуясь песней и комментариями

1. Please **forgive** me (for) **spilling** the juice. When I **pour** juice or water, I always **spill** it.

2. My sisters **are**[1] (sometimes) **so irrational**: sometimes they **sing** constantly and **prevent me from** working, but I **forgive** these "**nightingales**."

3. Sleep **is**[2] **always so tempting** during a **rest-stop** when we are on a **hike**.

4. When I **leave** (from) home in the morning, I never **believe** the **weather**: after a sunny morning, (it) often **rains**.

5. In 1918 a civil war **raged** in Russia. The Reds and the **Whites** were **settling scores**. Many **men** were **going off to war**, **death** was everywhere, and **there was no escape** for many villages **from** bandits.

6. In **spring** the **nightingales scream throughout the gardens**, fields and meadows. Their **songs end** only when (it) **rains**.

7. The baby walked (with) **uncertain steps** toward the **willow**.

8. Even if we **sing gallant songs**, **life** in the **infantry** is dangerous, and in wartime **there is no escape** for soldiers from fear and suffering.

9. Sergei **opened** the **door** and **left**. Ania **followed him with her eyes** and realized that their love (was) **finished**.

10. When war comes, **we will be doomed**.

11. "Is your **comrade** experiencing strong pain?" "No." "**Why then** is he **screaming**?" "He is a town crier: **screaming** is his **job**."

12. "**Only** children will **believe** in your **shaky** theory." "**Why then did** your **sister believe** in it?"

13. "Do you **believe** in the **salvation** of the soul?" "It's an **enticing** idea."

14. There was a **time** when pterodactyls circled[3] **above** the **earth**.

---

[1]Occasional "being" is involved here.
[2]**SEE** previous note.
[3]**SEE** "Примета."

15. The guru **teaches** his students[1] meditation and (how) **to live** peacefully.

16. If you value your **life**, don't walk under a **ladder**, especially if it is **shaky**.

17. **Death** came to her after a **prolonged** illness, and all her **comrades** were with her when she died.[2]

18. This translation is **finished**. I **always finish** everything quickly because **time** is money.

---

[1]"Студент" is used only with respect to a university/college setting.
[2]**SEE** "Бумажный солдат."

14 A (Blanks)

Я _ _ _ _ _(adv.) _ _ _(n.: gen.) _ _ _ _ _ _ _(n.) _ _ _ _(v.):
_ _ _ _ _(adv.) _ _ _ _ _ _ _ _(v.) и не _ _ _(adj.: short form) он.
И я _ _ _ _(v.) к себе _ _ _ _ _ _ _ _ _(substantivized adj.: acc.),
и _ _ _ _ _ _ _ _ _(v.: inf.) _ _ _ _ _ _ _(n.) _ _ _ _ _(v.).

Я _ _ _ _ _ _ _(v.) ему, _ _ _ _(verbal adv.),
« _ _ _ _ _ _ _ _ _ _ _(v.: imperat.) всё _ _ _ _ _(adv.).
_ _ _ _ _(v.) мне новые _ _ _ _ _(n.)
_ _ _ _ _ _ _ _ _ _(n.) _ _ _ _ _ _ _(n.: gen.) и _ _ _ _ _(n.: gen.)».

Я _ _ _ _ _ _ _ _(v.), а он _ _ _ _ _ _ _(n.)
_ _ _ _ _ _ _ _ _(adv.) так _ _ _ _ _ _ _ _ _ _ _(v.),
а сам так всё _ _ _ _ _ _ _ _ _ _ _(v.):
вдруг что не так[1] — такой _ _ _ _ _(n.)!

_ _ _ _(numeral) _ _ _ _ _ _ _(n.) _ _ _ _ _(adv.)
в его _ _ _ _ _ _ _ _(n.: prep.) _ _ _ _ _ _ _ _ _ _ _(adj.):
чтобы я _ _ _ _ _ _ _ _ _(v.) _ _ _ _ _ _ _ _ _ _ _(adj.: instr.)
в том _ _ _ _ _ _ _ _(n.: prep.), _ _ _ _(adv.) _ _ _ _(v.).

Он _ _ _ _ _ _ _ _ _ _ _ _ _(v.) это так:
_ _ _ _(adv.) _ _ _ _(particle) я _ _ _ _ _ _ _(n.) _ _ _ _ _ _ _ _(v.),
_ _ _ _ _(adv.) в твою _ _ _ _ _ _ _(n.) _ _ _ _ _ _(v.)...
Как бы не так[2] — такой _ _ _ _ _(n.)!

_ _ _ _ _(adv.) в твою _ _ _ _ _ _ _(n.) _ _ _ _ _ _(v.)...
Как бы не так — такой _ _ _ _ _(n.)!

---

[1]Вдруг что не так = what if something goes wrong?
[2]Как бы не так = no way!

14 B (Partial Blanks)

Я м_ _ _ _(adv.) л_ _(n.: gen.) _ _ _ _ _ _(n.) н_ _ _(v.):
Д_ _ _ _(adv.) пот_ _ _ _(v.) и не н_ _(adj.: short form) он.
И я з_ _ _(v.) к себе пор_ _ _ _ _(substantivized adj.: acc.),
и пере_ _ _ _(v.: inf.) _ _ _ _ _ _(n.) пр_ _ _(v.).

Я г_ _ _ _ _(v.) ему, ш_ _ _(verbal adv.),
« Перек_ _ _ _ _(v.: imperat.) всё ин_ _ _(adv.).
С_ _ _ _(v.) мне новые уд_ _ _(n.)
иск_ _ _ _ _ _(n.) кр_ _ _ _(n.: gen.) и ш_ _ _ _(n.: gen.)».

Я пош_ _ _ _(v.),[1] а он п_ _ _ _ _(n.)
сер_ _ _ _ _(adv.) так переш_ _ _ _ _(v.),[2]
а сам так всё переж_ _ _ _ _(v.):
вдруг что не так[3] — такой ч_ _ _ _(n.)!

О_ _ _(numeral) за_ _ _ _(n.) ная_ _(adv.)
в его ус_ _ _ии(n.: prep.) мол_ _ _ _ _ _ _(adj.):
чтобы я выг_ _ _ _ _(v.) сча_ _ _ _ _ _ _(adj.: instr.)
в том пи_ _ _ _ _(n.: prep.), п_ _ _(adv.) ж_ _ _(v.).

Он предс_ _ _ _ _ _ _(v.) это так:
е_ _ _(adv.) л_ _ _(particle) я пид_ _ _(n.) прим_ _ _(v.),
о_ _ _ _(adv.) в твою лю_ _ _ _(n.) по_ _ _ _(v.)...
Как бы не так[4] — такой чу_ _ _(n.)!

Оп_ _ _(adv.) в твою люб_ _ _(n.) пов_ _ _(v.)...
Как бы не так — такой чуд_ _(n.)!

---

[1]Same root as in the verbal adverb in the first line of the second stanza.
[2]Same root as the last noun in the previous stanza.
[3]Вдруг что не так = what if something goes wrong?
[4]Как бы не так = no way!

Song 14. Старый пиджак

Я много лет пиджак ношу.
Давно потёрся и не нов он.
И я зову к себе портного,
и перешить пиджак прошу.

Я говорю ему, шутя,
«Перекройте всё иначе.
Сулит мне новые удачи
искусство кройки и шитья».

Я пошутил, а он пиджак
серьёзно так перешивает,
а сам так всё переживает:
вдруг что не так — такой чудак!

Одна забота наяву
в его усердии молчаливом:
чтобы я выглядел счастливым
в том пиджаке, пока живу.

Он представляет это так:
едва лишь я пиджак примерю,
опять в твою любовь поверю...
Как бы не так — такой чудак!

Опять в твою любовь поверю...
Как бы не так — такой чудак!

Вопросы по тексту (ответы полными предложениями):
1) О каком виде одежды эта песня? 2) Сколько времени поэт носит свой пиджак? 3) В каком состоянии его пиджак? 4) Как поэт решает обновить пиджак? 5) Как поэт шутит с портным? 6) Чего не понимает портной? 7) Как он относится к своей работе? 8) Чего боится портной? 9) Как поэт называет портного из–за его отношения к работе? 10) Какая забота не покидает портного? 11) Как портной представляет результат своей работы? 12) К кому обращается поэт в этой песне? 13) Какая тема кроется за развеернутой метафорой, на которой основана эта песня, т.е., что это за пиджак?

Комментарии к тексту песни

- verb + time unit [acc.] (to do something **for** a time unit [**SEE** "ненадóлго/недóлго" in "О Володе Высоцком."])
  Я ношу пиджак пять лет. (I've been wearing the jacket for five years.)

•пиджак (jacket [dress jacket as opposed to a ski jacket])
•носи́ть || поноси́ть (to wear [in general, not just on a particular occasion])
  ношу́, но́сишь, но́сят
  Я ношу пиджак круглый год. (I wear a jacket all year round.)
  ••на + prep. + clothing/footwear [nomin.] (to be wearing something [on a particular occasion], to have something on)
  На нём [был] пиджак. (He is [was] wearing a jacket.)
  ••надева́ть || наде́ть (to put [clothing] on)
  надева́ю, –ешь, –ют || наде́ну, –ешь, –ут
  Мы надели сапоги и ушли. (We put on our boots and left.)
•примеря́ть || приме́рить (to try on [clothing/footwear])
  примеря́ю, –ешь, –ют || приме́рю, –ишь, –ят
•давно (for a long time, long ago [**SEE** "Шёл троллейбус по улице"])
•потере́ться (to become worn) perf.: потрётся (потёрся/потёрлась)
•звать || позва́ть (to summon / call / invite [**SEE** "Песенка старого шарманщика"])
•к + dat. (**to** someone's place or wherever someone is located [home, office])[1]
  Я привела к Любе портного. (I brought a tailor over to Liuba's place.)
  N.B. "Verb of motion + к + dat." often means "to go see / visit someone."
  Я пошёл к врачу. (I went to see a doctor.)
  ••у + gen. (**at** someone's place or wherever someone is located)
  У меня сейчас гости. (There are guests now at my place.)
•кройка и шитьё (dress-making, tailoring)
•перешива́ть || переши́ть (to alter [clothing])
  перешива́ю, –ешь, –ют || перешью́, –ёшь, –ю́т
  ••шить || сши́ть (to sew, to make [clothing], to tailor)
  шью, шьёшь, шьют || сошью́, –ёшь, –ю́т
•крои́ть || перекрои́ть (to cut [fabric; пере–: to recut, to change the cut])
  крою́, крои́шь, кроя́т
•проси́ть || попроси́ть (to ask [**SEE** "Чёрный кот"])
•говори́ть || сказа́ть (to speak / talk / tell [**SEE** "Чёрный кот"])
•шутя́ (jokingly, in jest)
•шути́ть || пошути́ть (to joke) шучу́, шу́тишь, шу́тят
•ина́че (differently, otherwise, in a different manner)
•сули́ть || посули́ть (to promise, to augur) сулю́, –и́шь, –я́т
•удача (luck, success)
•такой/ая (such, so [modifies nouns and adjectives; cf. какой])
  Помидор такой большой, что одному мне его не съесть.
  (The tomato is so big that I can't eat it by myself.)
•так (so, thus, this way [modifies verbs, short-form adjectives and adverbs)
  Мы так быстро бежали, что устали. (We ran so fast that we got tired.)
•а + сам/а́/са́ми (but)
  N.B. This construction indicates a contradiction in someone's behavior and/or thoughts, e.g., promises v. actions, statements v. thoughts etc.
  Он сказал ей что её любит, а сам знал, что это ложь!
  (He said to her that he loved her, but he knew that this was a lie.)
•всё + imperfective (to keep doing something)
  Портной всё переживает. (The tailor keeps worrying.)
•пережива́ть (to be upset, to anguish over something, to worry, to suffer emotionally)

---

[1]Cf. "chez quelqu'un / moi / soi" in French or "bei jemand" in German.

переживáю, –ешь, –ют
•вдруг что не так (what if something goes wrong!)
•забóта (care, concern)
•хотеть + чтобы + past tense form (to want someone to be / do something)
••хотéть || захотéть (to want) хочý, хóчешь, хóчет, хотúм, хотúте, –я́т
Я хочу, чтобы ты выглядел счастливым. (I want you to look happy.)
У меня только одна забота [i.e., я хочу] — чтобы ты выглядел счастливым. (I have only one care: that you look happy.)
•вы́глядеть + adv./instr. (to look [i.e., to appear: happy, stupid etc.])
вы́гляжу, вы́глядишь, вы́глядят
Мы выглядим счастливыми / хорошо. (We look happy / well.)
•счастливый (happy, lucky; рад: glad [**SEE** "Бумажный солдат"])
•пока (while, for the time being [**SEE** "Молитва (Франсуа Вийона)"])
•жить || поживúть (**SEE** "Песенка о голубом шарике")
•представля́ть || представúть (to imagine, to figure [often used with "себе"])
представля́ю, –ешь, –ют || представлю, представúшь, представят
•едва лишь (as soon as [either of these words can stand on its own])
•вéрить || повéрить (**SEE** "Солнышко сияет")
•как бы не так (no way, keep dreaming, you've got another think coming!)
Ты хочешь, чтобы я отстала от тебя? Как бы не так!
(You want me to leave you alone? No way!)
•чудáк (strange person, weirdo, oddball, eccentric)

Переведите на русский язык, пользуясь песней и комментариями

1. "He is a **such an eccentric**. For example, he **wears** the same[1] **jacket** and the same trousers (for) **so many years** that finally even the best **tailor** can't **alter** them. His last **jacket became so worn** that **for a long time** he avoided all his friends in the street." "Maybe that's why I haven't seen him **for a long time**." "No, he recently **asked** a **tailor** to **make** him a **new jacket**, and now he **looks happy** and proud."

2. Some kind of[2] **weirdo keeps** coming into our shop and **trying on** different **jackets** but he never buys anything.[3] **For the time being** we tolerate this.

3. The teacher **called** the **silent** pupil to the board. **She wanted him to** rewrite[4] the exercise, but he suddenly **said**: "**No way**!" Now probably the principal **will summon** him **to his** (office).

4. **While** the **tailor** was **cutting** and **sewing** my **new jacket**, I **tried on** another cut and decided to order it as well. Tomorrow I **will try on new** trousers too.

5. Yesterday, when the model **was wearing** a chic dress, she had only **one**

---

[1]**SEE** "Я вновь повстречался с надеждой."
[2]**SEE** "Шёл троллейбус по улице."
[3]**SEE** "ни[interrog. word]" in "Примета."
[4]Same prefix as in "to alter [clothing]."

concern: **what if something goes wrong**? She **worried so** (much) that she tripped on the catwalk and fell into the audience!

6. I **wanted** you to **believe** that I (was) **happy**. So when you **called** me (up), I **joked** and laughed, but **as soon as** you hung up,[1] I began to cry.[2]

7. When(ever) I **invite** Klava **to my place**, she always **tells** me that she has been invited[3] **to her friend's** (house) or **to her boss's** (house), etc. But I don't **believe** her, and I am always **so upset** afterwards. Is that **called love**?

8. I am **joking** when I **say** that I **believe** in ghosts.

9. **As soon as** Misha **jokingly said** "I love you," Masha **believed** in his **love**.

10. When(ever) my husband **wears** his **new jacket**, he always **asks** me how he **looks**. He **says** it **so seriously**, that I **tell** him that he **looks** good, and he **believes** me. **Otherwise** he **would be upset for a long time.**

11. **Art** requires **diligence**, **luck** and talent.

12. The **new** apprentice worked **silently at the old tailor's** (shop) (for) **many years**, but one day[4] he **asked the tailor** to pay him. He **said**: "**Otherwise** I will leave."[5] He did not **imagine** that the **tailor** (would) let[6] him leave. When he was leaving, he **looked** very perplexed.

13. When she **asked** her father (for) the **car once again**, he **told** her that when he **lived** with his parents, he never **asked them** (for) anything. Therefore, **while** she is **living** at home, she should behave **differently**.

14. **A long time ago** my boss **promised** me all kinds of things, but now he avoids me, and his **silent** shame **speaks** for itself.

15. "What does a **tailor** do first: **cuts** or **sews**?" "Are you **asking** me **seriously** or are you **joking**?"

16. The fortune-teller **promised success** to her client, **but**[7] (she) thought (to herself): "He (can't) even **imagine** what awaits him."

---

[1]To hang up = lit.: to hang the receiver [**SEE** "ве́шать" in "Чёрный кот"].
[2]**SEE** "Песенка о голубом шарике."
[3]Lit.: (they have) invited her.
[4]**SEE** "Ещё раз о дураках."
[5]**SEE** "Песенка о Моцарте."
[6]**SEE** "Я пишу исторический роман."
[7]There is a contradiction between the statements and thoughts of the speaker.

15 A (Blanks)

«Мой _ _ _ _(n.) _ _ _ _ _ _ _ _ _ _ _(v.),

_ _ _ _ _ _ _ _ _ _ _(v.) мои _ _ _ _ _ _ _ _(n.).

Куда же мне _ _ _ _ _(v.: inf.)? _ _ _ _ _ _ _ _(v. imperat.) мне,

_ _ _ _ _ _(v.: imperat.) _ _ _ _ _(adj.: short form)».[1]

« _ _ _ _ _(adv.) _ _ _ _ _ _ _ _(adj.) _ _ _ _(n.: gen.), моя _ _ _ _ _ _ _ _(n.),[2]

_ _ _ _ _(adv.) _ _ _ _ _ _ _ _(adj.) _ _ _ _(n.: gen.).

До _ _ _ _ _(adj.) _ _ _ _(n.: gen.), моя _ _ _ _ _ _ _ _(n.),

до _ _ _ _ _(adj.) _ _ _ _(n.: gen.)» .

«А где ж та _ _ _ _(n.) и _ _ _ _(n.)?

_ _ _ _ _ _ _ _ _ _ _(v.) мой _ _ _ _(n.).

_ _ _ _ _ _ _ _(v.: imperat.), пожалуйста, как мне

_ _ _ _ _ _ _ _ _(v.: inf.) _ _ _ _(adv.)?»

«На _ _ _ _ _(adj.) _ _ _ _ _(n.), моя _ _ _ _ _ _ _ _(n.),

на _ _ _ _ _(adj.) _ _ _ _ _(n.).

_ _ _ _ _(v.: imperat.)[3] на _ _ _ _ _(n.), моя _ _ _ _ _ _ _ _(n.),

_ _ _ _ _ _ _ _(v.) без _ _ _ _ _(n.: gen.)».

(continued)

[1]The last two words constitute an idiomatic construction.
[2]"Моя _ _ _ _ _ _ _(n.)" is an idiomatic construction.
[3]This is a colloquial imperative form of a verb of motion.

«А где ж этот _ _ _ _ _(adj.) _ _ _ _ _(n.)?
Почему не _ _ _ _ _(v.)?
_ _ _(numeral) _ _ _(n.: gen.) _ _ _ _ _ _ _ _ _(v.) я _ _ _ _(n.)
_ _ _ _ _ _(adj.) _ _ _ _ _ _(n.: instr.)» ...

« _ _ _ _ _ _ _ _ _(n.) был _ _ _ _ _ _(short-form adj.) _ _ _ _ _ _(v.: inf.),
да[4] _ _ _ _ _ _ _ _ _(n.) вот _ _ _ _(v.).
_ _ _ _ _ _ _ _ _(n.)–то _ _ _ _(v.), моя _ _ _ _ _ _ _ _(n.),
а я ни при чём» .[5]

И _ _ _ _ _(adv.) он _ _ _ _(v.) _ _ _ _(adj.)
без _ _ _ _ _ _(n.: gen.) во _ _ _ _(n.: acc.).
Куда же он _ _ _ _(v.), _ _ _ _(conj.) _ _ _ _(n.)
_ _ _ _ _ _ _ _ _ _ _(v.) к _ _ _ _ _ _(n.: dat.)!

« Ты что _ _ _ _ _ _ _(v.), моя _ _ _ _ _ _ _(n.)?» —
_ _ _ _ _(v.) я ему.
И он _ _ _ _ _ _ _ _ _(v.): « Ах если б(ы)
я _ _ _ _(v.) это _ _ _(pron.)».
« Ты что _ _ _ _ _ _ _(v.), моя _ _ _ _ _ _ _(n.)?» —
_ _ _ _ _(v.) я ему.
И он _ _ _ _ _ _ _ _ _(v.): « Ах если б(ы)
я _ _ _ _(v.) это _ _ _(pron.)»...

---

[4]Here “да” = “but.”
[5]“Я ни при чём” is an idiomatic construction.

15 B (Partial Blanks)

«Мой _ _ _ь(n.) при_ _ _ _ _ _ _(v.),
ст_ _ т_ _ _сь(v.) мои баш_ _ _ _(n.).
Куда же мне е_ _ _ _(v.: inf.)? С_ _ _ _ _ _(v. imperat.) мне,
б_ _ь_ _(v.: imperat.) до_ _ _(adj.: short form)».[1]

« _ _ _ _ь(adv.) к_ _ _ _ _ _(adj.) _ _ _ _(n.: gen.), моя _ _ _ _ _ _ _(n.),[2]
в_ _ _ь(adv.) кр_ _ _ _ _(adj.) р_ _ _(n.: gen.).
До _ _ _ _ _(adj.) _ _ _ _(n.: gen.), моя _ _ _ _ _ _ _(n.),
до с_ _ _ _(adj.) г_ _ _(n.: gen.)».

«А где ж та го_ _(n.) и ре_ _(n.) ?
прит_ _ _ _ся(v.) мой к_ _ь(n.).
Ск_ _ _ _ _(v.: imperat.), пожалуйста, как мне
про_ _ _ _ _(v.: inf.) т_ _ _(adv.)?»

«На _ _ _ _ _(adj.) _ _ _ _ _(n.), моя _ _ _ _ _ _ _(n.),
на я_ _ _ _(adj.) _ _ _ _ _(n.).
ез_ _ _(v.: imperat.)[3] на о_ _ _ _(n.), моя _ _ _ _ _ _ _(n.),
най_ _ _ _(v.) без тр_ _ _(n.: gen.)».

(continued)

---

[1]The last two words constitute an idiomatic construction.
[2]"Моя _ _ _ _ _ _ _(n.)" is an idiomatic construction.
[3]This is a colloquial imperative form of a verb of motion.

«А где ж этот яс_ _ _(adj.) ог_ _ _(n.)?
Почему не го_ _ _(v.)?
С_ _(numeral) л_ _(n.: gen.) подп_ _ _ _(v.) я н_ _ _(n.)
н_ _н_ _(adj.) пл_ _ _ _(n.: instr.)»...

«Ф_ _ _ _ _ _ _(n.) был д_ _ _ _ _(short-form adj.) за_ _ч_(v.: inf.),
да[4] фо_ _ _ _ _ _(n.) вот _ _ _ _(v.).
Фон_ _ _ _ _(n.)–то с_ _ _(v.), моя _ _ _ _ _ _ _ _(n.),
а я ни при чём».[5]

И сн_ _ _(adv.) он _ _ _ _(v.) о_ _ _(adj.)
без до_ _ _ _(n.: gen.) во ть_ _(n.: acc.).
Куда же он е_ _ _(v.), в_ _ _(conj.) н_ _ _(n.)
подст_ _ _ _ _(v.) к гл_ _ _ _(n.: dat.)!

«Ты что по_ _ _ _ _(v.), моя _ _ _ _ _ _ь(n.)?» —
к_ _ _ _(v.) я ему.
И он от_ _ _ _ _ _(v.): « Ах если б(ы)
я _ _ _ _(v.) это _ _ _(pron.)».
«Ты что пот_ _ _ _(v.), моя р_ _ _ _ _ь(n.)?» —
кр_ _ _(v.) я ему.
И он отв_ _ _ _ _(v.): « Ах если б(ы)
я з_ _ _(v.) это с_ _(pron.)»...

---

[4]Here “да” = “but.”
[5]“Я ни при чём” is an idiomatic construction.

Song 15. Ночной разговор

«Мой конь притомился. Стоптались мои башмаки.
Куда же мне ехать? Скажите мне, будьте добры».
« Вдоль красной реки, моя радость, вдоль красной реки.
До синей горы, моя радость, до синей горы».

«А где ж та гора, и река? Притомился мой конь.
Скажите, пожалуйста, как мне проехать туда?»
«На ясный огонь, моя радость, на ясный огонь.
Езжай на огонь, моя радость, найдёшь без труда».

«А где ж этот ясный огонь? Почему не горит?
Сто лет подпираю я небо ночное плечом»...
«Фонарщик был должен зажечь, да фонарщик вот спит.
Фонарщик–то спит, моя радость, а я ни при чём».

И снова он едет один без дороги во тьму.
Куда же он едет, ведь ночь подступила к глазам!
«Ты что потерял, моя радость?» — кричу я ему.
И он отвечает: «Ах если б я знал это сам».

«Ты что потерял, моя радость?» — кричу я ему.
И он отвечает: «Ах если б я знал это сам»...

<u>Вопросы по тексту (ответы полными предложениями)</u>:
1) Кто с кем разговаривает? 2) На что жалуется всадник? 3) Что он хочет узнать? 4) Куда его посылает собеседник? 5) Почему всадник не удовлетворяется ответами собеседника? 6) Виден ли ясный огонь? 7) Давно ли длится "ночь" всадника? 8) Как воспринимает всадник эту ночь? 9) Почему не горит огонь? 10) Почему фонарщик не зажёг огонь? 11) Считает ли собеседник всадника себя причастным к тому, что не горит огонь? 12) Что решает сделать всадник? 13) Чему удивляется его собеседник? 14) Что ищет всадник? 15) Кто этот всадник и его собеседник?

<u>Комментарии к тексту песни</u>
•конь (horse [usually male], stallion, steed) лошадь (horse [male or female])
•притомля́ться || притоми́ться (to grow <u>tired</u> / <u>weary</u>)
    притомля́юсь, –ешься, –ются || притом<u>л</u>ю́сь, притоми́шься, притомя́тся
•ста́птывать[ся] || стопта́ть[ся] (to wear down at the heel [-<u>ся</u>: to become worn])
    ста́птываю, –ешь, –ет[ся] –ют[ся] ||
    стоп<u>ч</u>у́, сто́пчешь, сто́пчет[ся], сто́пчут[ся]
    Мои башмаки стоптались. (My shoes have become worn at the heels.)
    Он стоптал свои башмаки. (He wore his shoes down at the heels.)
•где/куда (where [**SEE** "Он, наконец, явился в дом"])

•как мне проехать туда (how can I get there)
[**SEE** "interrog. word + dat. + inf." in "Ещё раз о дураках"])
•éхать || поéхать (to go/drive/ride [by some kind of transport: **uni**directional])
éду, –ешь, –ут
N.B. The standard imperative is "поезжáй," but the colloquial version is "езжáй."
N.B. The perfective with про– can mean "to get to." It is often used in requests for directions, e.g., "Как [мне] проехать / пройти на Тверскую улицу?" (How do I get to Tverskaia Street?).
N.B. When motion and reference to this motion are simultaneous, "éхать" can mean either "to come" or "to go."
Вот едет Аня. (Here comes / goes Ania [depending on the context].)
••éздить (to go/drive/ride [**multi**directional]) éзжу, éздишь, éздят
Я ездил туда часто. (I often went there [and came back every time].)
N.B. SEE "идти́ || пойти́" in "Шёл троллейбус по улице."
••verb of motion + на + means of transport [prep.] (to go by car/horse etc.)
Мы летим на самолёте. (We are traveling by plane.)
•verb of motion + на + acc. (to head for / in the direction of [some marker])
Она поéхала на огонь / звук. (She headed for the fire / sound.)
•говори́ть || сказáть (to speak / talk / tell [**SEE** "Чёрный кот"])
•бýдьте добры́ (would you be so kind as to, please)
Будьте добры: помогите мне перейти улицу.
(Would you be so kind as to / please help me cross the street.)
•моя́ рáдость (my dear ["радость" lit.: joy])
•ясный/ая (clear, bright [ясно: clearly, brightly])
•огóнь (fire [**SEE** "Ваше величество, женщина"])
•свет (light , world [**SEE** "Бумажный солдат"])
•горéть || сгорéть (to burn [**SEE** "Чёрный кот"])
•фонарь (streetlight, flashlight) фонарщик (lamplighter [the person who lights streetlights])
•находи́ть || найти́ (to find)
нахожý, нахóдишь, нахóдят || найдý, –ёшь, –ýт
•без труда (without difficulty / trouble, with ease ["труд" lit.: labor])
••с трудом (with difficulty, to have trouble doing something)
Я понимаю по–корейски без труда, но говорю с трудом.
(I understand Korean without trouble, but I have trouble speaking.)
•verb + time unit [acc.] (to do something **for** a time unit [**SEE** "ненадóлго/недóлго" in "О Володе Высоцком"])
Сто лет я подпираю небо плечом.
(I've been propping up the sky with my shoulder **for** a hundred years.)
•подпирáть || подперéть (to prop / hold up)
подпирáю, –ешь, –ют || подопрý, –ёшь, –ýт
•должен/должна (must, should, is supposed to, have to [**SEE** "Шёл троллейбус по улице"])
•зажигáть || зажéчь (to ignite, to light, to turn on [usually: electric light])
зажигáю, –ешь, –ют ||
зажгý, зажжёшь, зажжёт, зажжём, зажжёте, зажгýт (зажёг/зажглá)
•спать || уснуть (to sleep [**SEE** "Часовые любви"])
•я тут ни при чём (I have nothing to do with it, it's not my responsibility)
Мы тут [были] ни при чём. (We have [had] nothing to do with this.)
N.B. "Тут" = "this."
•один (alone, one, a certain [**SEE** "Бумажный солдат"])
•тьма/темнота (darkness, the dark [**SEE** "Ваше величество, женщина"])

•ведь (after all [**SEE** "Шёл троллейбус по улице"])
•ночь (**SEE** "Дежурный по апрелю"])
•подступа́ть || подступи́ть + к + dat. (to approach)
  подступа́ю, –ешь, –ют || подступлю́, подсту́пишь, подсту́пят
  Армия подступила к крепости. (The army approached the fortress.)
  У меня к глазам подступили слёзы.
  (I was on the verge of tears [lit.: tears approached my eyes].)
  N.B. This verb is often used with respect to an army approaching a military objective or the aggressive movement (approaching) by one person toward another.
•теря́ть || потеря́ть (to lose) теря́ю, –ешь, –ют
•крича́ть || закрича́ть (to shout/yell/scream) кричу́, –и́шь, –а́т
•отвеча́ть || отве́тить (to reply/answer)
  отвеча́ю, –ешь, –ют || отве́чу, отве́тишь, отве́тят
•если + б[ы] + past tense form (if only [**SEE** "Песенка старого шарманщика"])
  Если б[ы] я знал это сам. (If only I myself knew this.)
•знать || узна́ть (to know [у–: to find out, to recognize]) зна́ю, –ешь, –ют
•сам/а́/о́/са́ми (myself, yourself, herself etc. [**SEE** "Чёрный кот"])

Переведите на русский язык, пользуясь песней и комментариями

1. The novice **lamplighter** asked the old **lamplighter**: "**How do I**[1] **light** the **streetlights**?" The old **lamplighter answered**: "You need (some) matches." "**Where do I get**[2] the matches?" "**Ride** to our warehouse. You will **have no trouble finding** it." The novice **said**: "Yes, but **how (do I) get there**?" "You **should** already **know yourself how to get there**! And anyway, you **were supposed** to **light** the **streetlights** a long time ago."[3] "Yes, but I always **have trouble finding** the warehouse at **night** in the **dark**. **After all**, if I **ride** to the wrong place,[4] you will **scream** at me, but **it's not going to be my responsibility**," replied the novice and shrugged his **shoulders**. All **red** from indignation, the old **lamplighter approached** him and **said** with deliberate amiability: "**My dear** (fellow), **would you be so kind as to ride along the river** and (up) **to** that **road**. From there **go** toward the tallest church in the city. There the warehouse is **clearly** visible." The novice **rode (for)** four hours and **did not find** anything.[5] **He was on the verge of tears**. He **(had) become very tired**; therefore, he stopped, **fell asleep** and **slept (for)** an hour, and then **once again** he **rode** (all) **alone** into the **darkness**. He did not return,[6] and the old **lamplighter lit the streetlights** (by) **himself**.

---

[1]**SEE** "interrog. word + dat. + inf." above: watch for this construction elsewhere in this translation.
[2]Lit.: take. **SEE** previous note.
[3]**SEE** "Шёл троллейбус по улице."
[4]To / at the wrong place = не туда / там; the wrong book = не та книга.
[5]**SEE** "ни[interrog. word]" in "Примета."
[6]**SEE** "Песенка о голубом шарике."

2. Petrov-Vodkin painted a painting called[1] "The Bathing of a **Red Stallion**."

3. I **will sleep** (for a while) and then, if I wake up from the cold, I **will light a fire**.

4. She **clearly** saw that only a few beams **were propping** up the house. She thought: "**If only** I had brought (some) cement! I don't **know where I should**[2] go for cement."

5. "Volia's **shoes** (have) **become worn at the heel**. **How can**[3] **he** fix them?" "**My dear**, **I have nothing to do with this**: I didn't **wear down** his shoes."

6. I feel such **joy** when I **ride** (my) motorcycle in the **mountains**.

7. Last **night** I was **riding** (my) **horse** when I heard **screams** in the **darkness**. Someone[4] was **screaming**. "**If only** I could[5] see in the **dark**," I thought. In order to[6] **find out** who (was) **screaming**, I **headed in the direction of** the **screams**. When I **arrived** there, I (could) not believe my **eyes**. It was a sight that I will not forget **(for) a hundred years**. **Along** the **river blue** and **red fires were burning** and witches were dancing under the **night sky**. I did not stay there for a long time,[7] but the next day I **found out** that the forest (had) **burned down**.

8. If we don't extinguish the **fire**, the house will **burn down**.

9. I **fell asleep with difficulty**, but I woke up **with ease**.

10. "**If only I knew where** the matches are!" "What would you do then?" "I would **light a fire again**."

11. **Would you be so kind as to tell** (me) **how I** (can) **get**[8] **to the river**?

---

[1]**SEE** "Чёрный кот."

[2]See note 1 on the previous page.

[3]See previous note.

[4]**SEE** "Шёл троллейбус по улице."

[5]**SEE** "мочь" in "О Володе Высоцком."

[6]**SEE** "Примета."

[7]**SEE** "Шёл троллейбус по улице."

[8]This person is driving.

16 A (Blanks)

О Володе Высоцком я _ _ _ _ _(n.: acc.)

_ _ _ _ _ _ _ _ _(v.: inf.) _ _ _ _ _(v.).

Вот ещё _ _ _ _ _ _(numeral: dat.) не _ _ _ _ _ _ _ _ _(v.: inf.)

_ _ _ _ _(adv.) из _ _ _ _ _ _(n.: gen.).

_ _ _ _ _ _ _(v.), что _ _ _ _ _ _(v.),

что не к _ _ _ _ _(n.: dat.) _ _ _ _ _(n.: acc.) _ _ _ _ _ _ _(v.)...

Как _ _ _ _(v.), так и _ _ _(v.),

а _ _ _ _ _ _ _ _ _ _(substantivized adj.: acc.)

не _ _ _ _ _(v.) _ _ _ _ _ _ _(n.).

_ _ _ _ _ _ _(v.), что _ _ _ _ _ _(v.),

что не к _ _ _ _ _(n.: dat.) _ _ _ _ _(n.: acc.) _ _ _ _ _ _ _(v.)...

Как _ _ _ _(v.), так и _ _ _(v.),

а _ _ _ _ _ _ _ _ _ _(substantivized adj.: acc.)

не _ _ _ _ _(v.) _ _ _ _ _ _ _(n.).

_ _ _ _ _ _ _ _ _(adv.) _ _ _ _ _ _ _(n.) —

всего лишь[1] на _ _ _(n.),

а _ _ _ _ _(adv.) _ _ _ _ _ _ _ _ _ _ _ _(v.: inf.) и нам

по _ _ _ _ _ _(n.: dat.) по его по[2] _ _ _ _ _ _ _(adj.).

_ _ _ _ _(particle) _ _ _ _ _ _(v.) над _ _ _ _ _ _ _(proper n.: instr.)

_ _ _ _ _ _ _ _(participle) его _ _ _ _ _ _ _(n.).

Ну а мы _ _ _ _ _ _(adv.) с ним _ _ _ _ _ _ _ _ _(v.)

и _ _ _ _ _ _(adv.) _ _ _ _ _ _ _ _(v.).

_ _ _ _ _(particle) _ _ _ _ _ _(v.) над _ _ _ _ _ _ _(proper n.: instr.)

_ _ _ _ _ _ _ _(participle) его _ _ _ _ _ _ _(n.).

Ну а мы _ _ _ _ _ _(adv.) с ним _ _ _ _ _ _ _ _ _(v.)

и _ _ _ _ _ _(adv.) _ _ _ _ _ _ _ _(v.).

---

[1]"Всего лишь" is an idiomatic construction.

[2]Of the three "по" in this line, the last two are there only for rhythm.

О Володе Высоцком я _ _ _ _ _(n.: acc.)

_ _ _ _ _ _ _ _ _(v.: inf.) _ _ _ _ _(v.),

но _ _ _ _ _ _ _(v.) _ _ _ _(n.) и _ _ _ _ _(n.)

со _ _ _ _ _ _(n.: instr.) не _ _ _ _ _ _ _ _(v.).

_ _ _ _ _(adj.) _ _ _ _(n.) _ _ _ _ _ _ _ _ _ _ _(adj.)

на _ _ _ _ _(adj.) _ _ _ _(n.) _ _ _ _ _ _ _(v.),

_ _ _ _ _ _(adj.) _ _ _ _(n.) _ _ _ _ _ _ _ _ _ _ _(adj.)

на _ _ _ _ _ _(adj.) _ _ _ _ _(n.: acc.) _ _ _ _ _ _ _ _ _(v.).

_ _ _ _ _(adj.) _ _ _ _(n.) _ _ _ _ _ _ _ _ _ _ _(adj.)

на _ _ _ _ _(adj.) _ _ _ _(n.) _ _ _ _ _ _ _(v.),

_ _ _ _ _ _(adj.) _ _ _ _(n.) _ _ _ _ _ _ _ _ _ _ _(adj.)

на _ _ _ _ _ _(adj.) _ _ _ _ _(n.: acc.) _ _ _ _ _ _ _ _ _(v.)

16 B (Partial Blanks)

О Володе Высоцком я п_ _ _ _(n.: acc.)
пр_ _ _ _ _ _ _(v.: inf.) р_ _ _ _(v.).
Вот ещё од_ _ _ _(numeral: dat.) не ве_ _ _ _ _ _ _(v.: inf.)
д_ _ _ _(adv.) из по_ _ _ _(n.: gen.).
Г_ _ _ _ _ _(v.), что г_ _ _ _ _(v.),
что не к _ _ _ _ _(n.: dat.) с_ _ _ _(n.: acc.) за_ _ _ _ _(v.)...
Как _ _ _ _(v.), так и _ _ _(v.),
а без_ _ _ _ _ _ _(substantivized adj.: acc.)
не _ _ _ _ _(v.) пр_ _ _ _ _(n.).
Го _ _ _ _ _(v.), что гр _ _ _ _(v.),
что не к с_ _ _ _(n.: dat.) св_ _ _(n.: acc.) зат_ _ _ _(v.)...
Как у_ _ _(v.), так и _ _ _(v.),
а безгр_ _ _ _ _(substantivized adj.: acc.)
не з_ _ _ _(v.) при_ _ _ _(n.).

Ненад_ _ _ _(adv.) раз_ _ _ _(n.) —
всего лишь[1] на м_ _(n.),
а п_ _ _ _(adv.) отпр_ _ _ _ _ _ _ _(v.: inf.) и нам
по сл_ _ _ _(n.: dat.) по его по[2] гор_ _ _ _(adj.).
П_ _ _ _(particle) к_ _ _ _ _(v.) над М_ _ _ _ _ _(proper n.: instr.)
ох_ _ _ _ _ _(participle) его б_ _ _ _ _ _(n.).
Ну а мы _ _ _ _ _ _(adv.) с ним по_ _ _ _ _ _ _(v.)
и _ _ _ _ _ _(adv.) по_ _ _ _ _ _(v.).
Пу_ _ _(particle) кр_ _ _ _(v.) над Мо_ _ _ _ _(proper n.: instr.)
охр_ _ _ _ _(participle) его ба_ _ _ _ _(n.).

---

[1]"Всего лишь" is an idiomatic construction.
[2]Of the three "по" in this line, the last two are there only for rhythm.

Ну а мы в_ _ _ _ _(adv.) с ним посм_ _ _ _ _(v.)
и вм_ _ _ _(adv.) попл_ _ _ _(v.).

О Володе Высоцком я пе_ _ _(n.: acc.)
прид_ _ _ _ _(v.: inf.) х_ _ _ _(v.).
Но др_ _ _ _ _(v.) р_ _ _(n.) и мо_ _ _(n.)
со ст_ _ _ _(n.: instr.) не сх_ _ _ _ _ _(v.).
_ _ _ _ _(adj.) _ _ _ _(n.) _ _ _ _ _ _ _ _ _ _ _(adj.)
на _ _ _ _ _(adj.) _ _ _ _(n.) вз_ _ _ _ _(v.),
_ _ _ _ _ _(adj.) _ _ _ _(n.) _ _ _ _ _ _ _ _ _ _ _(adj.)
на _ _ _ _ _ _(adj.) з_ _ _ _(n.: acc.) сп_ _ _ _ _ _ _(v.).
Б_ _ _ _(adj.) а_ _ _(n.) м_ _ _ _ _ _ _ _ _ _(adj.)
на бе_ _ _(adj.) н_ _ _(n.) взл_ _ _ _(v.),
Ч_ _ _ _ _(adj.) аи_ _(n.) мо_ _ _ _ _ _ _ _(adj.)
на чё_ _ _ _(adj.) зе_ _ _(n.: acc.) спус_ _ _ _ _(v.)

Song 16. О Володе Высоцком

О Володе Высоцком[1] я песню придумать решил.
Вот ещё одному не вернуться домой из похода.
Говорят, что грешил, что не к сроку свечу затушил...
Как умел, так и жил, а безгрешных не знает природа.
Говорят, что грешил, что не к сроку свечу затушил...
Как умел, так и жил, а безгрешных не знает природа.

Ненадолго разлука — всего лишь на миг, а потом
отправляться и нам по следам по его по горячим.
Пусть кружит над Москвою охрипший его баритон.
Ну а мы вместе с ним посмеёмся и вместе поплачем.
Пусть кружит над Москвою охрипший его баритон.
Ну а мы вместе с ним посмеёмся и вместе поплачем.

О Володе Высоцком я песню придумать хотел,
но дрожала рука и мотив со стихом не сходился...
Белый аист московский на белое небо взлетел.
Чёрный аист московский на чёрную землю спустился.
Белый аист московский на белое небо взлетел.
Чёрный аист московский на чёрную землю спустился.

Вопросы по тексту (ответы полными предложениями):
1) О ком идёт речь? 2) Что посвящает поэт умершему певцу? 3) С чем сравнивается смерть Высоцкого [4 метафоры]? 4) Какие слухи ходят о Высоцком? 5) С какой птицей сравнивается Высоцкий? 6) Как выражается двойственность натуры Высоцкого? 7) Как поэт оправдывает "грешность" певца? 8) Что нас связывает с умершим певцом? 9) Что нам напоминает о Высоцком после его смерти? 10) Какие реакции вызывает музыка Высоцкого у слушателей? 11) Как давалась поэту песня о Высоцком? 12) Как объяснить эти трудности?
*Теперь давайте послушаем самого́ Высоцкого.

Комментарии к тексту песни
- приду́мывать || приду́мать (to invent/compose/fabricate/come up with)
  приду́мываю, –ешь, –ют || приду́маю, –ешь, –ют
- реша́ть || реши́ть (to decide/ [re]solve [**SEE** "Он, наконец, явился в дом"])
- dat. + не + inf. (cannot, will not)
  Ему не вернуться из похода. (He won't / can't return from the war.)
  Мне не вы́учить этот язык. (I can't learn this language.)

[1]Владимир Высоцкий (1937—1980): популярнейший русский певец, поэт, композитор, бард и актёр, прославившийся своим "блатным" песенным стилем, хриплым голосом и "богемным" образом жизни. Высоцкий хорошо передал облатнённый дух советского общества в эпоху после Сталина. Его внезапная и безвременная смерть поразила всю страну, и данная песня является реакцией Окуджавы на это событие.

••dat. + inf. imperf. (one must / should / is supposed to; it is one's turn to...)
Нам сейчас петь. (We are supposed to / it is our turn to sing now.)
•возвраща́ть[ся] || верну́ть[ся] (**SEE** "Песенка о голубом шарике")
•домо́й (home [homeward: destination]) до́ма ([at] home: location)
Он ещё идёт домой, а я уже до́ма.
(He's still walking home, and I'm already [at] home.)
•похо́д (hiking trip, war, military expedition [**SEE** "Часовые любви"])
•говорят [что]... (an indefinite personal construction equivalent to "they say")
Говорят [что] тут есть пиво. (They say [that] beer is sold here.)
••говори́ть || сказа́ть (to speak / talk / tell [**SEE** "Чёрный кот"])
•греши́ть || согреши́ть (to sin [from "грех": sin]) грешу́, –и́шь, –а́т
•к сроку (on / in time [не к сроку: not on time; too early / late])
Работу нужно кончить к сроку. (The job must be finished on time.)
•туши́ть || затуши́ть (to extinguish, to put out [a fire])
тушу́, ту́шишь, ту́шат
•уме́ть (can [to have the skill to..., i.e., to know how to do something])[1]
уме́ю, –ешь, –ют
Я умею плавать, а ты умеешь шить. (I can swim, and you can sew.)
••мочь || смочь (can [to have the physical ability to do something][2]
могу́, мо́жешь, мо́гут (мог/могла́)
Я могу купить лыжи хоть сейчас, но я не умею на них кататься.
(I can buy skis even now, but I can't [don't know how to] ski.)
•как уме́ть так и + verb (to do something as well as one can)
Я как умею, так и спою. (I'll sing as well as I can.)
•жить || вы́жить (вы́–: to survive [**SEE** "Песенка о голубом шарике"])
•знать || узна́ть (to know [у–: to find out, to recognize]) зна́ю, –ешь, –ют
•ненадо́лго/недо́лго (not for long; for a short while / period of time
[cf. "надолго/долго": for a long time])
••на + time unit [acc. if indicated by a noun][3] (proposed / intended duration)
Он приехал ненадолго / на месяц, но прожил у нас два года / долго.
(He came for a short while / for a month but stayed with us
for two years / for a long time.)
N.B. When the time span in question begins after the action expressed by the verb, "for + time unit" is rendered in Russian by "на + time unit" (cf. 1st clause of the above example: his arrival precedes his stay). If the time span in question and the verb's action coincide, then "for + time unit" is translated into Russian without "на" (cf. 2nd clause of the above example: his living with us and the period of his stay coincide in time). Generally, на + time unit is used with verbs of motion.
•разлука (separation, parting, being apart)
Я страдаю от нашей разлуки. (I suffer because we are apart.)
•всего лишь (merely/only [either of these words can stand on its own])
•отправля́ться || отпра́виться (to set out / leave / depart for)
отправля́юсь, –ешься, –ются || отпра́влюсь, отпра́вишься, отпра́вятся
Она отправилась в Курск. (She left for Kursk.)
•verb of motion + по следам + gen. (to follow someone, to go in someone's footsteps, to track [по горячим следам = to be right behind someone])
Мы пойдём по следам этого жирафа. (We will track this giraffe.)
•пусть (let + verb [**SEE** "Часовые любви")

---

[1]Cf. "savoir faire..." in French.
[2]Cf. "pouvoir faire..." in French.
[3]Cf. "pour" in French.

•кружи́ть || покружи́ть (**SEE** "Примета")
•охрипший/ая (hoarse [past active participle])
••хри́пнуть || охри́пнуть (to become hoarse)
хри́пну, –ешь, –ут (past perf.: охри́п/охри́пла)
Мы / наши голоса охри́пли от крика.
(We / our voices became hoarse from screaming.)
•смея́ться || посмея́ться (to laugh [**SEE** "Солнышко сияет"])
•пла́кать || запла́кать (to cry [**SEE** "Песенка о голубом шарике"])
•хоте́ть || захоте́ть (to want) хочу́, хо́чешь, хо́чет, хоти́м, хоти́те, хотя́т
•дрожа́ть || задрожа́ть (to tremble, to shake [intransitive]) дрожу́, –и́шь, –а́т
•стих (a line in a poem [стихи́: plural noun→ lyrics, verse, poetry])
•сходи́ться || сойти́сь (to come together)
схожу́сь, схо́дишься, схо́дятся || сойду́сь, –ёшься, –у́тся
•взлета́ть || взлете́ть (to fly up, to take off)
взлета́ю, –ешь, –ют || взлечу́, взлети́шь, взлетя́т
•спуска́ть[ся] || спусти́ть[ся] (to go down, [without -ся: to bring / take down; to lower])
спуска́ю[сь], –ешь[ся], –ют[ся] || спущу́[сь], спу́стишь[ся], спу́стят[ся]
Сначала я спустил свои вещи на верёвке, а потом сам спустился.
First I lowered my things on a rope, and then I went down myself.

Переведите на русский язык, пользуясь песней и комментариями

1. Here is a note that a mountain climber left to his children: "Dear Mika and Grunia, I am **setting out** on a **hike**, (for) a **week**. Because I am going (for) a **short time**, I don't **want** to take many things (along): **one** person **cannot** carry much. So I will take **only** a few things. If I don't **come down** from the mountain and don't **return home from** the **hike on time**, I hope that **together** you will **track** your poor father and find him. You **know** that because I **cannot** hunt (very) well, I **will survive** in **nature** (for) **a short while**: I am sure that I **cannot survive**[1] (for) **even a week**. Of course I will hunt **as well as I can**. Mika, **let** your sister call[2] the **Moscow** police before[3] you (two) **set out for** the mountains. While you are **at home**, don't tell the neighbors where I am: I hope that you **will invent** some kind[4] (of) a story. You are probably **laughing** at my premature fears, but if something happens, you **will be crying**. I hope that our **separation will not be for a long time**.[5] Your father."

2. "**It's our turn** to taxi,"[6] said the pilot to the copilot. "You will probably **have a** (good) **laugh** at me, but I have **decided** to tell you a secret about

---

[1]I cannot: dative construction.
[2]Call the police = call + в + acc. (**SEE** "Песенка старого шарманщика").
[3]Before / after + verb = перед тем / после того + как + verb.
[4]**SEE** "Шёл троллейбус по улице."
[5]First the act of parting takes place, and only then does "being apart" begin.
[6]This is a term from aviation: find its Russian equivalent.

myself. No one[1] is **sinless**, and I **sin** every day. My **sin** is fear. When(ever) my airplane **takes off**, I **tremble** when I look at the **earth** below us. Yesterday, when we were **circling over Moscow**, my **hands** were **shaking**, and, as we were **coming down**, I even closed (my) eyes **for an instant**."[2]

3. "My son **wants** to **know** how he appeared in our family." "Tell him that a **white stork** brought him **home**." "His favorite color is **black**." "Fine, **let** (it) be a **black stork**."

4. I **know** the **tune** and the **lyrics** of this **song**. But who is the **baritone** that[3] is singing it?

5. Don't play (with) **candles**, children. If a fire[4] starts, who will **put it out**?

6. "Why did your voice **become hoarse**?" "Because I tried to sing an aria for a soprano, and[5] I am a **baritone**." "(They) **say** that this **can** damage your voice."

7. Only when all the threads of the crime **come together**, will the detective **solve** the riddle of this murder.

---

[1]**SEE** "Примета."
[2]First you close your eyes, and only then begins the period of "shut eyes."
[3]**SEE** "тот + кто/который" in "Я вновь повстречался с надеждой."
[4]**SEE** "Ваше величество, женщина."
[5]**SEE** "Песенка о голубом шарике."

17 A (Blanks)

Моцарт на _ _ _ _ _ _ _ _ _ _ _(adj.: dimin.)
_ _ _ _ _ _ _(n.: prep.) _ _ _ _ _ _(v.).
Моцарт _ _ _ _ _ _(v.), а _ _ _ _ _ _ _(n.) _ _ _ _(v.).
Моцарт _ _ _ _ _ _ _ _ _(n.: gen.) не _ _ _ _ _ _ _ _(v.) —
_ _ _ _ _ _(adv.) _ _ _ _ _ _(v.) всю _ _ _ _ _(n.) _ _ _ _ _ _ _ _(adv.).
Ах, _ _ _ _ _ _(adv.), что всегда, как _ _ _ _ _ _ _ _(adv.),
наша _ _ _ _ _ _(n.) — то _ _ _ _ _ _(n.), то _ _ _ _ _ _(n.)...
Не _ _ _ _ _ _ _ _ _ _(v.: imperat.) _ _ _ _ _ _ _ _(n.: gen.), маэстро!
Не _ _ _ _ _ _ _ _(v.: imperat.) _ _ _ _ _ _(n.: gen.) со _ _ _(n.: gen.)!
Не _ _ _ _ _ _ _ _ _ _(v.: imperat.) _ _ _ _ _ _ _ _(n.: gen.), маэстро!
Не _ _ _ _ _ _ _ _(v.: imperat.) _ _ _ _ _ _(n.: gen.) со _ _ _(n.: gen.)!

_ _ _-_ _ _ _ _ _(adv.) на _ _ _ _ _ _ _ _ _(n.: prep.)
_ _ _ _ _ _ _ _(adj.)
_ _ _ _ _ _(v.) спасибо и этой _ _ _ _ _ _(n.: dat.).
Но из _ _ _ _ _ _(n.: gen.) своей
_ _ _ _ _ _(n.: gen.) _ _ _ _ _ _(adj.)
не _ _ _ _ _ _ _ _ _(v.: inf.) бы _ _ _ _ _ _(n.: acc.) себе.
Ах, _ _ _ _ _ _(adv.), что всегда, как _ _ _ _ _ _ _ _(adv.),
наша _ _ _ _ _ _(n.) — то _ _ _ _ _ _(n.), то _ _ _ _ _ _(n.)...
Не _ _ _ _ _ _ _ _ _ _ _ _ _(v.: imperat.)
с _ _ _ _ _ _ _ _(n.: instr.), маэстро!
Не _ _ _ _ _ _ _ _(v.: imperat.) _ _ _ _ _ _(n.: gen.) со _ _ _(n.: gen.)!
Не _ _ _ _ _ _ _ _ _ _ _ _ _(v.: imperat.)
с _ _ _ _ _ _ _ _(n.: instr.), маэстро!
Не _ _ _ _ _ _ _ _(v.: imperat.) _ _ _ _ _ _(n.: gen.) со _ _ _(n.: gen.)!

_ _ _ _ _ _ _(adj.: short form) наши _ _ _ _(n.) _ _ _ _ _ _ _(adj.):
_ _ _(n.) — и _ _ _ _ _ _ _ _ _(v.), как на _ _ _ _ _ _ _(n.: prep.),
_ _ _ _ _ _ _(adj.) _ _ _ _ _ _(n.), _ _ _ _ _ _ _(n.) _ _ _ _ _ _ _(adj.),
_ _ _ _ _(adj.) _ _ _ _ _(n.), _ _ _ _ _ _(n.) в _ _ _ _ _ _ _ _(n.: prep.).
Ах, _ _ _ _ _ _(adv.), что всегда, как _ _ _ _ _ _ _ _(adv.),
наша _ _ _ _ _ _(n.) — то _ _ _ _ _ _(n.), то _ _ _ _ _ _(n.)...
Не _ _ _ _ _ _ _ _ _ _(v.: imperat.) _ _ _ _ _ _ _ _(n.: gen.), маэстро!
Не _ _ _ _ _ _ _ _(v.: imperat.) _ _ _ _ _ _(n.: gen.) со _ _ _(n.: gen.)!
Не _ _ _ _ _ _ _ _ _ _(v.: imperat.) _ _ _ _ _ _ _ _(n.: gen.),[1] маэстро!
Не _ _ _ _ _ _ _ _(v.: imperat.) _ _ _ _ _ _(n.: gen.) со _ _ _(n.: gen.)!

---

[1]The last two words constitute an idiomatic construction.

17 B (Partial Blanks)

Моцарт на ст_ _ _ _ _ _ _ _(adj.: dimin.)
ск_ _ _ _ _(n.: prep.) _ _ _ _ _ _(v.).
Моцарт и_ _ _ _ _(v.), а скр_ _ _ _(n.) п_ _ _(v.).
Моцарт от_ _ _ _ _ _ _(n.: gen.) не вы_ _ _ _ _ _(v.) —
пр_ _ _ _(adv.) иг_ _ _ _(v.) всю ж_ _ _ _(n.) напр_ _ _ _(adv.).
Ах, _ _ _ _ _ _(adv.), что всегда, как и_ _ _ _ _ _ _(adv.),
наша _ _ _ _ _ _(n.) — то _ _ _ _ _ _(n.), то _ _ _ _ _ _(n.)...
Не ос_ _ _ _ _ _ _ _(v.: imperat.) с_ _ _ _ _ _ _(n.: gen.), маэстро!
Не _ _ _ _ _ _ _ _(v.: imperat.) _ _ _ _ _ _(n.: gen.) со _ _ _(n.: gen.)!
Не ост_ _ _ _ _ _ _(v.: imperat.) ст_ _ _ _ _ _(n.: gen.), маэстро!
Не _ _ _ _ _ _ _ _(v.: imperat.) _ _ _ _ _ _(n.: gen.) со _ _ _(n.: gen.)!

Г_ _-н_ _ _ _ _(adv.) на ост_ _ _ _ _ _(n.: prep.)
ко_ _ _ _ _ _(adj.)
с_ _ _ _ _(v.) спасибо и этой _ _ _ _ _ _(n.: dat.).
Но из гр_ _ _ _(n.: gen.) своей
ро_ _ _ _(n.: gen.) ве_ _ _ _(adj.)
не сотв_ _ _ _ _(v.: inf.) бы ку_ _ _ _(n.: acc.) себе.
Ах, н_ _ _ _ _(adv.), что всегда, как из_ _ _ _ _ _(adv.),
наша с_ _ _ _ _(n.) — то г_ _ _ _ _(n.), то п_ _ _ _ _(n.)...
Не рас_ _ _ _ _ _ _ _ _ _(v.: imperat.)
с на_ _ _ _ _ _(n.: instr.), маэстро!
Не _ _ _ _ _ _ _ _(v.: imperat.) _ _ _ _ _ _(n.: gen.) со _ _ _(n.: gen.)!
Не расст_ _ _ _ _ _ _ _(v.: imperat.)
с над_ _ _ _ _(n.: instr.), маэстро!
Не _ _ _ _ _ _ _ _(v.: imperat.) _ _ _ _ _ _(n.: gen.) со _ _ _(n.: gen.)!

Ко_ _ _ _ _(adj.: short form) наши л_ _ _(n.) мо_ _ _ _ _(adj.):
м_ _(n.) — и разв_ _ _ _ _(v.), как на ко_ _ _ _ _(n.: prep.),
кр_ _ _ _ _(adj.) кам_ _ _(n.), баш_ _ _ _(n.) зо_ _ _ _ _(adj.),
бе_ _ _(adj.) па_ _ _(n.), ру_ _ _ _(n.) в кру_ _ _ _ _(n.: prep.).
Ах, ни_ _ _ _(adv.), что всегда, как изв_ _т_ _(adv.),
наша су_ _ _ _(n.) — то гу_ _ _ _(n.), то па_ _ _ _(n.)...
Не об_ _ _ _ _ _ _(v.: imperat.) вн_ _ _ _ _ _(n.: gen.), маэстро!
Не у_ _ _ _ _ _ _(v.: imperat.) л_ _ _ _ _(n.: gen.) со _ _ _(n.: gen.)!
Не обра_ _ _ _ _(v.: imperat.) вни_ _ _ _ _(n.: gen.),[1] маэстро!
Не уб_ _ _ _ _ _(v.: imperat.) ла_ _ _ _(n.: gen.) со л_ _(n.: gen.)!

---

[1]The last two words constitute an idiomatic construction.

Song 17. Песенка о Моцарте

Моцарт на старенькой скрипке играет.
Моцарт играет, а скрипка поёт.
Моцарт отечества не выбирает —
просто играет всю жизнь напролёт.
Ах, ничего, что всегда, как известно,
наша судьба — то гульба, то пальба...
Не оставляйте стараний, маэстро!
Не убирайте ладони со лба.
Не оставляйте стараний, маэстро!
Не убирайте ладони со лба.

Где–нибудь на остановке конечной
скажем спасибо и этой судьбе.
Но из грехов своей родины вечной
не сотворить бы кумира себе.
Ах, ничего, что всегда, как известно,
наша судьба — то гульба, то пальба...
Не расставайтесь с надеждой, маэстро!
Не убирайте ладони со лба.
Не расставайтесь с надеждой, маэстро!
Не убирайте ладони со лба.

Коротки наши лета молодые:
миг — и развеются, как на кострах,
красный камзол, башмаки золотые,
белый парик, рукава в кружевах.
Ах, ничего, что всегда, как известно,
наша судьба — то гульба, то пальба...
Не обращайте внимания, маэстро!
Не убирайте ладони со лба.
Не обращайте внимания, маэстро!
Не убирайте ладони со лба.

<u>Вопросы по тексту (ответы полными предложениями)</u>:
1) О ком эта песня? 2) На чём играет композитор? 3) Какая у Моцарта скрипка? 4) С чем сравнивается звучание скрипки? 5) Как выражается общечеловеческая, а не узко национальная сущность музыки Моцарта? 6) Как долго играет Моцарт? 7) Из чего складывается наша жизнь? 8) О чём поэт просит Моцарта [3 разные просьбы] вопреки жизненным

конфликтам? 9) На что Моцарту не следует обращать внимания? 10) Что символизирует ладонь на лбу? 11) Чего опасается поэт? 12) Как из грехов родины делают кумиров [примеры]? 13) Сколько времени длится наша молодость? 14) С чем сравнивается краткость молодости? 15) Как одет Моцарт? 16) Чему в этой песне противопоставляется искусство?

Комментарии к тексту песни

•игра́ть || заигра́ть (to play [в + acc.: games/sports; на + prep.: musical instruments])
 игра́ю, –ешь, –ют
 Я час поиграю на скрипке, а потом буду играть в теннис.
 (I'll play the violin for an hour, and then I'll play tennis.)
•петь || спеть (to sing [**SEE** "Песенка старого шарманщика"])
•выбира́ть || вы́брать (to choose, select) выбира́ю, –ешь, –ют || вы́беру, –ешь, –ут
•весь/всё/всю + time unit [acc.] + напролёт (all [TIME UNIT] long)
 Он играет всю ночь / весь день напролёт.
 (He has been playing all night / day long.)
•ничего, что (it's O.K. that / if)
 Ничего, что у нас денег нет — лишь бы счастье было.
 (It's O.K. that we have no money: as long as we are lucky / happy.)
•как известно (as we know, as is known [parenthetical phrase])
 Как известно, у слона есть хобот.
 (As we know, an elephant has a trunk.)
•судьба (fate, life, life story)
•то..., то... (sometimes..., sometimes...; alternately... and...; to go from... to...)
 Он то плачет, то смеётся. (He keeps going from tears to laughter.)
•гульба́ (loud / wild partying [**SEE** "гуля́ть" in "Дежурный по апрелю"])
•пальба́ (intensive / indiscriminate shooting [from "пали́ть || пальну́ть"])
 палю́, –и́шь, –я́т || пальну́, –ёшь, –у́т (**SEE** "стреля́ть" in "Примета")
•оставля́ть || оста́вить + verbal noun (to cease / stop an activity)
 Оставьте разговоры и займитесь работой. (Stop talking and get to work.)
 ••оставля́ть || оста́вить (to leave [transitive])
 оставля́ю, –ешь, –ют || оста́влю, оста́вишь, оста́вят
 ••уходи́ть || уйти́, уезжа́ть || уе́хать (to leave [intransitive], to go away)
 ухожу́, ухо́дишь, ухо́дят || уйду́, –ёшь, –у́т (ушёл/ушла)
 уезжа́ю, –ешь, –ют || уе́ду, –ешь, –ут
 В 1917 г. многие оставили всё имущество и уехали из России.
 (In 1917 many people left [behind] all their property and left Russia.)
 N.B. The idea of "leaving a place" [departing from somewhere] is conveyed by the transitive "to leave" in English, e.g., I left London. In Russian a preposition, such as "из" or "с," is required: Я уехал из Лондона or Игрок ушёл с площадки (The player left the court).
•старание (hard work, effort [often in the plural])
 ••стара́ться || постара́ться + inf. (to try / strive / endeavor)
 стара́юсь, –ешься, –ются
•убира́ть || убра́ть (to remove; to take / put away; to clean up [a house, a room])
 убира́ю, –ешь, –ют || уберу́, –ёшь, –у́т
•[кто/где/как/что/какой]-нибудь (some-[one/where/how/thing/kind of]; **SEE** "Шёл троллейбус по улице")
•конечная остановка (terminus [end point in a transportation route])
•говори́ть || сказа́ть (to speak / talk / tell [**SEE** "Чёрный кот"])
•сказа́ть спасибо (to thank)

••благодари́ть || поблагодари́ть (to thank) благодарю́, –и́шь, –я́т

•не + inf. perf. + бы (I hope that something won't happen to me, I hope that I won't do something)

Не ошиби́ться бы. (I hope I won't make a mistake.)

•твори́ть || сотвори́ть (to create / make [**SEE** "Молитва (Франсуа Вийона)"])

•куми́р (idol [a person whom one reveres])

•себе ([for] myself / [for] yourself etc.)

Он себе сделал бутерброд. (He made [for] himself a sandwich.)

•расстава́ться || расста́ться (to part with [**SEE** "Солнышко сияет"])

•лета́ (poetic/archaic variant of "годы")

•молодой (young)

N.B. "Молодой" can be used only in reference to adults. A young child is not "молодой ребёнок" but "маленький ребёнок." A young woman is "молодая женщина."

•разве́ивать[ся] || разве́ять[ся] (to dissipate [about smoke etc.], to dispel [about illusions, misconceptions etc.]; –ся: intransitive)

разве́иваю, –ешь разве́ивает[ся], –ют[ся] ||

разве́ю, –ешь, разве́ет[ся], -ят[ся]

•костёр (fire [**SEE** "Ваше величество, женщина"])

•не обраща́ть || обрати́ть + внимание/я + на + acc. (not to notice; not to pay attention to; to ignore; not to let something bother oneself / get to oneself)

обраща́ю, –ешь, –ют || обращу́, обрати́шь, обратя́т

Не обращайте внимания на шум.

(Don't pay [any] attention to the noise / don't let the noise get to you.)

••обраща́ть || обрати́ть внимание на + acc. (to direct one's attention to..., to notice, to note)

Обратите внимание на эту картину. (Have a look at this painting.)

Переведите на русский язык, пользуясь песней и комментариями

1. Here is what the child psychologist **said** to the conductor: "**Maestro, it's O.K. if** your little son is **sometimes** a demon and **sometimes** an angel. He is still **young! It's O.K. if** he doesn't **clean up** his room. **As** (we) **know**, everyone grows up. One day[1] your son will **stop** (his) **games**, will roll up (his) **sleeves** and will start doing **something** serious. Childhood is not **eternal**. **It's O.K. that** he **plays** soccer **all** day **long** now: it's not a **sin**. **It's O.K. that** his **idols** are hairy rock stars and not violinists. **Don't let that get to you. Don't give up hope.** Continue doing your parental duty: your **hard work** will bear fruit one day. Even if he doesn't like the **violin,** let[2] him continue his lessons. One day he will **thank you**. Who knows what kind of **life**[3] awaits him? In[4] thirty or forty **years**, **somewhere** far away, when he is no longer **young**, he will remember[5] his **old**

---

[1]**SEE** "Ещё раз о дураках."

[2]**SEE** "Часовые любви."

[3]Do not use "жизнь."

[4]**SEE** "verb + че́рез" in "Песенка старого шарманщика."

[5]**SEE** "Дежурный по апрелю": forgotten information recalled.

parents with fondness and will see his childhood as a **golden** age. By the way, last night[1] your orchestra **played** marvelously. You **chose** an excellent program, and you **left** just enough time for an encore. And the guest singer **sang** beautifully! I clapped so loud that the **palms** (of my hands) still hurt! You should[2] take your son to these concerts more often."

2. Maybe **someone somewhere** wears[3] **wigs** today, but I think that wearing a **wig** is[4] like wearing a **camisole**: an anachronism. However, **lace** is still in fashion: recently at a streetcar **stop** I **noticed** a **young** woman with **lace** on (her) **sleeves**.

3. I **don't pay** (any) **attention to** fashion. Life is so **short**, that worrying about things like **shoes** and **lace** is a waste of time. I **try to direct my attention to** more important matters.[5]

4. When the **shooting** stopped and the smoke **dissipated**, I saw Zhenia, who was lying on the ground with a scratched **forehead** but unhurt.

5. The forester **said**: "Excuse me, but why are you **removing** the sign with the inscription: 'No **(camp)fires**[6] in the park.'?" The tourist replied: "O.K., I'll **leave** the sign and will simply **ignore it**."

6. When the train (had) **left** the station the passenger thought: "**I hope** (I) **won't miss** my **stop** or I won't end up at the **terminus**."

7. The **young** spouses **parted** because the husband thought only about **living it up** with his buddies and always **left** his wife alone with the kids. At first she **ignored** this, but then she lost (all) **hope** and **left**.

8. **Fate** is such a fickle thing: it can change in one **moment**. **Sometimes** we **party** and **drink**, (and) **sometimes** we **shoot** and die.

9. Ask not what your **motherland** can do for you; ask what you can do for your **motherland**.

10. **As we know**, according to the Old Testament, God **made** the world in six[7] days.

11. These **young** children will soon grow up and **stop** their games. They **will choose** a profession, and then their **fate** will be in their hands. But for now I am not **paying** (any) **attention** to their silliness.

12. The war **dispelled** all his illusions, but he **never lost hope** that it would stop. Nothing[8] is **eternal**.

13. "I **will dispel** all your illusions about your **idol**: he is a drunk and a criminal!"

---

[1]**SEE** "Дежурный по апрелю."
[2]**SEE** "Примета."
[3]**SEE** "Старый пиджак."
[4]Here the verb "to be" is best rendered by "это."
[5]**SEE** "Он, наконец, явился в дом."
[6]Lit.: campfires are forbidden.
[7]**SEE** "verb + за + time unit [acc.]" in "Песенка старого шарманщика."
[8]**SEE** "Примета."

18 A (Blanks)

В _ _ _ _ _(n.) на _ _ _ _ _(adj.) _ _ _ _ _ _(n.: acc.)

_ _ _ _ _ _ _ _ _ _(v.) _ _ _ _ _ _(n.).

Ему _ _ _ _ _ _ _ _ _(n.) _ _ _ _ _ _(n.)

_ _ _ _ _ _ _ _(n.: gen.) _ _ _ _ _ _ _ _ _(v.)

и _ _ _ _ _ _(adj.) _ _ _ _ _ _(n.: acc.)

так _ _ _ _ _ _ _ _ _ _(adv.) _ _ _ _ _ _(v.).

_ _ _ _(v.) ему _ _ _ _ _(n.: acc.) _ _ _ _ _ _ _ _(n.: gen.)

и в _ _ _ _ _ _ _ _ _(n.: prep., dimin.) _ _ _ _(n.).

И _ _ _ _(n.) свои _ _ _ _ _ _(n.: dat.)

_ _ _ _ _ _ _ _ _(v.) на _ _ _ _ _(n.).

_ _ _ _ _ _ _ _(v.) ему, _ _ _ _ _ _ _ _ _(verbal adv.) его

_ _ _ _ _ _(n.: instr.) _ _ _ _ _ _ _ _ _(adj.):

« _ _ _ _ _ _ _ _(adv.) их _ _ _(v: imperat.), а не то[1]

_ _ _ _ _ _ _ _ _ _ _(v.) _ _ _ _ _ _ _ _ _ _ _(n.: instr.).

И _ _ _ _ _ _ _ _ _(n.: gen.) _ _ _ _ _ _ _ _(adj.)

_ _ _ _ _ _(v.: inf.) у _ _ _ _ _(n.: gen.) не _ _ _ _ _ _(v.: imperat.)».

И _ _ _ _ _(v.) _ _ _ _ _ _(n.) — его _ _ _ _ _ _(n.)

_ _ _ _ _(v.) средь _ _ _ _ _(n. gen.):

_ _ _ _(numeral) _ _ _ _ _ _ _ _ _(adj.) _ _ _ _ _ _(n. gen.),

_ _ _ _(numeral) _ _ _ _ _ _ _ _(adj.) _ _ _ _ _ _(n. gen.)

и _ _ _ _ _ _ _ _ _(n.).

_ _ _ _ _ _(v.) им _ _ _ _ _ _(n.): «Не _ _ _ _ _ _ _ _(adj.: short form) нам

ни _ _ _ _ _ _(n.) ни _ _ _ _ _(n.)!

_ _ _ _ _(n.: acc.) мы _ _ _ _ _ _(v.) и с _ _ _ _ _ _ _ _(n.: instr.)

_ _ _ _ _ _(v.) и ура!»

(continued)

[1]А не то = idiomatic construction.

И вот _ _ _ _ _ _ _ _ _ _(v.) _ _ _ _ _ _ _ _ _ _ _ _(adj.) _ _ _ _ _(n.: gen.)

_ _ _ _ _ _ _ _ _ _(n.→ subj. of sentence).

В _ _ _ _ _ _(n.: prep.) _ _ _ _ _ _(n.) свою _ _ _ _ _(n.: acc.)

_ _ _ _ _ _ _ _ _ _ _(v.):

_ _ _ _ _ _ _(adj.) _ _ _ _ _ _(n. acc.)

_ _ _ _ _ _ _ _ _ _ _ _ _(n.: instr.) сразу _ _ _ _ _ _ _ _ _(v.),

а _ _ _ _ _ _ _ _ _(adj.: acc.) _ _ _ _ _ _ _(v.) в _ _ _ _ _ _ _ _ _(n. prep.) —

_ _ _ _ _(particle) _ _ _ _ _ _(pron.)...

_ _ _ _ _ _ _ _ _ _ _ _(v.: imperat.) себе —

_ _ _ _ _ _ _ _ _ _(v.) _ _ _ _ _ _ _ _ _(adj.) _ _ _(n.).

_ _ _ _(numeral) _ _ _ _ _ _ _ _ _(adj.) _ _ _ _ _ _(n. gen.)

не _ _ _ _ _ _ _ _ _ _(v.) из _ _ _ _ _ _ _(n.: gen.) _ _ _ _ _ _ _(adj.).

_ _ _ _ _ _ _ _ _(n.), _ _ _ _ _ _ _ _ _(adv.) не _ _ _ _ _ _ _(adj.),

_ _ _ _ _ _ _(v.) на _ _ _ _ _ _ _(substantivized adj.: prep.),

но _ _ _ _ _ _ _ _(n.: gen.) _ _ _ _ _(adj.) _ _ _ _ _(n.)

_ _ _ _ _ _ _ _ _ _(v.) они.

_ _ _ _ _ _ _(v: imperat.), _ _ _ _ _ _ _ _ _(n.)!

_ _ _ _ _ _ _(v.: imperat.), и _ _ _ _ _(n.) и _ _ _ _(n.)!

_ _ _ _ _ _ _ _ _(adj.) _ _ _ _ _ _(n.: dat.) не _ _ _ _ _(v.), _ _ _ _ _ _(n.),

_ _ _ _ _ _ _ _ _ _ _ _(v.: inf.).

Ведь _ _ _ _ _ _ _ _(adj.) _ _ _ _ _ _ _ _ _(n.: dat.)

нет _ _ _ _ _ _(n.: gen.) в _ _ _ _ _(substantivized adj.: prep.)

_ _ _ _ _ _ _ _ _ _ _(v.: inf.),

и _ _ _ _ _ _ _ _ _(n.: gen.), _ _ _ _ _ _(adv.),

всегда не _ _ _ _ _ _ _(v.) на всех.

18 B (Partial Blanks)

В п_ _ _ _ на чу_ _ _(adj.) ст_ _ _ _(n. acc.)
соб_ _ _ _ся(v.) _ _ _ _ _ь(n.).
Ему к_ _ _ _ _ _ _(n.) м_ _ _ _(n.)
су_ _ _ _ _(n.: gen.) нас_ _ _ _ _(v.)
и с_ _ _ _ _(adj.) м_н_ _ _(n.: acc.)
так акк_ _ _ _ _ _(adv.) за_ _ _ _(v.).
Д_ _ _(v.) ему п_ _ _ _(n.: acc.) мах_ _ _ _(n.: gen.)
и в тр_ _ _ч_е(n.: prep., dimin.) с_ _ь(n.).

И р_ _ _(n.) свои _ _ _ _ _ю́ (n.: dat.)
по_ _ _ _ _ _(v.) на гр_ _ь(n.).
_ _ _ _ _ _ _(v.) ему, обл_ _ _ _ _(verbal adv.) его
вз_ _ _ _(n.: instr.) лу_ _ _ _ _м(adj.):
«Пол_ _ _ _(adv.) их б_ _(v: imperat.), а не то[1]
просл_ _ _ _ь(v.) па_ _ _ _ _ _ _ _(n.: instr.).
И _ _ _ _ _ _ _ _(n.: gen.) сл_ _ _ _ _(adj.)
от_ _ _ _(v.: inf.) у вр_ _ _(n.: gen.) не за_ _ _ _(v.: imperat.)».

И в_ _ _ _(v.) _ _ _ _ _ь(n.) — его в_ _с_ _(n.)
_ _ _ _ _(v.) средь дв_ _ _(n. gen.):
_ _ _ _(numeral) _ _ _ _ _ _ _ _ _(adj.) _ _ _ _ _ _(n. gen.),
_ _ _ _(numeral) в_ _ _ _ _ _(adj.) _ _ _ _ _ _(n. gen.)
и е_ _ _ _ _ _ _(n.).
С_ _ _ _ _(v.) им ко_ _ _ь(n.): «Не стр_ _ _ _(adj.: short form) нам
ни п_ _ _ _ _(n.) ни ве_ _ _(n.)!
Вр_ _ _(n.: acc.) мы по_ _ _ _(v.) и с по_ _ _ _ _(n.: instr.)
п_ _ _ _ _(v.) и ура!»

(continued)

[1]А не то = idiomatic construction.

И вот отгр_ _ _ _ _(v.) про_ _ _ _ _ _ _ _(adj.) р_ _ _ _(n.: gen.)
тор_ _ _ _во(n.→ subj. of sentence).
В по_ _ _ _(n.: prep.) кор_ _ь(n.) свою а_ _ _ _(n.: acc.)
переин_ _ _ _(v.):
ве_ё_ _ _(adj.) _ _ _ _ _ _ _(n. acc.)
инт_ _ _ _ _ _ _ _ _ _(n.: instr.) сразу наз_ _ _ _ _(v.),
а г_ _ _ _ _ _ _ _(adj.: acc.) ос_ _ _ _ _(v.) в _ _ _ _ _ _ах(n.: prep.) —
а_ _ _ь (particle) н_ _ _ _ _(pron.)...

Предс_ _ _ь_ _(v.: imperat.) себе —
нас_ _ _ _ _ _(v.) поб_ _ _ _ _ (adj.)[1] д_ _(n.).
П_ _ _(numeral) гр_ _ _ _ _ _(adj.) с_ _ _ _ _(n. gen.)
не ве_ _ _ _ _ _ _ _(v.) из сх_ _ _ _ _(n.: gen.) во_ _ _ _ _(adj.).
Еф_ _ _ _ _ _(n.), м_ _ _ _ _ _ _ _(adv.) не ст_ _ _ _ _(adj.),
же_ _ _ся(v.) на пл_ _ _ _ _(substantivized adj.: prep.),
но пр_ _ _ _ _ _(n.: gen.) ц_ _ _ _(adj.) ме_ _ _(n.)
зах_ _ _ _ _ _(v.) они.

И_ _ _ _ _ _(v.: imperat.), ор_ _ _ _ _ _(n.)!
Зв_ _ _ _ _(v.: imperat.), и п_ _ _ _(n.) и с_ _ _(n.)!
Ми_ _ _н_ _(adj.) пе_ _ _ _(n.: dat.) не с_ _ _ _(v.), _ _ _ _ _ _ _(n.),
пред_ _ _ _ _ся(v.: inf.).
Ведь гр_ _т_ _м(adj.) со_ _ _ _ам(n.: dat.)
нет см_ _ _ _(n.: gen.) в ж_ _ _ _(substantivized adj.: prep.)
ос_ _ _ _ _ _ся(v.: inf.),
и пря_ _ _ _ _(n.: gen.), к_ _ _ _ _(adv.),
всегда не хв_ _ _ _ _(v.) на всех.

---

[1]Same root as in the second-last blank on the previous page.

Song 18. Песенка о старом короле

В поход на чужую страну собирался король.
Ему королева мешок сухарей насушила
и старую мантию так аккуратно зашила.
Дала ему пачку махорки и в тряпочке соль.

И руки свои королю положила на грудь.
Сказала ему, обласкав его взором лучистым:
«Получше их бей, а не то прослывёшь пацифистом.
И пряников сладких отнять у врага не забудь».

И видит король — его войско стоит средь двора:
пять грустных солдат, пять весёлых солдат и ефрейтор.
Сказал им король: « Не страшны нам ни пресса, ни ветер!
Врага мы побьём и с победой придём, и ура!»

И вот отгремело прощальных речей торжество.
В походе король свою армию переиначил:
веселых солдат интендантами[1] сразу назначил,
а грустных оставил в солдатах — авось ничего...

Представьте себе — наступили победные дни.
Пять грустных солдат не вернулись из схватки военной.
Ефрейтор, морально нестойкий, женился на пленной,
но пряников целый мешок захватили они.

Играйте, оркестры! Звучите, и песни и смех!
Минутной печали не сто́ит, друзья, предаваться.
Ведь грустным солдатам нет смысла в живых оставаться,
и пряников, кстати, всегда не хватает на всех.

Вопросы по тексту (ответы полными предложениями):
1) Куда собирался король? 2) Как королева его подготовила к походу? 3) О чём она его предупредила? 4) Что она его попросила принести домой? 5) Опишите войско короля. 6) Как король изменил свою армию? 7) Кто вернулся с войны? 8) Как ефрейтор проявил свою моральную слабость? 9) Как король выполнил просьбу королевы? 10) Стоит ли печалиться о грустных солдатах? 11) Почему грустным солдатам нет смысла оставаться в живых? 12) Кто такие грустные солдаты? 13) В чём главная мысль этой песни?

---

[1]Supply officer (in charge of provisions and material support).

Комментарии к тексту песни

•похóд (hiking trip, war, military expedition [**SEE** “Часовые любви”])
•чужой/ая (someone else’s, foreign [**SEE** “Примета”])
•собирáться || собрáться (to intend / get ready to)
собирáюсь, –ешься, –ются || соберýсь, –ёшься, –ýтся
Мы собрались [идти] в школу. (We got ready to go to school)
Нина собирается вы́купаться. (Nina intends to take a bath.)
•сухарь (rusk, biscuit)
•суши́ть || насуши́ть (to dry [with rusks: by roasting]) сушý, сýшишь, сýшат
•аккуратно (carefully, neatly, meticulously)
•так (thus, so, this way [такой→ such, so; **SEE** “Старый пиджак”])
•зашивáть || заши́ть (to darn, mend [fabric])
зашивáю, –ешь, –ют || зашью́, –ёшь, –ю́т
•давáть || дать (to give)
даю́, даёшь, даю́т || дам, дашь, даст, дади́м, дади́те, дадýт
•класть || положи́ть (to put/place [for objects in a **non-upright** position])
кладý, –ёшь, –ут || положý, полóжишь, полóжат
••лежáть || полежáть (to be/lie [for objects in a **non-upright** position])
лежý, –и́шь, –áт
Деньги лежат в копилке, потому что я их туда положила.
(The money is in the piggy-bank because I put it there.)
••стáвить || постáвить (to put/place [for objects in an **upright** position])
стáвлю, стáвишь, стáвят
••стоя́ть || постоя́ть (to be/stand [for objects in an **upright** position])
стою́, –и́шь, –я́т (**SEE** “Часовые любви”)
Книги стоят на полке потому, что я их туда поставил.
(The books are / are standing on the shelf because I put them there.)
•possessor [dat.] + preposition + possessed thing (on one’s..., to one’s... etc.)
Она положила руки ему на грудь. (She put her hands on his chest.)
Он бросил письмо мне в портфель. (He threw a letter in my briefcase.)
Она надела шапку Гале на голову. (She put a hat on Galia’s head.)
•говори́ть || сказáть (to speak / talk / tell [**SEE** “Чёрный кот”])
•ласкáть || обласкáть + acc. (to caress/fondle, to be tender with someone [об–: to show kindness to someone]) ласкáю, –ешь, –ют
Она всегда ласкает дочку. (She is always tender with her daughter.)
У них меня так обласкали! (I was shown so much kindness at their place.)
N.B. In the song the queen’s radiant gaze “caresses” the king.
•получше + verb (to do something well / better)
Ешь получше, и ты всегда будешь здоровым.
(Eat well / better, and you’ll always be healthy.)
•бить || поби́ть (to beat / hit / strike / vanquish) бью, бьёшь, бьют
•а не то (otherwise, or else)
•слыть || прослы́ть + instr. (to be known as [про-: to become known as])
слывý, –ёшь, –ýт
Он прослыл пацифистом. (He became known as a pacifist.)
•пряник (honey biscuit [similar to the German *Pfeffernuß*])
•отнимáть || отня́ть + acc. + у + gen. (to take something away from someone)
отнимáю, –ешь, –ют || отнимý, отни́мешь, отни́мут
Он отнял сухари у врага. (He took the rusks away from the enemy.)
•забывáть || забы́ть (to forget) забывáю, –ешь, –ют || забýду, –ешь, –ут
•войско/армия (army [войско: more archaic; plur. “войска”: armed forces])

•двор (courtyard, court [physical court or royal court, but not a court of law])
•средь/среди + gen. (among, in the middle of [a space])

N.B. "Средь" is less common than "среди."

•весёлый/ая (jolly, joyful, in a good mood, optimistic, happy)

N.B. The short form "вéсел/веселá" is used as a predicate that implies someone's jolly state at a given point in time, e.g., Он сегодня очень вéсел (He is [acting] very jolly today). The full form "весёлый/ая," **when used as a predicate,** can refer to a more permanent kind of jolliness, such as a character trait, e.g., Миша — весёлый парень (Misha is a jolly fellow).

•солдат (soldier, private [irregular genitive plural: много солдат)
•ефрейтор (lance-corporal or private 1st class)
•dat. + не страшен/на (not to be afraid of something)

Нам не страшен серый волк. (We are not afraid of the big bad wolf.)

•не... ни... ни... (neither... nor, either... or)

Я не знаю ни его ни её. (I know neither him, nor her.)

•вернуться с победой (to come back victorious/triumphant [from war etc.])
•гремéть || отгремéть (to thunder [от–: to stop thundering; to die down]) гремит, –ят
•переинáчивать || переинáчить (to change/alter)

переинáчиваю, –ешь, –ют || переинáчу, –ишь, –ат

•назначáть || назнáчить + acc. + instr. (to appoint/name [to a post])

назначáю, –ешь, –ют || назнáчу, –ишь, –ат
Я назначила её председателем. (I appointed her chairperson.)

•оставлять || остáвить + acc. + в + prep. [plural] (to leave in the capacity of)

оставляю, –ешь, –ют || остáвлю, остáвишь, остáвят
Я оставил его в председателях. (I left him in the capacity of chairperson.)
••оставáться || остáться + в + prep. [plur.] (stay in the capacity of)
остаюсь, –ёшься, –ются || остáнусь, –ешься, –утся
Он остался в солдатах. (He stayed in the rank of private.)

•остаться в живых (to survive)

Он остался в живых после чистки. (He survived the purge.)

•авóсь ничегó (hopefully it'll be O.K. ["не случится" is implicit here])

Кажется, я пересолил суп — авось ничего [не случится]. (It seems I have put too much salt in the soup: hopefully, it'll be O.K. [i.e., hopefully, the guests won't notice].)

•представлять || представить (to imagine [**SEE** "Старый пиджак"])
•наступáть || наступить (to come/begin [regarding a time period or a state])

наступáет, –ют || наступит, –ят
Наступили победные дни. (The days of victory arrived.)
Наступила весна. (Spring came.)

•возвращáть[ся] || вернуть[ся] (**SEE** "Песенка о голубом шарике")
•схвáтка (battle [has more emotional coloration than "бой"])
•стóйкий (steadfast, tough)
•жениться на + prep. (to marry [a **man** marrying a **woman**])

женюсь, жéнишься, жéнятся (imperf. || perf. = same form)
Вчера он на ней женился. (Yesterday he married her.)
••выйти замуж за + acc. (to marry [a **woman** marrying a **man**])
Надежда вышла замуж за Владимира. (Nadezhda married Vladimir.)
••поженить[ся] (to marry [without –ся: to marry two people; with –ся: to marry **each other**, to get married)
Владик и Лариса поженились год назад. Их поженил священник. (Vladik and Larissa [got] married a year ago. They were married by a priest.)

•плéнный/ая (captured [when not modifying a noun: prisoner of war])
Пленного офицера расстреляли. (The captured officer was shot.)
Пленного допросили. (The prisoner of war was interrogated.)
•целый/ая (a whole) весь/вся (the whole)
Целый поезд полетел под откос. Потом весь поезд отправлили по частям в мастерскую. (A whole train fell off a cliff. Then the whole train was sent in pieces to a repair shop.)
•захвáтывать || (to capture) захвáтываю, -ешь, -ют ||
•звучáть || зазвучáть (to sound [intransitive]) звучý, –и́шь, –áт
Песня звучала хорошо. (The song sounded good.)
•dat. + стóит + inf. (one should...; it's worth doing something)
[Ему] стóит подумать о будущем.
(He [one] should think about the future.)
Туда стóит/стóило съездить. (It is/was worth going there.)
N.B. With a negative particle this can be translated as "there is no point in + verb."
•предавáться || предáться + dat. (to be carried away by [an emotion, dreams...])
предаю́сь, –ёшься, –ются ||
предáмся, –дáшься, –дáстся, –дади́мся, –дади́тесь, –даду́тся
Не предавайся печали.
(Don't get carried away by sadness / don't let sadness get to you.)
•ведь (after all [**SEE** "Шёл троллейбус по улице"])
•dat. + нет смы́сла + imperf. inf. (there is no point in doing something)
[Мне] нет смысла это делать. (There is no point [for me] in doing this.)
•gen. + хватáет || хвáтит [хватáло || хвати́ло] + на + acc. (enough [left] for)
Одежды хватает на всех. (There are enough clothes [left] for everyone.)
N.B. This construction is normally used when something is being distributed.
••dat. + хватáет || хвáтит [хватáло || хвати́ло] + gen. (to be / have enough)
Мне не хвати́ло дéнег; их всегдá не хватáет.
(I didn't have enough money; there is never enough [of it].)
N.B. This construction can be used with "на + time unit [acc.]," e.g., Этой одежды нам хватило на неделю (These clothes sufficed [were enough] for us for a week).

Переведите на русский язык, пользуясь песней и комментариями

1. Why are you **putting** a compress **on this soldier's leg**?[1] He is a **prisoner of war**! **There will not be enough** compresses left **for all** the **soldiers** in our (own) **army**. Let[2] our **captured enemies** recover (by) themselves. **Hopefully, it'll be O.K.** **You should**[3] think about what our **press** will say about such unpatriotic behavior.

2. I **intend to put** the bottle on the table, and then I **intend to put** the **rusk** in the **sack**.

3. The teacher said to the class bully: "You say that you will **take away** all the **rusks** and **honey biscuits from** these children. You certainly know how to take children **in a good mood** and make them **sad**. But I cannot

[1]Use "possessor [dat.] + preposition + possessed thing": **SEE** above.
[2]**SEE** "Часовые любви."
[3]Do not use "надо/нужно" or "должен."

imagine that you can be so **morally** base: they are your little **friends**! And regardless of the **moral** question, **there is no point in** creating a conflict for the sake of **momentary** gratification. Besides, I will **tell** your father, and he will certainly **beat** you at home."

4. "You are **getting ready** (to go) to a **foreign country**, and you have **forgotten** (your) passport!" "I don't need to take it: **hopefully, it'll be O.K.**"

5. "**By the way**, why are you **giving** me **someone else's mantle**?" **said** the **king** to the **queen**.

6. "The **king** directed[1] his **radiant gaze** at his **army** and he **said**: "**Friends**, we have **beaten** the **enemy**! **We are not afraid** of **either** external **enemies or** internal (ones). I will **appoint** (to the rank of) officers the **soldiers** who **will come back victorious** from future **battles**." **The whole army** cheered.

7. After the **victorious campaign, songs** will **sound**, and everyone will scream: "**Hurray**!" We will have to overcome our **sadness** when we remember[2] those who[3] **will not have survived.**[4]

8. "How many[5] **enemies** will you **capture** in **battle**?" "**A whole** regiment! **There is no point in capturing** fewer (than that)." "Will you interrogate **the whole** regiment or just the officers?"

9. The **tough prisoner of war** did not **tell** anything[6] to the **enemy** even when **salt** was sprinkled **on his**[7] wounds.

10. "He **married** her. She **married** him. **A whole orchestra played** at their wedding, and **among** the guests **laughter** and **joy** reigned." "And who **married** them?" "A ship's captain. They rented **a whole** ship."

11. If the **soldiers** continue eating the **honey biscuits**, we will **have enough honey biscuits for** a day, but tomorrow **there will not be enough honey biscuits** [left] **for everyone**, and we will have to buy **five** more **packs**.

12. **Imagine**, Klara had been a **steadfast pacifist**, but then she met an **old supply officer**, they **got married**, and she **became known as a military** enthusiast!

13. These boys **are not afraid** of the **wind** or the rain, so **there is no point** in keeping them indoors.

14. **There is no point** in **getting carried away** by dreams[8] when reality is so interesting.

---

[1]**SEE** "Я вновь повстречался с надеждой."
[2]**SEE** "Дежурный по апрелю."
[3]**SEE** "тот + <u>кто/который</u>" in "Я вновь повстречался с надеждой."
[4]Future tense (Russian has no equivalent of the future perfect).
[5]**SEE** "Ещё раз о дураках."
[6]**SEE** "ни[interrog. word]" in "Примета."
[7]"Possessor [dat.] + preposition + possessed thing." Lit.: (they) sprinkled salt...
[8]**SEE** "мечта́ть || помечта́ть о + prep." in "Он, наконец, явился в дом."

15. **Don't forget** to cover (your) **chest, or else** you will get sick.[1] **Sometimes** (it's) **worth** dressing more warmly than usual.
16. I will **name** Nikolai minister of **war**. If he refuses, he will **stay a lance-corporal**.
17. I think that very few **privates** will **survive** the **battle**.
18. I never **forget** that a good professor **should alter** his lectures every year. Those who don't do it **are known as** bores **among** the students.
19. The stingy fatalist said: "I will not buy a new parachute. Instead of that I will **mend** the old (one) (and) **hopefully, it'll be O.K.**"
20. If the **military orchestra is playing a victory** march, why is the king saying a **good-bye speech** to his **court**?
21. I hope that you **will dry** enough **rusks** before[2] the famine **begins**. (It's) always **worth** thinking about the **day** when there **will not be enough** food **for everyone**.
22. According to the **press, the king** proclaimed **victory** even before the **thunder of the battle had died down**.[3]
23. The **king** was in a very **good mood** yesterday because his son and the daughter of his former **enemy got married**. This means that now a time of peace **will come**.
24. **I (can) never have enough** sugar. This is why **I am known** as a sweet tooth. You (cannot) **imagine** how many candies **are**[4] in this drawer.
25. There is **a whole** encyclopedia of errors in this essay. **You should** write **carefully**! And use **your** dictionary **better**. You have **five** dictionaries: two **are** on your bookshelf and three **are**[5] in your desk.
26. You should wipe **the whole** table with this **rag**. When you finish, you will **put the rag in my sack**,[6] and then you will **give the sack** to me.
27. The **jolly** clown **put** a bottle **on** the **sad** clown's head.[7]
28. The **queen showed** (much) **kindness to the lance-corporal** who had **taken** the flag **away from the enemy**.
29. Our **king is tender with** his dogs, but he doesn't care how many **soldiers** in his **army will survive** in **battle**.
30. If you are a true **pacifist**, you should be **tough** and refuse to fight even if you are punished.

---

[1]"Get sick" is one verb: find the right aspect.
[2]Before / after + verb = перед тем / после того + как + verb.
[3]Lit.: the battle stopped thundering.
[4]Think of the position of these candies and use the correct "position" verb.
[5]**SEE** previous note.
[6]"Possessor [dat.] + preposition + possessed thing."
[7]**SEE** previous note.

19 A (Blanks)

_ _ _ _(adv.) _ _ _ _ _(n.) ещё _ _ _ _ _ _ _ _ _(v.),
_ _ _ _(adv.) ещё _ _ _ _(adj.: short form) _ _ _ _(n.),
_ _ _ _ _ _ _ _(n.), _ _ _(v.: imperat.) же ты
_ _ _ _ _ _ _ _(substantivized adj.: dat.), чего у него нет.

_ _ _ _ _ _(substantivized adj.: dat.) _ _ _(v.: imperat.) _ _ _ _ _ _(n.: acc.).
_ _ _ _ _ _ _ _ _ _ _(subst. adj.: dat.) _ _ _(v.: imperat.) _ _ _ _(n.: acc.).
_ _ _(v.: imperat.) _ _ _ _ _ _ _ _ _ _ _ _(subst. adj.: dat.) _ _ _ _ _(n.: gen.)...
и не _ _ _ _ _ _(v.: imperat.) про меня.

_ _ _ _(adv.) _ _ _ _ _(n.) ещё _ _ _ _ _ _ _ _ _(v.),
_ _ _ _ _ _ _ _(n.), — твоя _ _ _ _ _ _(n.)!
_ _ _(v.: imperat.) рвущемуся к _ _ _ _ _ _(n.: dat.)
навластвоваться _ _ _ _ _ _ _(adv.).
_ _ _(v.: imperat.) _ _ _ _ _ _ _ _ _ _(n.: acc.) _ _ _ _ _ _ _(subst. adj.: dat.),
_ _ _ _(conj.) до исхода _ _ _(n.: gen.).
_ _ _ _ _(proper noun: dat.)[1] _ _ _(v.: imperat.) _ _ _ _ _ _ _ _ _ _(n.)...
и не _ _ _ _ _ _(v: imperat.) про меня.

Я _ _ _ _(v.) — ты всё _ _ _ _ _ _(v.).
Я _ _ _ _ _(v.)[2] в _ _ _ _ _ _ _ _ _(n.) твою,
как _ _ _ _ _(v.)[3] _ _ _ _ _ _(n.) _ _ _ _ _ _(past passive participle),
что он _ _ _ _ _ _ _ _ _ _(v.) в _ _ _(n.: prep.),
как _ _ _ _ _(v.) каждое _ _ _(n.)
_ _ _ _ _(adj.) _ _ _ _ _(n.: dat.) твоим,
как _ _ _ _ _ _(v.) и мы сами,
не ведая, что творим![4]

_ _ _ _ _ _ _ _(n.), мой _ _ _ _(n.),
_ _ _ _ _ _ _ _ _ _ _ _ _(substantivized adj.) мой,
_ _ _ _(adv.) _ _ _ _ _(n.) ещё _ _ _ _ _ _ _ _ _(v.),
и это ей _ _ _ _ _ _ _(adv.) самой,
_ _ _ _(adv.) ещё _ _ _ _ _ _ _ _(v.) _ _ _ _ _ _ _ _(n.) и _ _ _ _(n.: gen.)...
_ _ _(v.: imperat.) же ты _ _ _ _(pron.: dat.) _ _ _ _ _ _ _ _ _ _(adv.)
и не _ _ _ _ _ _(v.: imperat.) про меня...
_ _ _(v.: imperat.) же ты _ _ _ _(pron.: dat.) _ _ _ _ _ _ _ _ _ _(adv.)
и не _ _ _ _ _ _(v.: imperat.) про меня.

---

[1]Name of a biblical character (Genesis 4).
[2]This is an archaic form of the verb (used in religious contexts): it has one extra vowel which is missing from its modern counterpart.
[3]This is the modern version of the verb referred to in the previous note.
[4]Biblical phrase.

19 B (Partial Blanks)

_ _ _ _(adv.) _ _ _ _ _(n.) ещё в_ _ _ _ _ _ _(v.),
_ _ _ _(adv.) ещё я_ _ _(adj.: short form) с_ _ _(n.),
_ _ _ _ _ _и(n.), _ _ _(v.: imperat.) же ты
ка_ _ _ _ _(substantivized adj.: dat.), чего у него нет.

Ум_ _ _ _(subst. adj.: dat.) _ _ _(v.: imperat.) го_ _ _ _(n.: acc.).
Тру_ _ _ _ _ _ _(subst. adj.: dat.) _ _ _(v.: imperat.) к_ _ _(n.: acc.).
_ _ _(v.: imperat.) сч_ _т_ _ _ _ _ _(subst. adj.: dat.) д_ _ _ _(n.: gen.)...
и не _ _ _ _ _ _(v.: imperat.) про меня.

_ _ _ _(adv.) з_ _ _ _(n.) ещё ве_ _ _ _ _ _(v.),
Г_ _ _ _ _ _(n.), — твоя _ _ _ _ _ _(n.)!
_ _ _(v.: imperat.) рвущемуся к в_ _ _ _ _(n.: dat.)
навластвоваться вс_ _ _ _ _(adv.).
_ _ _(v.: imperat.) пер_ _ _ш_ _(n.: acc.) ще_ _ _ _ _(subst. adj.: dat.),
х_ _ _(conj.) до исхода д_ _(n.: gen.).
К_ _ _ _(proper noun: dat.)[1] _ _ _(v.: imperat.) рас_ _я_ _ _(n.)...
и не _ _ _ _ _ _(v: imperat.) про меня.

Я з_ _ _(v.) — ты всё у_ _ _ _ _(v.).
Я _ _ _ _ _(v.)[2] в м_д_ _ _ _ _(n.) твою,
как _ _ _ _ _(v.)[3] со_ _ _ _(n.) уб_ _ _ _(past passive participle),
что он про_ _ _ _ _ _(v.) в р_ _(n.: prep.),
как в_ _ _ _(v.) каждое _х_(n.)
т_ _ _ _(adj.) ре_ _ _(n.: dat.) твоим,
как в_ _у_ _(v.) и мы сами,
не ведая, что творим![4]

Го_ _ _ _и(n.), мой Б_ _ _(n.),
зе_ _ _огл_ _ _ _(substantivized adj.) мой,
_ _ _ _(adv.) зе_ _ _(n.) ещё вер_ _ _ся(v.),
и это ей ст_ _ _ _ _(adv.) самой,
п_ _ _(adv.) ещё хв_ _ _ _ _(v.) вр_ _ _ _ _(n.) и о_ _ _(n.: gen.)...
_ _ _(v.: imperat.) же ты _ _ _ _(pron.: dat.) по_ _ _ _ _ _ _(adv.)
и не з_ _ _ _ _(v.: imperat.) про меня...
Д_ _(v.: imperat.) же ты в_ _ _(pron.: dat.) по_ _ _н_ _ _(adv.)
и не за_ _ _ _(v.: imperat.) про меня.

[1]Name of a biblical character (Genesis 4). Hint: "Am I my brother's keeper?"
[2]This is an archaic form of the verb (used in religious contexts): it has one extra vowel which is missing from its modern counterpart.
[3]This is the modern version of the verb referred to in the previous note.
[4]Biblical phrase.

Song 19. Молитва (Франсуа Вийона)

Пока земля ещё вертится,
пока ещё ярок свет,
Господи, дай же ты каждому,
чего у него нет.

Умному[1] дай голову.
Трусливому дай коня.
Дай счастливому денег...
и не забудь про меня.

Пока земля ещё вертится,
Господи, — твоя власть.
Дай рвущемуся к власти
навластвоваться всласть.
Дай передышку щедрому,
хоть до исхода дня.
Каину дай раскаяние...
и не забудь про меня.

Я знаю — ты всё умеешь.
Я верую в мудрость твою,
как верит солдат убитый,
что он проживает в раю,
как верит каждое ухо
тихим речам твоим,
как веруем и мы сами,
не ведая, что творим!

Господи, мой Боже,
зеленоглазый мой,
пока земля ещё вертится,
и это ей странно самой,
пока ещё хватает времени и огня...
дай же ты всем понемногу
и не забудь про меня...
Дай же ты всем понемногу
и не забудь про меня.

François Villon (1431- after 1463) was a famous French poet who led a very turbulent life: he associated with criminals, committed murder, spent time in prison and was almost hanged.

---

[1] "Мудрому" in the Frumkin edition.

Вопросы по тексту (ответы полными предложениями):
1) Какой это речевой жанр, т.е., диалог, монолог, рассказ и т.д.? 2) К кому обращается поэт? 3) Какая просьба поэта — самая главная? 4) Что надо дать умному и счастливому? 5) Как объяснить эти две странные просьбы? 6) Что надо дать остальным людям, за которых молится поэт? 7) О ком поэт все время просит не забыть Бога? 8) Во что верит поэт? 9) С чем поэт сравнивает свою веру в мудрость Бога? 10) Какого цвета глаза у Бога, и как это объяснить? 11) Чему земля удивляется и что означает этот образ? 12) Какой срок поэт даёт Богу для удовлетворения своих просьб? 13) Что произойдёт когда земля перестанет вертеться и почему тогда будет поздно ответить на молитву поэта?

Комментарии к тексту песни:
•пока (while, as long as, for the time being [пока не: until])
Пока у нас есть еда, но завтра может начаться голод.
(For the time being we have food, but tomorrow famine might start.)
Пока есть еда, ешь её: завтра она может исчезнуть.
(While / as long as there is food, eat it: tomorrow it might disappear.)
Пока ты не прочтёшь эти пять страниц, я тебя не выпущу гулять.
(Until you finish reading these five pages, I won't let you go outside.)
•ещё (still, again) ещё не (not yet)
•верте́ть[ся] || заверте́ть[ся] (to turn / spin [–ся: intransitive])
верчу́[сь], ве́ртишь[ся], ве́ртят[ся]
Этот пропеллер сам вертится или его вертит ветер?
(Is this propeller turning by itself or is the wind spinning it?)
•я́рок/я́рка (bright [full-form adj.: яркий/ая; adv.: я́рко])
•свет (light, world [**SEE** "Бумажный солдат"])
•дава́ть || дать (to give [**SEE** "Песенка о старом короле"])
•Го́споди (Oh, Lord [form of address; cf. Господь: Lord, i.e., God])
•Бо́же (Oh, God [form of address; cf. Бог: God])
•каждый (every, each [when not modifying a noun: everyone, all])
•у + possessor [gen.] + нет + gen. (someone doesn't have something)
"Чего у вас нет? " "У меня нет хлеба."
("What do you not have?" "I don't have [any] bread.")
••у + possessor [gen.] + есть + nomin. (someone has something)
У меня есть / была / будет вода. (I have / had / will have water.)
N.B. With body parts and things related to the body the word "есть" is normally left out, e.g., У неё рыжие ресницы (She has red eyelashes) or На губах у неё улыбка (She has a smile on her face).
It is also left out when the existence of the thing in question has already been established, e.g., Я потерял матрас. У тебя мой матрас? (I've lost my mattress. Do you have my mattress?). The past and future tense equivalents of "есть" (был/будет) can never be left out.
•конь (horse [usually male], stallion, steed) лошадь (horse [male or female])
•счастливый (happy, lucky; рад: glad [**SEE** "Бумажный солдат"])
•деньги (money)
N.B. Nouns that refer to things or substances of indefinite quantity appear in the partitive genitive form when acting as direct objects, e.g., Дай мне денег/воды

(Give me [some] money/water).[1]

•забыва́ть || забы́ть (to forget) забыва́ю, –ешь, –ют || забу́ду, –ешь, –ут

•рвущийся к власти ([someone] yearning for power])

••рва́ться || дорва́ться (to yearn/seek [intensely]; to be unable to wait to... [до–: to get / reach / get to one's object of yearning])

рвусь, рвёшься, рву́тся

Мида́с рвался к золоту. (Midas sought gold [coveted gold etc.].)

Они рвутся на фронт. (They can't wait to go to the front.)

•наVERBся (to get one's fill of doing something, e.g., навластвоваться)

Я наелся и напился. (I've had enough / my fill of food and drink.)

•вла́ствовать || повла́ствовать (to be in power) вла́ствую, –ешь, –ют

•передышка (pause, break [to catch one's breath, i.e., "a breather")

•хоть / хотя́ + бы (at least [with "хоть" the particle "бы" may be dropped])

•исход (end, outcome)

•раскаяние (remorse) покая́ние (repentance [often religious connotation])

••ка́яться || пока́яться + в + prep. (to repent) ка́юсь, –ешься, –ются

Грешники покаялись в своих грехах. (The sinners repented their sins.)

••раска́яться || раска́иваться + в + prep. (to feel remorse, to regret)

Я раскаялся в этом поступке. (I felt remorse about this action.)

•знать || узна́ть (to know [у–: to find out, to recognize]) зна́ю, –ешь, –ют

•уме́ть, мочь || смочь (can [**SEE** "О Володе Высоцком"])

•ве́ровать || уве́ровать + в + acc. (to believe in... [religious usage only; у–: to come to believe in, to start believing in])

ве́рую, –ешь, –ют (variant of "ве́рить" [**SEE** "Солнышко сияет"])

•убит/а (killed, murdered [**SEE** "Батальное полотно"])

•прожива́ть (to reside) прожива́ю, –ешь, –ют

•рай (heaven [prepositional case: в раю́; cf. сад: в саду́])

•сам/а́/о́/са́ми (myself, yourself, herself etc. [**SEE** "Чёрный кот"])

•они не ведают, что творят (they know not what they do [biblical])

••твори́ть || сотвори́ть (to create [usually regarding a divine act: God creating the world]; to do [archaic]; to create [a work of art])

творю́, –и́шь, –я́т

••натворить (to do something which causes damage/harm)

N.B. This verb is used chiefly in two expressions:

1) Что + nomin. + натворил!? (What has someone done?!)

Что вы натворили!? (What have you done!? [said in reaction to some harm or mischief done by the culprit])

2) Натворить много дел/глупостей. (To do many harmful / stupid things.)

•dat. + adv. (to feel strange / cold / embarrassed etc.; to find something strange / interesting / boring etc.)

Ему [было/будет] странно, что вода так быстро кончилась.

(He finds [found / will find] it strange that the water ran out so quickly.)

Мне [было/будет] здесь так хорошо. (I feel [felt/will feel] so good here.)

•хвата́ет || хва́тит (to be / have enough [**SEE** "Песенка о старом короле"])

•время (time [irregular declension: cf. вымя, знамя, пламя, темя, племя: add the suffix -ен- in all the oblique cases and in the nomin. plural])

•огонь (fire [**SEE** "Ваше величество, женщина"])

•понемногу (a little at a time, a little to everyone / each)

Дай всем понемногу. (Give a little bit to everyone / each.)

Ешь понемногу. (Eat a little at a time.)

[1]Cf. "du, de la, de l' " in French.

Переведите на русский язык, пользуясь песней и комментариями

1. My aunt always **forgets** everything and **knows** very well that she is forgetful. But yesterday she **herself found it strange** that she (had) **forgotten** her **money** at home. **She had no money**, but **she had** a credit card. She was **glad** that she **could** buy **at least** a few things.

2. Oh **Lord**, these **cowardly** people do not **believe** in your **power** on **earth** and in **heaven**! Please **give** them **wisdom** and show them the way to **repentance**, for they **know not what they do**.

3. The wheels of the car were **spinning**, but the car **itself** was not moving. The children **found** (it) **interesting**, but the parents **knew** that they were stuck. **They had enough** food **until** the next **day** when a tow truck finally came from the city. They were all so **happy**: the truck driver was like an angel from **heaven**.

4. Although the sun is shining **brightly for the time being**, **don't forget** your umbrella.

5. "Did you notice[1] the **horse** that the soldier was riding?"[2] "No, but I noticed that the soldier (was) **green-eyed** and handsome."

6. According to the Old Testament, Cain **killed** Abel and did not **repent**.

7. "You **can't wait** (to get to) the water, but **can** you swim?" "You are right. **Can** you teach[3] me to swim **while** you are **still** here?"

8. Don't you **believe** that **everyone** needs[4] a **break** sometimes?

9. **While we had enough money**, we were very **generous**, but unfortunately we **did many stupid things** with our **money**.

10. **Because we did not have enough time** to light[5] a **fire**, we ate a cold supper.

11. "**I have** a hat on (my) **head** and **I have** an earring in (my) **ear**. **For the time being** this is all that **I have** in the **world**."

12. The **outcome** of the battle is unclear, and I don't **believe** the **soldiers** who say that victory is ours.

13. "**Do you have** my matches?" "No, **I have no** matches." "**As long as I don't have fire**, I **can't** cook." "Good: you need a **break** from cooking."

14. According to the Old Testament, **God created light**, the **earth** and **every** living creature on **earth**.

---

[1]**SEE** "Песенка о Моцарте."
[2]**SEE** "Ночной разговор."
[3]**SEE** "Ещё раз о дураках."
[4]**SEE** "Примета."
[5]**SEE** "Чёрный кот."

15. When the **soldier** saw his **killed** comrade, he said to the killer: "What have you **done**?![1] You have **killed** him!"

16. **While** the tsar **was in power,**[2] he **did many stupid things**, but afterwards, when he thought about that **time**, he **felt remorse** about his behavior. Before death he **repented** his sins and died **happy**.[3] Of course such **wisdom** is rare.

17. According to the New Testament, St. Paul **came to believe in God** on the road to Damascus.

18. When the boy **will have** (had) **his fill of** playing, I **will give** him his homework. **For the time being**, let[4] him play.

19. A **quiet** man **resided** in this house. We had **forgotten about** him **until** he died. Then we **found out** that **he had** a lot of **money** in the house.

20. "Please **give** me **(some) money**!" "If I **give** you all the **money**, I **know** that you will spend it quickly, and you **will not have enough money until** the end of the month. You will think that I am not very **generous**, but, **for the time being, I can give** you **money** only **a little at a time** because very often you are like a child and **'know not what you do**.' **Until** you stop drinking and start using your **head**, **forget** about financial independence."

21. This great composer **creates** great music **every** day.

22. My daughter will be **happy** only when she finally **gets to the horses** whom she loves more than anything on **earth**.

23. The king **had** (had) **his fill of power** and abdicated, but when he saw that his son **could** not rule **wisely**, he thought: "**What have I done**!?"

24. Because **everyone** in politics **yearns for power**, we don't **believe** politicians.

25. Is he a pacifist because he is a **coward** or because he is **smart**?

---

[1]Do not use the verb "делать."
[2]To be in power = one word (verb).
[3]Instrumental.
[4]**SEE** "Часовые любви."

20 A (Blanks)

Ах, _ _ _ _ _(n.), что ж(е) ты _ _ _ _ _ _ _(v.), _ _ _ _ _ _(adj.)?
_ _ _ _ _(v.) _ _ _ _ _ _(adj.: instr.) наши _ _ _ _ _(n.).
Наши _ _ _ _ _ _ _ _(n.) _ _ _ _ _ _(n.) _ _ _ _ _ _ _ _(v.) —
_ _ _ _ _ _ _ _ _ _ _ _(v.) они до _ _ _ _(n.: gen.).
На _ _ _ _ _ _(n.: prep.) _ _ _ _(adv.) _ _ _ _ _ _ _ _ _ _(v.)
и _ _ _ _(v.) за _ _ _ _ _ _ _ _ _(n.: instr.) _ _ _ _ _ _(n.)...

До свидания, _ _ _ _ _ _ _ _(n.)!
_ _ _ _ _ _ _ _(n.), _ _ _ _ _ _ _ _ _ _ _ _ _(v.: imperat.)
_ _ _ _ _ _ _ _ _ _(v.: inf.) _ _ _ _ _(adv.).

Нет, не _ _ _ _ _ _ _ _ _ _(v.: imperat.) вы,
будьте _ _ _ _ _ _ _ _ _(adj.: instr.).
Не _ _ _ _ _ _ _(v.: imperat.)
ни _ _ _ _(n.: gen.) ни _ _ _ _ _ _(n.: gen.).
И себя не _ _ _ _ _ _(v.: imper.) вы... И _ _ _-_ _ _ _(conj.)
_ _ _ _ _ _ _ _ _ _ _ _ _(v.: imperat.) _ _ _ _ _ _ _ _ _ _(v.: inf.) _ _ _ _ _(adv.).

Ах, _ _ _ _ _(n.), что ж(е) ты _ _ _ _ _ _(adj.) _ _ _ _ _ _ _ _(v.)?
_ _ _ _ _ _(preposition) _ _ _ _ _ _(n.: gen.) —
_ _ _ _ _ _ _(n.) и _ _ _(n.).
Наши _ _ _ _ _ _ _(n.) _ _ _ _ _ _ _ _ _(n.: dimin.) _ _ _ _ _(adj.)
_ _ _ _ _ _ _ _ _ _(v.) _ _ _ _ _ _ _ _ _ _ _(n.: dat., dimin.) своим.

_ _ _ _ _ _(n.)! Ну куда от них _ _ _ _ _ _ _ _(v.)?
Да[1] _ _ _ _ _ _ _ _(adj.) _ _ _ _ _ _(n.) _ _ _ _ _(n.: gen.)...
Вы _ _ _ _ _ _ _ _(v.: imperat.) на _ _ _ _ _ _ _ _ _ _ _(n.: acc.), _ _ _ _ _ _ _ _(n.).
Мы _ _ _ _ _ _(v.) с ними _ _ _ _ _(n.) _ _ _ _ _(adv.).

_ _ _ _ _(particle) _ _ _ _ _ _ _(v.),
что _ _ _ _ _ _(v.: inf.) вам нé во что,
что _ _ _ _ _(v.) _ _ _ _ _ _(n.: instr.) _ _ _ _ _ _(adv.)...

До свидания, _ _ _ _ _ _ _(n.)!
_ _ _ _ _ _ _(n.), _ _ _ _ _ _ _ _ _ _ _ _ _(v.: imperat.)
_ _ _ _ _ _ _ _ _ _(v.: inf.) _ _ _ _ _(adv.).
До свидания, _ _ _ _ _ _ _(n.)!
_ _ _ _ _ _ _(n.), _ _ _ _ _ _ _ _ _ _ _ _ _(v.: imperat.)
_ _ _ _ _ _ _ _ _ _(v.: inf.) _ _ _ _ _(adv.).

[1]Here “да” = “и.”

20 B (Partial Blanks)

Ах, в_ _ _ _(n.), что ж(е) ты с_ _ _ _ _ _(v.), по_ _ _ _(adj.)?
С_ _ _ _(v.) т_ _ _ _ _(adj.: instr.) наши дв_ _ _(n.).
Наши м_ _ _ _ _ _ _(n.) го_ _ _ _(n.) под_ _ _ _(v.) —
повзр_ _ _ _ _ _(v.) они до п_ _ _(n.: gen.).
На по_ _ _ _(n.: prep) е_ _ _(adv.) пом_ _ _ _ _ _(v.)
и у_ _ _(v.) за с_ _ _ _ _ _ _(n.: instr.) со_ _ _ _(n.)...

До свидания, ма_ _ _ _ _ _(n.)!
Маль_ _ _ _(n.), по_ _ _ _ _ _ _ _ _ь(v.: imperat.)
в_ _ _ _ _ _ _ _(v.: inf.) _ _ _ _ _(adv.).

Нет, не пр_ _ь_ _ _ _(v.: imperat.) вы,
будьте вы_ _ _ _ _ _(adj.: instr.).
Не ж_ _ _ _ _ _(v.: imperat.)
ни п_ _ _(n.: gen.) ни гр_ _ _ _(n.: gen.).
И себя не щ_ _ _ _ _(v.: imper.) вы... И _ _ _-_ _ _ _(conj.)
пос_ _ _ _ _ _ _ _ _(v.: imperat.) ве_ _ _ _ _ _ _(v.: inf.) н_ _ _ _(adv.).

Ах, во_ _ _(n.), что ж(е) ты под_ _ _(adj.) сд_ _ _ _ _(v.)?
Вм_ _ _ _(prepeposition) св_ _ _ _(n.: gen.) —
раз_ _ _ _(n.) и д_ _(n.).
Наши _ _ _ _ _ _ _(n.) пл_ _ь_ _ _(n.: dimin.) б_ _ _ _(adj.)
разд_ _ _ _ _(v.) сес_ _ _ _ _ _ _(n.: dat., dimin.) своим.

Са_ _ _ _(n.)! Ну куда от них де_ _ _ь_ _(v.)?
Да[1] зе_ _ _ _ _(adj.) кр_ _ _ _(n.) по_ _ _(n.: gen.)...
Вы напл_ _ _ _(v.: imperat.) на спл_ _ _ _ _ _ _(n.: acc.), _ _ _ _ _ _ _(n.).
Мы св_ _ _ _(v.) с ними сч_ _ _(n.) по_ _ _(adv.).

П_ _ _ь(particle) бол_ _ _ _(v.),
что в_ _ _ _ _(v.: inf.) вам нé во что,
что и_ _ _ _(v.) в_ _ _ _ _(n.: instr.) нау_ _ _(adv.)...

До свидания, _ _ _ _ _ _ _(n.)!
Д_ _ _ _ _ _(n.), пос_ _ _ _ _ _ _ _ь(v.)
вер_ _ _ _ _ _(v.: inf.) н_ _ _ _(adv.).
До свидания, де _ _ _ _ _(n.)!
Дев _ _ _ _(n.), пост_ _ _ _ _ _ _ь(v.)
верн_ _ _ _ _(v.: inf.) на_ _ _(adv.).

---

[1]Here “да” = “и.”

Song 20. До свидания, мальчики!

Ах, война, что ж(е) ты сделала, подлая?
Стали тихими наши дворы.
Наши мальчики головы подняли —
повзрослели они до поры.
На пороге едва помаячили
и ушли за солдатом солдат...

До свидания, мальчики!
Мальчики, постарайтесь вернуться назад.

Нет, не прячьтесь вы, будьте высокими.
Не жалейте ни пуль ни гранат.
И себя не щадите вы...
И всё-таки постарайтесь вернуться назад.

Ах, война, что ж(е) ты, подлая, сделала?
Вместо свадеб — разлуки и дым.
Наши девочки платьица белые
Раздарили сестрёнкам своим

Сапоги! Ну куда от них денешься?
Да зелёные крылья погон...
Вы наплюйте на сплетников, девочки.
Мы сведем с ними счёты потом.

Пусть болтают, что верить вам нé во что,
что идёте войной наугад...

До свидания, девочки!
Девочки, постарайтесь вернуться назад.
До свидания, девочки!
Девочки, постарайтесь вернуться назад.

Вопросы по тексту (ответы полными предложениями):
1) К какому “подлецу” обращается поэт? 2) Что изменилось во дворах и почему? 3) Как изменились мальчики и почему? 4) Что поэт просит сделать и мальчиков и девочек? 5) Что поэт просит не делать мальчиков, и в чём парадоксальность этой просьбы? 6) Как война изменила жизнь девочек? 7) Что и почему отдали девочки? 8) От чего теперь нéкуда деваться? 9) С кем будут сводиться счёты и почему? 10) В чём девочек обвиняют сплетники? 11) Как девочкам следует реагировать на сплетников? 12) Что имеет в виду поэт, когда он просит девочек вернуться назад?

Комментарии к тексту песни

•де́лать || сде́лать (to do/make) де́лаю, –ешь, –ют

•по́длый/ая (base, rotten [morally]; подлец: scoundrel)

•станови́ться || стать + instr. (to become)

становлю́сь, стано́вишься, стано́вятся || ста́ну, –ешь, –ут

•быть + instr. (to be [no present tense]) бу́ду, –ешь, –ут

Он раньше был либералом, а теперь стал консерватором.

(He had been a liberal but has now become a conservative.)

•двор (courtyard, court [physical court or royal court, but not a court for trials])

•подня́ть[ся] || поднима́ть[ся] (to raise/lift [with –ся: to rise, to go / get up])

поднима́ю[сь], –а́ешь[ся], –а́ют[ся] ||

подниму́[сь], подни́мешь[ся], подни́мут[ся]

•взросле́ть || повзросле́ть (to mature / get older [about a child/teenager])

взросле́ю, –ешь, –ют

•до поры́ (before one's time)

Он сильно состарился до поры. (He really aged before his time.)

•порог (threshold, doorway [на пороге: in the doorway])

•едва́ (barely)

Га́лина нога уже срослась, и ее хромота́ едва заметна.

(Galia's leg has already mended, and her limp is barely noticeable.)

Хотя он едва отобедал, ему уже опять захотелось есть.

(Even though he had barely dined, he was already hungry again.)

•мая́чить || помая́чить (to be visible in the distance)

мая́чу, –ишь, –ат

•уходи́ть || уйти́ (to leave [**SEE** "Песенка о Моцарте" and "идти́ || пойти́" in "Шёл троллейбус по улице"])

•стара́ться || постара́ться (to try [**SEE** "Песенка о Моцарте"])

•возвраща́ть[ся] || верну́ть[ся] (to return [**SEE** "Песенка о голубом шарике")

•пря́тать[ся] || спря́тать[ся] (to hide [**SEE** "Чёрный кот"])

•не жале́ть + gen. (not to spare, to use without regard for thrift)

Пиши, не жалея бумаги! (Write without sparing paper!)

••жале́ть || пожале́ть (to feel sorry for; to have regrets about; to regret; to be stingy with; to use sparingly) жале́ю, –ешь, –ют

Он её пожалел и помог ей. (He felt sorry for her and helped her.)

Она пожалела о своём решении. (She regretted her decision.)

Он жалел денег/деньги и никому никогда не давал.

(He was stingy with his money and never gave any to anyone.)

•щади́ть || пощади́ть (to spare [usually: to forego the chance to harm someone])

щажу́, щади́шь, щадя́т

•и всё-таки (but still, and yet)

•разлука (separation, parting, being apart [**SEE** "О Володе Высоцком"])

•дари́ть || раздари́ть (to give [as a gift; раз–: to give away many things])

дарю́, да́ришь, да́рят

Марина раздарила свои марки друзьям.

(Marina gave her stamps [away] to friends)

•сестрёнка (sister [diminutive: often means "little / younger sister")

•свой (my, your, his, her, its, our, their [**SEE** "Бумажный солдат"])

•куда + dat. + дева́ть[ся] / деть[ся] (where is one supposed to put something [with –ся: where is one supposed to go])

Куда им [было/будет] девать / деть перчатки?

(Where are they [were they / will they be] supposed to put their gloves?)

Куда ему [было/будет] деваться / деться без денег?
(Where is he [was he / will he be] supposed to go without any money?)
N.B. Only the infinitive (either aspect) can be used in this construction. This construction implies the presence of an impediment to the action in question.
N.B. "Де́нешь[ся]" can replace "дева́ть[ся] / деть[ся]" in an indefinite personal construction, e.g., Куда от работы денешься? (How can you avoid work [lit.: where is one supposed to go from work]?)
••куда + dat. + дева́ться / деться + от + gen. (how can one escape from something [duty, obligation, an unavoidable phenomenon etc.])
Куда мне деваться от своих обязанностей?
(How can I escape from my responsibilities?)
••дева́ть[ся] || деть[ся] (to misplace [with –ся: to disappear→ intrans.])
дева́ю[сь], –ешь[ся], –ют[ся] || де́ну[сь], –ешь[ся], –ут[ся]
Куда я девал / дел перчатки? (Where did I put my gloves?)
Куда девались / делись мои перчатки? (Where did my gloves go [disappear]?)
Куда Лёня девался / делся. (Where did Lionia go [disappear]?)
Я всегда куда-то деваю кошелёк.
(I always misplace my wallet somewhere.)
N.B. This verb can be translated by "put," but only if it connotes misplacement.

•плева́ть || наплева́ть + на + acc. ([colloquial: lit.→ to spit on] to ignore, not to care about, not to give a darn about) плюю́, –ёшь, –ю́т
Я плюю на этих дураков. (I ignore these idiots [I don't care about them].)

•сплé тник/сплé тница (gossip [a person who gossips])
••сплетни (gossip [what talkative people spread])

•своди́ть || свести́ счёты (to settle scores [**SEE** "Простите пехоте"])

•пусть (let + verb [**SEE** "Часовые любви")

•болта́ть || сболтну́ть (to blabber, to say nonsense, to natter, to chatter [with с–: to let out / blab something one should not have said])
болта́ю, –ешь, –ют || сболтну́, –ёшь, –у́т
Хватит болтать. За работу! (Stop chattering and get to work.)
Я сболтнул, что я богат, и теперь у меня все просят денег.
(I blabbed / let out that I was rich, and now everyone begs me for money.)

•ве́рить || пове́рить (**SEE** "Солнышко сияет")

•dat. + не́ [interrog. word] + inf. (to have nothing / nowhere etc. [**SEE** "Примета"])
Говорят, что верить вам не́ во что.
(They say that you have nothing to believe in.)

•наугáд (blindly, by guess-work, at random)
Он открыл газету наугад и увидел свою фамилию в некрологах. (He opened the paper at random and saw his last name in the obituaries.)

Переведите на русский язык, пользуясь песней и комментариями

1. I think that because of our family tragedy my **little sister** will **mature before** (her) **time**.

2. This poor little **boy has nowhere to go, he has nothing to do** and **he has no one to talk with**. That is why he **quietly** sits in **his yard** and **doesn't do anything**.

3. “Where did she **put her green boots**?” “**I will try** to find them.”

4. Do you see the **tall boy** who[1] is standing in the **doorway**? Maybe you won’t **believe** me, but he is a real **scoundrel** and a terrible **gossip**. Everything that he **does** is **base**. I did not **spare** money and time when he needed[2] my help, but now he **doesn’t give a darn about me**!

5. The **soldier** said to his fiancée: “I hope that you will **ignore the war, the bullets, the grenades, the smoke** and our unavoidable **separation**, and I hope that you will not postpone our **wedding**.”

6. It seemed as if Mila had **barely** put on[3] **her white dress**, and the **wedding** ended.[4]

7. When my father **returns**[5] from the **war**, he will **settle his scores** with these **rotten gossips**. And **I will not feel sorry** (for) them.

8. Our house burned down[6] and **we had nowhere to live**, so we pitched a tent in the **yard.** But we didn’t know **where we were supposed to put** our things. Therefore, we temporarily **hid** them in a shed.

9. This colonel is such a **scoundrel**. He is even **stingy** (with) **bullets** when **his soldiers** need them in battle. **Instead** (of) **bullets**, he gives them advice: **do not raise** (your) **head**(s) when the enemy shoots.

10. The battleship was **barely visible** on the horizon when the pilot launched a torpedo and saw **smoke** in[7] a few seconds. But then he **spared** the people in the lifeboats.

11. When the **war** finished, the **soldiers gave away** all **their boots** and **epaulets**, and they did not **regret** this.

13. “Why do you **lift** dumbbells every day? You always **hide your** muscles anyway.” “**I don’t give a darn about** your remarks. **Where did I put** my dumbbells?” “I don’t know **where they have disappeared**.”

14. “Do you believe in fairies?” “Fairies? Are they[8] **girls** with **white wings**?”

15. Children always want to **become adults** and independent, but childhood will never **come back**, and when they **get older**, they will **regret** their haste.

16. I always **feel sorry** (for) all the **girls** and **boys** whose fathers have gone[9] to **war**.

---

[1]**SEE** “тот + кто/который” in “Я вновь повстречался с надеждой.”
[2]**SEE** “Примета.”
[3]**SEE** “Старый пиджак.”.
[4]**SEE** “Часовые любви.”
[5]**SEE** “Песенка о голубом шарике.”
[6]**SEE** “Чёрный кот.”
[7]**SEE** “Песенка старого шарманщика.”
[8]Lit.: (Is) this.
[9]**SEE** “Идти́ || пойти́” in “Шёл троллейбус по улице.”

17. First we **mature** and then we **become** old. Time is a **scoundrel**, but **how can** (one) **escape from it**!?

18. **"Where did all her dresses disappear**?" "I have **given them away** because I really **believed** that she (would) not **return**." "But she had **barely** worn[1] them! What a **rotten** person you are!" "I am sorry. I will **return** her **dresses**, and **believe** me: I **will not spare** (any) effort (in order) to[2] find them."

19. Feofan **got up** and said: "I am **leaving**." Mila exclaimed: "**Where am I to go** when you **leave**?"

20. The bird is so tired that it is **barely lifting** (its) **wings, and yet** it is still **trying to lift** them.

21. First the little **boy hid his** toys and then he **hid** in the closet.

22. My **sister randomly** took a **white dress** out of the laundry pile and put it on.

---

[1]**SEE** "Старый пиджак," perf.
[2]**SEE** "Примета."

21 A (Blanks)

В _ _ _ _ _ _ _(n.: prep.) _ _ _ _ _ _ _(adj.) _ _ _ _ _ _(n.: gen.) из–под
_ _ _ _ _ _ _ _ _ _ _(adj.) _ _ _ _(n: gen.).
_ _ _ _(n.) _ _ _ _ _ _ _ _(adj.) _ _ _ _ _(v.)
_ _ _ _ _(adv.) и _ _ _ _ _ _ _ _ _ _ _ _(adv.).
_ _ _ _ _ _ _ _ _ _ _ _ _(adj.) _ _ _ _ _(n.)
_ _ _ _ _ _ _(v.) я _ _ _ _ _ _ _ _ _ _(adv.),
_ _ _ _ _ _ _ _ _ _ _(verbal adv.), как в _ _ _ _ _(n.),
от _ _ _ _ _ _ _(n.: gen.) к _ _ _ _ _ _ _(n.: dat.).

_ _ _ _ _ _(substantivized adj.) _ _ _ _ _(v.), что он _ _ _ _ _ _(v.).
_ _ _ _ _ _(substantivized adj.) _ _ _ _ _ _(v.), как он _ _ _ _ _(v.).
Как он _ _ _ _ _(v.), так и _ _ _ _ _(v.),
не _ _ _ _ _ _ _ _ _ (verbal adv.) _ _ _ _ _ _ _(v.: inf.).
Так _ _ _ _ _ _ _ _(n.) _ _ _ _ _ _ _ _ _(v.). Почему — не наше _ _ _ _(n.).
Для чего — не нам с_ _ _ _ _(v.: inf.).

Были _ _ _ _(n.) _ _ _ _ _ _(adj.: short form),
было _ _ _ _ _ _ _(n.: gen.) в _ _ _ _ _ _ _(n.: prep.)[1]
и из _ _ _ _ _ _ _ _ _ _ _ _(adj.) _ _ _ _ _ _(n.: gen.)
я _ _ _ _ _ _ _ _ _ _ _(v.) по _ _ _ _ _(n.: dat.).
В _ _ _ _(n.) _ _ _ _ _ _(n.: acc.) _ _ _ _ _ _ _ _ _(v.),
_ _ _ _ _ _ _(v.) о _ _ _ _ _ _ _(n.: prep.) _ _ _ _ _ _ _(n.)
и _ _ _ _ _ _ _ _ _(n.: instr.) в _ _ _ _ _ _ _ _(n.: prep.) сам себя _ _ _ _ _ _ _ _ _(v.).

_ _ _ _ _ _(substantivized adj.) _ _ _ _ _(v.), что он _ _ _ _ _ _(v.).
_ _ _ _ _ _(substantivized adj.) _ _ _ _ _ _(v.), как он д_ _ _ _(v.).
Как он _ _ _ _ _(v.), так и _ _ _ _ _(v.),
не _ _ _ _ _ _ _ _ _(verbal adv.) _ _ _ _ _ _ _(v.: inf.).
Так _ _ _ _ _ _ _ _(n.) _ _ _ _ _ _ _ _ _(v.). Почему — не наше _ _ _ _(n.).
Для чего — не нам _ _ _ _ _ _(v.: inf.).

_ _ _ _ _ _ _(n.) не есть _ _ _ _ _(n.).
_ _ _ _ _ _ _(n.) — ещё не _ _ _ _ _(n.).
_ _ _ _ _(v.: imperat.) _ _ _ _ _ _ _ _ _(v.: inf.) _ _ _ _ _(n.)
до _ _ _ _ _ _ _ _ _ _ _(adj.) _ _ _ _ _ _ _ _ _(n.: gen., dimin.).
И _ _ _ _(adv.) ещё _ _ _ _(adj.: short form)
_ _ _ _(n.) _ _ _ _ _ _ _ _(adj.) в _ _ _ _ _ _ _ _(n.: prep.),
_ _ _ _ _(v.: imperat.) _ _ _ _ _ _ _ _ _ _ _(v.: inf.) _ _ _ _ _(n.),
что _ _ _ _ _(adv.) _ _ _ _ _(v.) в _ _ _ _ _ _ _ _(n.: prep.)!

_ _ _ _ _ _(substantivized adj.) _ _ _ _ _(v.), что он _ _ _ _ _ _(v.).
_ _ _ _ _ _(substantivized adj.) _ _ _ _ _ _(v.), как он _ _ _ _ _(v.)...

[1]В _ _ _ _ _ _ _(n.: prep.)= idiomatic construction.

21 B (Partial Blanks)

В скл_ _ _ _(n.: prep.) тё_ _ _ _ _(adj.) ст_ _ _ _(n.: gen.) из-под
им_ _ _т_ _ _ _(adj.) п_ _ _(n: gen.).
_ _ _ _(n.) к_ _ _ _ _ _(adj.) ц_ _ _ _(v.)
г_ _ _ _(adv.) и нетор_ _ _ _ _ _(adv.).
Ист_ _ _ _ _ _ _ _ _(adj.) р_ _ _ _(n.)
соч_ _ _ _(v.) я поне_ _ _ _ _(adv.),
проб_ _ _ _сь(verbal adv.), как в т_ _ _ _(n.),
от про_ _ _ _(n.: gen.) к эп_ _ _ _ _(n.: dat.).

_ _ _ _ _ _(substantivized adj.) _ _ _ _ _(v.), что он _ _ _ _ _ _(v.).
_ _ _ _ _ _(substantivized adj.) _ _ _ _ _ _(v.), как он _ _ _ _ _(v.).
Как он _ _ _ _ _(v.), так и _ _ _ _ _(v.),
не ст_ _ _ _ _ь(verbal adv.) у_ _ _ _ _ _(v.: inf.).
Так п_ _ _ _ _ _(n.) за_ _ _ _ _ _(v.). Почему — не наше _ _ _ _(n.).
Для чего — не нам с_ _ _ _ _(v.: inf.).

Были д_ _ _(n.) го_ _ _ _(adj.: short form),
было вы_ _ _ _ _(n.: gen.) в из_ _ _ _ _n.: prep.)[1]
и из собст_ _ _ _ _ _(adj.) су_ь_ _(n.: gen.)
я выд_ _ _ив_ _(v.) по н_ _ _ _(n.: dat.).
В п_ _ _(n.) ге_ _ _ _(n.: acc.) снар_ _ _ _(v.),
нав_ _ _ _(v.) о пр_ _ _ _ _(n.: prep.) спр_ _ _ _(n.)
и пор_ _ _ _ _ _(n.: instr.) в отст_ _ _ _(n.: prep.) сам себя воо_ _ _ _ _ _(v.).

_ _ _ _ _ _(substantivized adj.) _ _ _ _ _(v.), что он _ _ _ _ _ _(v.).
_ _ _ _ _ _(substantivized adj.) _ _ _ _ _ _(v.), как он д_ _ _ _(v.).
Как он _ _ _ _ _(v.), так и _ _ _ _ _(v.),
не ста_ _ _сь(verbal adv.) уго_ _ _ _(v.: inf.).
Так пр_ _ _ _ _(n.) зах_ _ _ _ _(v.). Почему — не наше д_ _ _(n.).
Для чего — не нам су_ _ _ _(v.: inf.).

Вым_ _ _ _(n.) не есть об_ _ _(n.).
За_ _ _ _ _(n.) — ещё не т_ _ _ _(n.).
_ _ _ _ _(v.: imperat.) до_ _ _ _ _ _(v.: inf.) ро_ _ _(n.)
до пос_ _ _ _ _ _ _(adj.) ли_ _ _ _ _ _(n.: gen., dimin.).
И п_ _ _(adv.) ещё ж_ _ _(adj.: short form)
р_ _ _(n.) кр_ _ _ _ _(adj.) в бу_ _ _ _ _(n.: prep.),
д_ _ _ _(v.: imperat.) вык_ _ _ _ _ _ _(v.: inf.) с_ _ _ _(n.),
что д_ _ _ _(adv.) л_ _ _ _(v.) в коп_ _ _ _(n.: prep.)!

К_ _ _ _ _(substantivized adj.) п_ _ _ _(v.), что он с_ _ _ _ _(v.).
Ка_ _ _ _(substantivized adj.) сл_ _ _ _(v.), как он ды_ _ _(v.)...

---

[1]В из_ _ _ _ _(n.: prep.)= idiomatic construction.

Song 21. Я пишу исторический роман

Василию Аксёнову[1]

В склянке тёмного стекла из–под импортного пива
роза красная цвела гордо и неторопливо.
Исторический роман сочинял я понемногу,
пробиваясь, как в туман, от пролога к эпилогу.

Каждый пишет, что он слышит.
Каждый слышит, как он дышит.
Как он дышит, так и пишет, не стараясь угодить.
Так природа захотела. Почему — не наше дело.
Для чего — не нам судить.

Были дали голубы, было вымысла в избытке
и из собственной судьбы я выдёргивал по нитке.
В путь героев снаряжал, наводил о прошлом справки
и поручиком в отставке сам себя воображал.

Каждый пишет, что он слышит.
Каждый слышит, как он дышит.
Как он дышит, так и пишет, не стараясь угодить.
Так природа захотела. Почему — не наше дело.
Для чего — не нам судить.

Вымысел не есть обман.
Замысел — ещё не точка.
Дайте дописать роман до последнего листочка.
И пока ещё жива роза красная в бутылке,
дайте выкрикнуть слова, что давно лежат в копилке.

Каждый пишет, что он слышит.
Каждый слышит, как он дышит...

Вопросы по тексту (ответы полными предложениями):

1) О ком эта песня? 2) Какой цветок стоит перед глазами писателя? 3) В чём стоит цветок? 4) Какую роль играет эта роза для писателя? 5) Что он пишет? 6) Легко ли ему пишется? 7) Кому писатель не должен угождать? 8) Как описывается творческий процесс, и почему он именно такой а не иной? 9) Где писатель находит материал для своего романа (два источника)? 10) Кем себя воображает писатель и почему? 11) О чём просит писатель? 12) С чем сравниваются слова писателя?

[1]Василий Аксёнов — русский писатель–модернист, ставший знаменитым в 60–ые годы. Аксёнов отказывался идти на поводу у советского режима, выражал своё несогласие с системой, печатался нелегально и, наконец, эмигрировал в США.

Комментарии к тексту песни

•noun + из + name of material [gen.] (something made of something)
Ваза из стекла. (A glass vase / a vase made of glass [из: sometimes left out.])
•из–под + gen. (about a container that no longer contains its original contents)
Склянка / бутылка из–под пива. (Beer bottle.)
••container + gen. (container with its contents still inside)
Склянка / бутылка молока. (A bottle of milk.)
•цвести́ || расцвести́ (to bloom) цвету́, –ёшь, –у́т
•неторопли́во (slowly, unhurriedly)
•сочиня́ть || сочини́ть (to compose/write [a literary text, music], to make up)
сочиня́ю, –ешь, –ют || сочиню́, –и́шь, –я́т
•понемногу (a little at a time [**SEE** "Молитва (Франсуа Вийона)"])
•пробива́ться || проби́ться (to fight one's way somewhere [perf.: to break through]) пробива́юсь, –ешься, –ются || пробью́сь, –ёшься, –ю́тся
•каждый (every, each [when not modifying a noun: everyone, all])
•писа́ть || дописа́ть (to write [до–: to write to the end, to reach a (writing) goal, to finish writing]) пишу́, пи́шешь, пи́шут
Derived imperfective: допи́сываю, –ешь, –ют (**SEE** "лить || проли́ть" in "Простите пехоте")
•слы́шать || услы́шать (to hear) слы́шу, –ишь, –ат
••слу́шать || послу́шать (to listen) слу́шаю, –ешь, –ют
Я слышал его голос но его не слушал. (I heard his voice without listening **to** him [note that "to" is not translated].)
•слышать / видеть + как + verb. (to hear / see someone do something)
Я часто вижу, как она идёт домой. (I often see her going home.)
•дыша́ть || подыша́ть (to breathe) дышу́, ды́шишь, ды́шат
•как + verb + так и + verb (the way)
Как Боря жил, так и умер: в пьяном виде.
(Boria died the way he lived: drunk)
•стараясь (trying, striving, endeavoring)
••стара́ться || постара́ться (to try [**SEE** "Песенка о Моцарте"])
•так (thus, so, this way [такой→ such, so; **SEE** "Старый пиджак"])
•угожда́ть || угоди́ть + dat. (to please someone)
угожда́ю, –ешь, –ют || угожу́, угоди́шь, угодя́т
Маша угодила своей маме, сварив суп.
(By making soup, Masha pleased her mother.)
•хоте́ть || захоте́ть (to want) хочу́, хо́чешь, хо́чет, хоти́м, хоти́те, хотя́т
•не моё/твоё/его... + дело (none of my/your/his... business)
•для чего (what for, for what purpose)
•не dat. + inf. (it is not for / up to someone to do something)
Не нам судить. (It is not for us to judge.)
•суди́ть || осуди́ть (to judge, to try [in court]; о–: to condemn/sentence])
сужу́, су́дишь, су́дят
•gen. + в избытке (more than enough of something):
У меня бумаги [было/будет] в избытке [note the absence of "есть"].
(I have [had/will have] more than enough paper.)
•собственный/ая ([one's] own)
Я приехал на [своей] собственной машине. (I came in my own car.)
•судьба (fate, life, life story)

•выдёргивать || выдернуть (to pull out [abruptly])
 выдёргиваю, –ешь, –ют || вы́дерну, –ешь, –ут
•по + dat. (amount of something at a time)
 Я выдёргивал по нитке. (I was pulling out a thread at a time.)
•снаряжа́ть[ся] || снаряди́ть[ся] + в + acc. (to outfit / equip for a trip [-ся: intransitive])
 снаражáю[сь], –ешь[ся], –ют(ся] ||
 снаряжу́[сь], снаряди́шь[ся], снаряд́ят[ся]
 N.B. This construction is often used with “путь,” e.g., Я снарядился в путь и уехал. (I outfitted myself for the trip and left.)
•герой/героиня (hero/heroine [general sense], a character in a work of fiction)
•наводи́ть || навести́ + справки + о + prep. (to research, to make inquiries about)
 навожу́, наво́дишь, наво́дят || наведу́, –ёшь, –у́т
 Я навёл о ней справки и узнал, что она переехала.
 (I made inquires about her and found out that she had moved.)
•сам/а́/са́ми + себя/себе/собой (something done by one to oneself)
 Я сама себя ругаю. (I curse myself.)
 Он сам себе не доверяет. (He doesn’t trust himself.)
•отставка (retirement from military service [civil service before 1917])
 Я в отставке. (I am retired.)
 ••пенсия (pension, retirement from non-military work)
 Я на пенсии. (I am retired.)
•воображá́ть || вообрази́ть (to imagine)
 воображáю, –ешь, –ют || воображу́, вообрази́шь, вообразя́т
•воображá́ть || вообрази́ть + себя + instr. (to imagine oneself to be someone else)
 Я вообразил себя поручиком в отставке.
 (I imagined myself to be a retired lieutenant.)
•вы́мысел (fiction, artistic invention, product of the imagination/fantasy)
•за́мысел (in literature: the idea behind a given literary work)
•noun + есть + noun (something is something [used in definitions: bookish])
 Человек есть существо двуногое. (A human being **is** a biped.)
•жив/а (alive [full-form adj.: живой/ая→ living, lively])
 Жук — это живое существо. (A beetle is a living being.)
 Она всё еще жива. (She is still alive.)
•пока (while, for the time being [**SEE** “Молитва (Франсуа Вийона)”])
•дава́ть || дать + dat. + inf. (to let/allow [**SEE** “Примета”])
•выкри́кивать || вы́крикнуть (to scream out)
 выкри́киваю, –ешь, –ют || вы́крикну, –ешь, –ут
•лежа́ть || полежа́ть (to be / lie [**SEE** “Песенка о старом короле”])
•давно (for a long time, long ago [**SEE** “Шёл троллейбус по улице”])

Переведите на русский язык, пользуясь песней и комментариями

1. The hunter fired[1] his gun and then **listened**. The moose was **still alive**, since he **heard** the animal **breathing** nearby, but he did not see it because of the **fog**.

---

[1]**SEE** “Примета.”

2. "Do you see the **milk bottle** that **is**[1] on the table?" "Yes?" "I've **wanted** to ask you **for a long time** (now) what's in it: **beer**?" "**None of your business**!"
3. Some authors **write**[2] **little by little**: one page **at a time**.
4. **For a long time** our nation refused to **judge** its **own heroes**, but today we **try** to be more objective about our myths and idols.
5. Dasha wanted to **please** Semion who[3] loves money. Therefore, she gave[4] him a **piggy-bank**.
6. Why do you **imagine yourselves** to be writers? You are just hacks![5]
7. **Fate** did not **let** me **write** my historical **novel to the end**. I had **more than enough** ideas and **had done the research** about my **characters**. But I did not **please** the censor. I **fought my way through** the censorship system **for a long time**, but nothing helped. When I asked **why** my **novel** (had been) banned, (they) told me: "**None of your business**!" Then I decided that **while** I am (still) **alive**, while I (still) **breathe**, I **will write**, even if no one[6] reads my **words**. I am not a **hero**, but a decent person should behave only **this way**. So you see that my **life** has been a difficult one, and **for the time being** I have little hope that it will improve.
8. I **outfitted** Vitalik **for a trip**, and then I **made inquiries** about his destination.
9. My cat always **pulls thread**(s) out of my jacket.
10. You will probably **condemn** me for (my) drunkenness, and I promise to change, but **for the time being give** me another **bottle of dark beer**, please.
11. (There are) many **sheets** of paper **lying** on my desk, I have **more than enough** ink; I even have the (main) **idea** for my **novel**, but I just can't **finish writing** the first paragraph!
12. In the **past** people lived in harmony with **nature**. But then they became **proud** and decided to subdue **nature**. They forgot that it is **not for us** to play the role of God.
13 "(It is) **none of your business** what I **write**!" **screamed out** Nikolai and **proudly** left[7] the room.
14. "The professor could[8] not **compose** a sentence with the word '**period**.'

---

[1]**SEE** "лежа́ть" above.
[2]Do not use "писать."
[3]**SEE** "тот + кто/который" in "Я вновь повстречался с надеждой."
[4]Special "gift" verb [**SEE** "дари́ть" in "До свидания, мальчики"].
[5]Hack (a person who writes badly but with enthusiasm) = графоман.
[6]**SEE** "Примета."
[7]**SEE** "Песенка о Моцарте."
[8]**SEE** "О Володе Высоцком."

Can you?" "Of course: a **period is**[1] the **last** element of a sentence."

15. Although the soldiers **fought their way** through enemy lines (for) three days and did not **break through**, they are **heroes**, and it is not **up to us to judge them.**

16. The typist **heard** the **writer** but was not **listening** (to) **him.**

17. **Red roses** fade **the way** they **bloom**: **unhurriedly**.

18. **For what purpose** did you **pull** the **last sheet** of paper out of the notebook?

19. When I **write** a **novel** about **historical** persons,[2] I always **make inquiries** about their relatives.

20. Botany **is** a science about plants.

21. **Characters** in a **novel** are part of the author's **artistic invention**. Their actions illustrate the (central) **idea** of the **novel**.

22. **Everyone** knows that these books about "**historical**" events are one big **lie**.

23. This **lieutenant** (has been) retired **for a long time**, but his wife is not yet **retired**.[3] She sells **beer** and **imported** cigarettes at a street kiosk.

24. **While** Larissa is asleep, I **try to breathe** quietly.

25. Sometimes, if I **listen** very attentively, I **can hear** my **roses bloom**.

27. **Everyone** knows that good authors **write prologues** and **epilogues** only after[4] they **finish writing**[5] their **novels.**

27. I love **paper roses**. If they **are** (made) **of dark paper**, they look[6] almost real.

---

[1]Assume that this is a bookish formal definition.
[2]Use "лицо."
[3]She is not in the military.
[4]Before / after + verb = перед тем / после того + как + verb.
[5]Finish writing: one word.
[6]**SEE** "Старый пиджак."

22 A (Blanks)

Антон Павлович _ _ _ _ _(last name)
_ _ _ _ _ _ _(adv.) _ _ _ _ _ _ _(v.),
что _ _ _ _ _(substantivized adj.) _ _ _ _ _(v.) _ _ _ _ _ _ _(v.: inf.),
а _ _ _ _ _(n.) — _ _ _ _ _(v.: inf.).
_ _ _ _ _ _ _ _(interrogative adj.) _ _ _ _ _ _ _(n.: gen.)
в своей _ _ _ _ _(n.: prep.) я _ _ _ _ _ _ _ _(v.)!
Мне _ _ _ _ _(adv.) _ _ _ _(adv.) уже
_ _ _ _ _(n.) _ _ _ _ _ _ _ _(v.: inf.).

_ _ _ _ _ _(n.) _ _ _ _ _ _ _(v.)
_ _ _ _ _ _ _ _ _ _ _(v.: inf.) в _ _ _ _(n.: acc.):
_ _ _ _ _ _ _(adv.) — _ _ _ _ _ _ _(substantivized adj.)
во всей _ _ _ _ _(n.: prep.).
В _ _ _ _ _ _ _(n.: prep.) я _ _ _ _ _(v.), что
_ _ _ _ _ _ _(adv.) _ _ _ _ _ _(v.),
а _ _ _ _ _ _ _(n.: gen.) нету — _ _ _ _ _ _ _(v.) все.

Ах, _ _ _ _ _ _ _(adj.) _ _ _(n.) мои, — какая _ _ _ _ _ _(n.)!
В каких _ _ _ _ _ _ _(n.: prep.)
я по _ _ _ _ _ _ _ _(n.: dat.) _ _ _ _ _(v.)!
У _ _ _ _ _ _ _(n.: gen.) на _ _ _ _ _(n.: prep.)[1]
_ _ _ _ _ _ _ _(adj.) _ _ _ _ _ _(n.)...
_ _ _ _ _ _(adv.), чего–то я не _ _ _ _ _ _ _ _ _(v.).

А _ _ _ _ _(substantivized adj.) в _ _ _ _ _ _ _ _ _ _ _ _(n.: prep.)
_ _ _ _ _ _(v.) _ _ _ _ _ _ _(n.: instr.).
Он _ _ _ _ _(v.) _ _ _ _ _ _ _ _ _ _ _ _(n.) _ _ _ _ _ _ _(adv.) всего.
И его так _ _ _ _ _ _(adv.) _ _ _ _ _(v.: inf.)
_ _ _ _ _ _(adj.) _ _ _ _ _ _(n.: instr.):
_ _ _ _ _(adv.) их _ _ _ _ _ _ _ _ _(v.)
всех до _ _ _ _ _ _(numeral: gen.).[2]

(continued)

[1]Archaic/poetic.
[2]"Всех до _ _ _ _ _ _(numeral)" constitutes an idiomatic construction.

Когда ж(е) их всех _ _ _ _ _ _ _ _ _(v.),
_ _ _ _ _ _ _ _(v.) _ _ _ _ _(n.),
которую не _ _ _ _ _ _ _ _(v.: inf.) и не _ _ _ _ _ _ _(v.: inf.).
С _ _ _ _ _(substantivized adj.: instr.) _ _ _ _ _ _ _ _ _(adv.),
с _ _ _ _ _ _ _(n.: instr.) _ _ _ _ _(adv.).
Нужно что–то _ _ _ _ _ _ _(substantivized adj.) —
да где же его _ _ _ _ _(v.: inf.)?

_ _ _ _ _ _ _(n.: instr.) быть _ _ _ _ _ _ _(adv.),
да очень не _ _ _ _ _ _ _(v.).
_ _ _ _ _(substantivized adj.: instr.) — очень _ _ _ _ _ _ _(v.),
да[1] _ _ _ _ _ _ _ _(v.) _ _ _ _ _ _(n.: instr.).
У _ _ _ _ _ _ _(n.: gen.) на _ _ _ _ _(n.: prep.)
_ _ _ _ _ _ _ _(adj.) _ _ _ _ _ _ _ _ _ _ _ _(n.)...
Но _ _ _ _ _(v.) _ _ _ _(v: inf.)[2] _ _ _ _ _-_ _ _ _ _ _(adv.)
к _ _ _ _ _ _ _ _(substantivized adj.:dat.) _ _ _ _ _ _(v.).
Но _ _ _ _ _(v.) _ _ _ _(v: inf.) _ _ _ _ _-_ _ _ _ _ _(adv.)
к _ _ _ _ _ _ _ _(substantivized adj.: dat.) _ _ _ _ _ _(v.).

[1]Here “да” = “but.”
[2]The last two words constitute an idiomatic construction.

22 B (Partial Blanks)

Антон Павлович _ _ _ _ _(last name)
од_ _ _ _ _(adv.) зам_ _ _ _(v.),
что _ _ _ _ _(substantivized adj.) л_ _ _ _(v.) _ _ _ _ься(v.: inf.),
а _ _ _ _ _(n.) — у_ _ _ _(v.: inf.).
Ск_ _ _ _ _ _(interrogative adj.) _ _ _ _ _ _ _(n.: gen.)
в своей ж_ _ _ _(n.: prep.) я встр_ _ _ _(v.)!
Мне да_ _ _(adv.) п_ _ _(adv.) уже
ор_ _ _(n.) пол_ _ _ _ _(v.: inf.).

_ _ _ _ _ _(n.) об_ _ _ _ _(v.)
соб_ _ _ _ _ _ _(v.: inf.) в с_ _ _(n.: acc.):
вп_ _ _ _ _(adv.) — Гл_ _ _ _ _(substantivized adj.)
во всей кр_ _ _(n.: prep.).
В де_ _ _ _ _(n.: prep.) я ве_ _ _(v.), что
одн_ _ _ _(adv.) вст_ _ _(v.),
а д_ _ _ _ _ _(n.: gen.) нету — уле_ _ _ _(v.) все.

Ах, дет_ _ _ _(adj.) с_ _(n.) мои, — какая ош_ _ _ _(n.)!
В каких обл_ _ _ _(n.: prep.)
я по глу_ _ _ _ _(n.: dat.) ви_ _ _(v.)!
У пр_ _ _ _ _(n.: gen.) на у_ _ _ _(n.: prep.)[1]
ко_ _ _ _ _ _(adj.) ул_ _ _ _(n.)...
Ви_ _ _ _(adv.), чего–то я не рассч_ _ _ _(v.).

А _ _ _ _ _(substantivized adj.) в од_ _ _ _ _ _ _ _ _(n.: prep.)
гу_ _ _ _(v.) кру_ _ _ _(n.: instr.).
Он ц_ _ _ _(v.) оди_ _ _ _ _ _ _ _(n.) прев_ _ _(adv.) всего.
И его так пр_ _ _ _(adv.) вз_ _ _(v.: inf.)
го_ _ _ _(adj.) ру_ _ _ _(n.: instr.):
ск_ _ _(adv.) их пов_ _ _ _ _ _(v.)
всех до од_ _ _ _(numeral: gen.).[2]

(continued)

---

[1] Archaic/poetic.
[2] "Всех до _ _ _ _ _ _(numeral)" constitutes an idiomatic construction.

Когда ж(е) их всех повыл_ _ _ _(v.),
наст_ _ _ _(v.) эп_ _ _(n.),
которую не выд_ _ _ _ _(v.: inf.) и не оп_ _ _ _ _(v.: inf.).
С у_ _ _ _(substantivized adj.: instr.) хл_ _ _ _ _ _(adv.),
с ду_ _ _ _ _(n.: instr.) пл_ _ _(adv.).
Нужно что–то с_ _ _ _ _ _(substantivized adj.) —
да где же его вз_ _ _(v.: inf.)?

Дур_ _ _ _(n.: instr.) быть выг_ _ _ _(adv.),
да очень не х_ _ _ _ _ _(v.).
Ум_ _ _(substantivized adj.: instr.) — очень хо_ _ _ _ _(v.),
да[1] кон_ _ _ _ _(v.) би_ _ _ _(n.: instr.).
У при_ _ _ _(n.: gen.) на ус_ _ _(n.: prep.)
кова_ _ _ _(adj.) проро_ _ _ _ _ _(n.)...
Но м_ _ _ _(v.) _ _ _ _(v: inf.)[2] к_ _ _ _-ни_ _ _ _(adv.)
к ср_ _ _ _ _ _(substantivized adj.: dat.) п_ _ _ _ _(v.).
Но мо_ _ _(v.) б_ _ _(v: inf.) ко_ _ _-ниб_ _ _(adv.)
к сред_ _ _ _(substantivized adj.: dat.) пр_ _ _ _(v.).

[1]Here “да” = “but.”
[3]The last two words constitute an idiomatic construction.

Song 22. Ещё раз о дураках

Антон Павлович Чехов однажды заметил,
что умный любит учиться, а дурак — учить.[1]
Скольких дураков в своей жизни я встретил!
Мне давно пора уже орден получить.

Дураки обожают собираться в стаю:
впереди — Главный во всей красе.
В детстве я верил, что однажды встану,
а дураков нету — улетели все.

Ах детские сны мои, — какая ошибка!
В каких облаках я по глупости витал!
У природы на устах коварная улыбка...
Видимо, чего–то я не рассчитал.

А умный в одиночестве гуляет кругами.
Он ценит одиночество превыше всего.
И его так просто взять голыми руками:
скоро их повыловят всех до одного.

Когда ж(е) их всех повыловят, наступит эпоха,
которую не выдумать и не описать.
С умным хлопотно, с дураком плохо.
Нужно что–то среднее — да где ж его взять?

Дураком быть выгодно, да очень не хочется.
Умным — очень хочется, да кончится битьём.
У природы на устах коварные пророчества...
Но может быть когда–нибудь к среднему придём.
Но может быть когда–нибудь к среднему придём.

<u>Вопросы по тексту (ответы полными предложениями)</u>:
1) Чьи слова цитируются в этой песне? 2) О каких двух категориях людей здесь идёт речь? 3) Чем отличаются умные от дураков? 4) Почему поэту давно пора получить орден? 5) Чем дураки и умные отличаются в своём отношении к одиночеству? 6) Нужен ли дуракам вожак? 7) Какую ошибку поэт совершал в детстве? 8) Почему природа коварно улыбается? 9) Как поэт объясняет свою ошибку? 10) Почему скоро умных повыловят всех до одного, и кто это сделает? 11) Может ли поэт себе представить, как будет

---

[1] Эта цитата — из записных книжек А.П.Чехова: "Умный любит учиться, а дурак — учить". Песня — из кинофильма «Из жизни начальника уголовного розыска».

без умных? 12) В чём недостатки наличия дураков и умных? 13) Что лучше дураков и умных? 14) Каково быть дураком, и как дурак относится к своей глупости? 15) В чём заключается "горе от ума"? 16) На что надеется поэт? 17) Кто эти умные и дураки?

Комментарии к тексту песни

•однажды (once, one day, [normally in reference to an event in the past])
•когда–нибудь (one / some day [in reference to the future])
•замеча́ть || заме́тить (to notice, to make an observation [comment])
замеча́ю, –ешь, –ют || заме́чу, заме́тишь, заме́тят
•у́мный/ая (smart, intelligent [when not modifying a noun: smart person])
•по глупости (out of one's stupidity [глупость: stupidity, silliness])
••глупый/ая (stupid, silly)
•главный/ая (main, head, chief [**SEE** "Солнышко сияет"])
•средний/яя (average [when not modifying a noun: the average, something in-between])
•дурак/ду́ра (fool, idiot)
•люби́ть || полюби́ть (to like/love) люблю́, лю́бишь, лю́бят

N.B. "Любить" tends to indicate **general attraction**, e.g., Я люблю оперу (I like/love opera [in general]). "Полюби́ть" means "to come to like/love" e.g., Я полюбил оперу год назад (I came to like/love opera a year ago). When the attraction is very strong, "любить" **can indicate specific attraction** in the "love" sense, e.g., Она любит Ефима / эту картину (She loves Iefim / this picture [crazy about this picture]). In this case "полюбить" means "to fall in love."

••dat. + нра́виться || понра́виться (to like)
нра́влюсь, нра́вишься, нра́вятся
"Нра́виться" tends to indicate **specific** (moderate) **attraction**, e.g., Мне нравится эта опера (I like this [specific] opera). "Понравиться" means to like something specific **at a given point in time**, e.g., Вчера мне понравилась опера в Большом театре (I liked the opera I saw last night at the Bolshoi).

N.B. "To like to do / doing something" is rendered by любить + inf., e.g., Дурак любит учить (The fool likes/loves to teach).

•учи́ться + subject of study [dat.] (to study/learn [normally with a teacher and/or in an institutional setting, e.g., school])
учу́сь, у́чишься, у́чатся
Я учу́сь физике в университете. (I study physics at university.)
Она у́чится в школе. (She goes to school [lit.: studies at school].)
••научи́ться + inf. imperf. (to learn [how] to... [to acquire a skill])
Зина научилась нырять. (Zina has learned [how] to dive.)
••учи́ть || научи́ть + acc. + dat./inf. (to teach)
учу́, у́чишь, у́чат
Профессор нас учит математике. (The professor is teaching us math.)
Лёня научил Петю нырять. (Lionia has taught Petia [how] to dive.)
Не учи меня! (Don't lecture me [lit.: don't teach me]!)
••изуча́ть || изучи́ть + acc. (to study, to research [in depth, often at a high level])
изуча́ю, –ешь, –ют || изучу́, изу́чишь, изу́чат
Учёный изучает механику полёта стрекозы.
The scientist is studying/working on the mechanics of the dragonfly's flight.

N.B. When the issue is not research but classroom study, the difference between **a)**Я учусь русскому языку and **b)**Я изучаю русский язык is that in **a** Russian is being studied less in depth than in **b**, but this nuance is not always present, and the two verbs are sometimes interchangeable.

••занима́ться + instr. (to study)

N.B. This verb is often used in reference to study that is not done in a classroom, e.g., homework, independent study etc., e.g., Миша занимается в библиотеке (Misha is studying at the library). This verb can also be the equivalent of "учи́ться + dat." in an institutional setting, e.g., Мы занимаемся физикой в институте (We study physics at the institute). Furthermore, this verb can be the equivalent of "изуча́ть || изучи́ть + acc." with respect to high-level research, e.g., Я занимаюсь магнетизмом (I am studying magnetism.)

•сколько/их/им/ими (how many/much)

N.B. When "сколько," acts as subject or direct object, it is followed by **a)**the genitive singular if it refers to **non-countable** entities (water, sand), e.g., Сколько здесь было воды? (How much water was there here?) and by **b)**the genitive plural if it refers to **countable inanimate** entities, e.g., Сколько стульев ты купил? (How many chairs did you buy?).
When "сколько" cannot play the role of subject or direct object, it is replaced by **a)** "какое количество + gen. singular" in reference to **non-countable** entities, e.g, Каким количеством воды вы пользуетесь по утрам? (How much water do you use in the morning?), or by **b)**the modifier "скольк_" in reference to **countable** entities, e.g., Со ско́лькими писателями вы знакомы? (How many authors are you acquainted with?).
Countable animate entities in the accusative case can be modifed either by "скольких" or by "сколько," e.g., Скольких / сколько дураков ты знаешь? (How many fools do you know?).

•свой (my, your, his, her, its, our, their [**SEE** "Бумажный солдат"])

•встреча́ть || встре́тить (to meet/encounter)
встреча́ю, –ешь, –ет || встре́чу, встре́тишь, встре́тят

•давно (for a long time, long ago [**SEE** "Шёл троллейбус по улице"])

•dat. + пора + inf. (it's time for someone to do something, one should be doing something [by now / then])

N.B. With "давно" this construction means something like "it's high time."
Вам давно пора научиться плавать.
(It's high time that you learned how to swim.)
Ей было пора учиться. (It was time for her to go to school.)
Мне пора [идти] домой. (It's time for me to go / I should be going home.)

•получа́ть || получи́ть (to receive)
получа́ю, –ешь, –ют || получу́, полу́чишь, полу́чат

•орден (decoration [military; получить орден = to be decorated])

•обожа́ть (to adore) обожа́ю, –ешь, –ют

•собира́ть[ся] || собра́ть[ся] (to gather [–ся: "to come / get together"])
собира́ю[сь], –ешь[ся], –ют[ся] || соберу́[сь], –ёшь[ся], –у́т[ся]
Мы собрали свои вещи и ушли. (We gathered our things and left.)
Мы собрались на террасе. (We gathered [got together] on the terrace.)

•впереди́ (ahead, in front [**SEE** "Шёл троллейбус по улице"])

•ве́рить || пове́рить (to believe [**SEE** "Солнышко сияет"])

•во всей [своей] красе (in all one's beauty)

•встава́ть || встать (to get / stand up, to get up out of bed, to get up in the

morning) встаю́, –ёшь, –ю́т || вста́ну, –ешь, –ут
•gen. + нет[у] (something isn't there [**SEE** "Песенка о голубом шарике"])
•лете́ть || улете́ть (to fly [**SEE** "Песенка о голубом шарике"])
•какой/какая (which [one], what a, what)
Какую я сделал ошибку**?** (What mistake have I made**?**)
Какую я сделал ошибку**!** (What a mistake I have made**!**)
Какой дом вам нужен? (Which / what house do you need?)
•вита́ть в облаках (to have illusions, to have one's head up in the clouds)
вита́ю, –ешь, –ют
•у + gen. possessor (someone has [**SEE** "Молитва (Франсуа Вийона)"])
•[кто/где/как/что/какой]–нибудь (some-[one/where/how/thing/kind of]; **SEE** "Шёл троллейбус по улице")
N.B. After negation the genitive "чего–нибудь/–то" is often used instead of the accusative.
N.B. In the song "нужно что–то среднее" is used for the purpose of rhythm, whereas "нужно что–нибудь среднее" would have been more idiomatic.
•ви́димо (apparently, must, one must have done something)
Вот его пальто — видимо он здесь.
(Here is his coat: he must be here [he is apparently here].)
•рассчи́тывать || рассчита́ть (to calculate [не: to miscalculate])
рассчи́тываю, –ешь, –ют || рассчита́ю, –ешь, –ют
•одиночество (being alone, loneliness, privacy, [в одиночестве: alone])
•гуля́ть || погуля́ть (to stroll/walk [**SEE** "Дежурный по апрелю"])
•verb of motion + instr. (to move in a certain manner)
Он ходит кругами. (He is walking in circles.)
•цени́ть || оцени́ть (to value) ценю́, це́нишь, це́нят
•[пре]выше всего (more than anything [пре–: for emphasis])
•так (thus, so, this way [такой→ such, so; **SEE** "Старый пиджак"])
•брать || взять + голыми руками (to take/catch [prey] with one's bare hands)
беру́, –ёшь, –у́т || возьму́, –ёшь, –у́т
•повы́ловить (to catch every single one [action affecting many objects/beings])
повы́ловлю, повы́ловишь, повы́ловят
•все до одного (every single one [**SEE** "Примета"])
•наступа́ть || наступи́ть (to begin [about a time period or state of being])
наступа́ет, –ют || насту́пит, –ят
•эпо́ха (age, epoch, time period [in history])
•не + inf. perf. (it is impossible to do something, something cannot be done)
Это не описать. (This cannot be described.)
•выду́мывать || вы́думать (to invent, to come up with, to make up, to fabricate)
выду́мываю, –ешь, –ют || вы́думаю, –ешь, –ют
•опи́сывать || описа́ть (to describe)
опи́сываю, –ешь, –ют || опишу́, опи́шешь, опи́шут
•с + instr. + adv. (it's... around someone, someone is...., to find someone...)
С ними так приятно.
(It's so pleasant to be around them [I find them / they are so pleasant].)
С ним очень хлопотно. (He is / I find him troublesome.)
•хло́потно (troublesome [adj.: хло́потный/ая])
•ну́жен/ну́жно (to need [**SEE** "Примета"])
•interrog. word + dat. + inf.
(how/where/when etc. can one / does one / is one supposed to do something)
Где взять лёд в пустыне? (Where does one get ice in the desert?)

С кем ему [было / будет] поговорить в одиночке?
(With whom is he [was he / will he be] supposed to talk in solitary confinement?)
Куда мне бежать? (Where am I supposed to / should I / can I run?)

•выгодно (advantageous[ly] / profitab[ly]; adj.: выгодный/ая)
•хотéться || захотéться (to feel like [**SEE** "Примета"])
•кончáться || кóнчиться + instr. (to end with)
кончáется, –ются || кóнчится, –атся
Их встреча кóнчилась дракой. (Their meeting ended with a fight.)
•ковáрный (devious, insidious, perfidious, crafty, sly)
•пророчество (prophecy [пророк: prophet])
•приходи́ть || прийти́ (to arrive)
прихожу́, прихóдишь, прихóдят || приду́, –ёшь, –у́т
N.B. With the preposition "к" this verb can mean "to arrive at" in such constructions as "to arrive at a conclusion" etc.

Переведите на русский язык, пользуясь песней и комментариями

1. "**I have no** more[1] bread: **it's time for me to** buy (some) bread..." Ring... "**Do you have** (any) bread?" "Yes." "**How much** bread **do you have**?" "Let me check... Oh, I've made a **mistake**: we **must have** sold everything. We often **miscalculate** and don't make enough." "A **smart** entrepreneur who **values** his customers always has enough merchandise." "But **we need** to sell what **we have**; if we keep too much, everything **will end in** bankruptcy, and that is not very **profitable**! **I don't feel like** losing my store. I am not a **fool**." "Well, then **you need something in-between**. It's very **simple**. **With how much** bread do you start (out) every day?" "Look, this is a **stupid** conversation. Are you **teaching** me (how) to sell bread? **I don't like** pushy people." "I don't **believe** my ears! ! **How many** customers have you lost **this way**? **One day** you **will notice** that your old customers **are not there** anymore. Good-bye!"
2. "You **will not believe** me, but **one day** I **met Chekhov,** whom[2] I **adored** (back) then. **I found him so interesting**, and he **liked** me." "**What a** story! You are **making this up**! You **love to make up** stories." "No, it's true! **Some day I will describe** this meeting to you. But (for) now **I don't have** (any) time. **It's time for me** to go."
3. **Out of** (my) **stupidity** I always **believe** every **idiot** that I **meet**. **Maybe** I myself am **stupid**, but I **like** people and trust them.
4. You **must have your head up in the clouds** because you never **notice** the **head** doctor and never **get up** when he **arrives**. Don't you **value** your position?[3] **It's high time that you received**[4] a premium for your good work, but you

---

[1]**SEE** "Примета."
[2]**SEE** "тот + кто/который" in "Я вновь повстречался с надеждой."
[3]**SEE** "Простите пехоте."
[4]Not past tense.

haven't **received** it. **Don't you feel like** moving **ahead**? Don't you **like** your job? You are making a **mistake** that a **smart** person would not make. I know you are not a **fool**, and you are not **stupid**. If you **learn** (how) **to calculate** your actions, you will **arrive at something average** between grovelling and defiance. Maybe a **smile** at the right moment is all that **you need**. If you don't listen to me, everything **will end in** your dismissal **one day**. In our cynical **age** we **need** to do what is **profitable** and not what **we feel like** (doing). **Maybe a time will come** when **we won't need** all this **calculation** and scheming.

5. Boris never **notices** that I **love** to be **in front**, and he goes **to the front** himself.

6. Some birds **miscalculate** and **fly** so close to the ship that the sailors **take** them **with** (their) **bare hands**. Some passengers think that if this continues, **soon** they **will** (have) **caught every single one**[1] in this area.

7. "If you **have been studying** Hebrew **for a long time** at university, **you should** know it **by now**. Why do you know it **so poorly**?" "I **study for a long time** every evening at home, but nothing helps." "At **what** university are you **studying** now?" "At Columbia University. My professor is a very famous linguist; he used to **work on** the stylistics of **prophecy** in the Old Testament. Now he is **studying** the etymology of biblical Hebrew." "**Apparently** his brilliance is not helping your Hebrew." "I **arrived at** the same[2] conclusion **a long time ago**."

8. "**How many fools believe smart people**?" "I don't know: **how many fools have I met in my life**?"

9. The swan was **flying in all its beauty in front of the flock**.

10. After the birth of his son, the happy[3] father strolled around[4] the park with a **stupid smile** on (his) face.

11. **I have valued privacy for a long time** (now) **more than anything**.

12. (It is) very **advantageous** to be the **chief**, but sometimes it (is) **troublesome**.

13. I **really do not feel like inventing** all kinds of **silly** sentences.

14. **Maybe someday** you will **describe your life** to me. I **like** biographies, and I am sure that I **will like** your autobiography especially.

15. Alik is a **smart** boy because he **values** his **childhood** years. **Childhood** is wonderful!

16. The **prophet had** a devious smile on (his) **lips**,[5] when he said that this **age** (would) **end**[6] **with** a war, and a new **age** (would) **begin**.

17. Where **does** (one) **get**[7] an **average fool**?

---

[1]Watch the gender of "one".
[2]**SEE** "Я вновь повстречался с надеждой."
[3]**SEE** "Бумажный солдат."
[4]**SEE** "verb of motion + по + dat." in "Шёл троллейбус по улице."
[5]Here the archaic word for "mouth" is appropriate.
[6]Future tense.
[7]Here use the "interrog. word + inf." construction: **SEE** above.

18. If a teacher **teaches his** students **poorly**, they **get together** and study (by) themselves.

19. For promotion in the army I **needed a decoration**, but **where was I supposed to get**[1] a **decoration** if all my superiors were **fools** and didn't **value** my courage and intelligence?

20. Even when **beating** was used in schools, when a good teacher **taught** good children, **he did not need** to use **beating** as punishment for **errors**.

21. **How many** planes were flying **in circles** at the air show?

22. Meteorologists **study** the structure of **clouds**. They **calculate** the distance between **clouds** and determine **how much** water each **cloud** releases.

23. "**What period** does this art historian **study**?" "He writes about the Renaissance." "**What an** interesting period! I **like** Raphael especially. **What a** painter! **How many** painters has the art historian written about?"

24. I am the **head** engineer here, and **I have** such a **troublesome** job because I am surrounded by **devious** scoundrels[2] and **fools**.

25. "On his nose the professor **has** a wart." "Tell me **something** more interesting."

26. "**How many** people did he phone?" "**It is impossible to** count them all!"

27. Every day Larissa **gets up** (in the morning) and **studies for a long time**.

---

[1]**SEE** previous note.
[2]**SEE** "До свидания, мальчики."

Song 23 A (Blanks)

Я _ _ _ _ _(adv.) _ _ _ _ _ _ _ _ _ _ _ _ _(v.)
с _ _ _ _ _ _ _ _ _(n.: instr.) —
_ _ _ _ _ _ _ _ _(adj.) _ _ _ _ _ _ _(n.).
Она _ _ _ _ _ _ _ _ _ _(v.) всё там же — (э)то я был далéче.[1]
Всё то же на ней из _ _ _ _ _ _ _(n.: gen.)
_ _ _ _ _ _ _ _ _ _ _(adj.) _ _ _ _ _ _(n.).
Всё так же _ _ _ _ _(adj.: short form) её _ _ _ _(n.),
_ _ _ _ _ _ _ _ _ _ _ _ _(participle) в _ _ _ _(n.).

Ты наша _ _ _ _ _ _(n.), мы твои
_ _ _ _ _ _ _ _ _ _ _(adj.) _ _ _ _ _ _(n.),
и _ _ _ _ _ _(adv.) _ _ _ _ _ _ _ _ _(v.: inf.), что _ _ _ _ _(n.)
_ _ _ _ _ _ _(adj.: short form).
Ты наша _ _ _ _ _ _(n.), мы твои
_ _ _ _ _ _ _ _ _ _ _(adj.) _ _ _ _ _ _(n.),
и _ _ _ _ _ _(adv.) _ _ _ _ _ _ _ _ _(v.: inf.), что _ _ _ _ _(n.)
_ _ _ _ _ _ _(adj.: short form).

А _ _ _ _ _(particle) ты нам _ _ _ _ _ _ _(v.)
_ _ _ _ _ _ _(n.) златые?[2]
Мы сами себе их _ _ _ _ _ _(v.), _ _ _ _(conj.) _ _ _ _ _ _ _(adj.).
Мы сами себе _ _ _ _ _ _ _ _ _(v.) и _ _ _ _ _(n.)
и _ _ _ _ _ _(n.).
И _ _ _ _(n.) тому, кто _ _ _ _ _ _ _ _(v.)
не _ _ _ _ _ _ _(adv.) нас.

Ты наша _ _ _ _ _ _(n.), мы твои
_ _ _ _ _ _ _ _ _ _ _(adj.) _ _ _ _ _(n.).
Нам _ _ _ _ _ _(v.) _ _ _ _ _ _ _(n.),
да _ _ _ _ _ _ _ _ _(v.) из _ _ _ _(n.: gen.).
Ты наша _ _ _ _ _ _(n.), мы твои
_ _ _ _ _ _ _ _ _ _ _(adj.) _ _ _ _ _(n.).
Нам _ _ _ _ _ _(v.) _ _ _ _ _ _ _(n.),
да _ _ _ _ _ _ _ _ _(v.) из _ _ _ _(n.: gen.).

(continued)

[1] Archaic form of “далеко.”
[2] Archaic/poetic form of “золотые.”

Когда бы[1] _ _ _ _ _ _(n.) и _ _ _ _ _ _ _(n.: acc.)
_ _ _ _ _ _ _(v.: inf.) _ _ _ _ _ _ _(adv.)!
Какая бы, _ _ _ _ _ _(adv.) _ _ _ _ _ _ _ _(v.: inf.),
_ _ _ _ _ _ _ _(v.) _ _ _ _ _ _ _(n.)!
Какие бы нас _ _ _ _ _ _ _ _(v.) _ _ _ _ _ _ _ _ _(adj.) _ _ _ _(n.)!
И _ _ _ _ _ _(particle) _ _ _ _ _ _ _ _ _ _(adj.) _ _ _ _(n.)
_ _ _ _ _ _ _(v.) б(ы) с чела[2]...

Ты наша _ _ _ _ _ _(n.), что ж(е) так _ _ _ _ _(adv.)
мы были в _ _ _ _ _ _ _(n.: prep.)?
Нас _ _ _ _ _ _(n.) _ _ _ _ _ _ _(v.),
да _ _ _ _ _ _ _ _(n.) _ _ _ _ _(v.).
Ты наша _ _ _ _ _ _(n.), что ж(е) так _ _ _ _ _(adv.)
мы были в _ _ _ _ _ _ _(n.: prep.)?
Нас _ _ _ _ _ _(n.) _ _ _ _ _ _ _(v.),
да _ _ _ _ _ _ _ _(n.) _ _ _ _ _(v.).

---

[1]Когда бы = если бы.
[2]Archaic/poetic form of "лоб," i.e., "brow."

Song 23 B (Partial Blanks)

Я в_ _ _ь(adv.) повс_ _ _ _ _ _ _ _(v.)
с н_ _ _ _ _ _ _(n.: instr.) —
при_ _ _ _ _(adj.) вст_ _ _ _(n.).[1]
Она прож_ _ _ _ _(v.) всё там же — (э)то я был далéче.[2]
Всё то же на ней из поп_ _ _ _(n.: gen.)
сч_ _т_ _ _ _ _(adj.) пл_ _ _ _(n.).
Всё так же г_ _ _щ(adj.: short form) её в_ _ _(n.),
устр_ _ _ _ _ _ _ _(participle) в в_ _ _(n.).

Ты наша _ _ _ _ _ _(n.), мы твои
мо_ _ _ _ _ _ _ _(adj.) б_ _ _ь_(n.),
и т_ _ _ _ _(adv.) по_ _ _ _ _ _(v.: inf.), что _ _ _нь(n.)
ко_ _ _ _ _(adj.: short form).
Ты наша _ _ _ _ _ _(n.), мы твои
молч_ _ _ _ _ _(adj.) бр_ _ь_(n.),
и тр_ _ _ _(adv.) пов_ _ _ _ _(v.: inf.), что _ _знь(n.)
кор_ _ _ _(adj.: short form).

А р_ _ _ _(particle) ты нам об_ _ _ _ _(v.)
чер_ _ _ _(n.) златые? [3]
Мы сами себе их р_ _ _ _ _(v.), п_ _ _(conj.) мо_ _ _ _ _(adj.).
Мы сами себе со_ _ _ _ _ _(v.) и п_ _ _ _(n.)
и с_ _ь_ _(n.).
И г_ _ _(n.) тому, кто од_ _ _ _ _(v.)
не вов_ _ _ _(adv.) нас.

Ты наша _ _ _ _ _ _(n.), мы твои
то_ _ _ _ _ _ _ _(adj.) _ _ _ь_(n.).
Нам вы_ _ _ _(v.) сч_ _ _ _ _(n.),
да ск_ _ _ _ _ _(v.) из г_ _ _(n.: gen.).
Ты наша с_ _ _ _ _(n.), мы твои
тор_ _ _ _ _ _ _(adj.) с_ _ь_(n.).
Нам вып_ _ _(v.) сч_ _т_ _(n.),
да скр_ _ _ _ _(v.) из гл_ _(n.: gen.).

(continued)

---

[1]This noun has the same root as the preceding verb.
[2]Archaic form of “далеко.”
[3]Archaic/poetic form of “золотые.”

Когда бы[1] л_ _ _ _ь(n.) и на_ _ _ _ _(n.: acc.)
св_ _ _ _ _(v.: inf.) вое_ _ _ _(adv.)!
Какая бы, тр_ _ _ _(adv.) пов_ _ _ _ _(v.: inf.),
воз_ _ _ _ _(v.) кар_ _ _ _(n.)!
Какие бы нас ми_ _ _ _ _ _(v.) нап_ _ _ _ _ _(adj.) _ _ _ _(n.)!
И т_ _ь_ _(particle) прек_ _ _ _ _ _(adj.) м_ _ _(n.)
гл_ _ _ _ _(v.) б(ы) с чела[2]...

Ты наша се_ _ _ _(n.), что ж(е) так д_ _ _ _(adv.)
мы были в ра_ _ _ _ _(n.: prep.)?
Нас ю_ _ _ _ _(n.) св_ _ _ _ _(v.),
да ст_ _ _ _ _ _(n.) с_ _ _ _(v.).
Ты наша сес_ _ _(n.), что ж(е) так до_ _ _(adv.)
мы были в разл_ _ _(n.: prep.)?
Нас юн_ _ _ _(n.) сво_ _ _ _(v.),
да[3] ста_ _ _ _ _(n.) св_ _ _(v.).[4]

---

[1]Когда бы = если бы.
[2]Archaic/poetic form of "лоб," i.e., "brow."
[3]Here "да" = "и."
[4]This is the perfective form of the preceding verb.

Song 23. Я вновь повстречался с надеждой

Я вновь повстречался с надеждой — приятная встреча.
Она проживает всё там же — (э)то я был далече.
Всё то же на ней из поплина счастливое платье.
Всё так же горящ её взор, устремлённый в века.

Ты наша сестра, мы твои молчаливые[1] братья,
и трудно поверить, что жизнь коротка.
Ты наша сестра, мы твои молчаливые братья,
и трудно поверить, что жизнь коротка.

А разве ты нам обещала чертоги златые?
Мы сами себе их рисуем, пока молодые.
Мы сами себе сочиняем и песни и судьбы.
И горе тому, кто одёрнет не вовремя нас.

Ты наша сестра, мы твои торопливые судьи.
Нам выпало счастье, да скрылось из глаз.
Ты наша сестра, мы твои торопливые судьи.
Нам выпало счастье, да скрылось из глаз.

Когда бы любовь и надежду[2] связать воедино!
Какая бы, трудно поверить, возникла картина!
Какие бы нас миновали напрасные му́ки!
И только прекрасные му́ки глядели б(ы) с чела...

Ты наша сестра, что ж(е) так долго мы были в разлуке?
Нас юность сводила, да старость свела.
Ты наша сестра, что ж(е) так долго мы были в разлуке?
Нас юность сводила, да старость свела.

Вопросы по тексту (ответы полными предложениями):
1) С кем долго не виделся поэт? 2) Изменился ли адрес надежды? 3) Какая мысль выражается фразой "(э)то я был далече"? 4) Как одета надежда? 5) Почему взор надежды устремлён в века? 6) С кем поэт сравнивает себя и себе подобных? 7) Как люди себя обманывают в молодости? 8) Как они реагируют, когда им напоминают о действительности? 9) Было ли счастье в жизни поэта? 10) О чём мечтает поэт? 11) К чему привело бы объединение любви и надежды? 12) О каких напрасных му́ках говорит поэт и почему они миновали бы людей? 13) О

[1] "Удивлённые" in the Frumkin edition.
[2] "Любовь" and "Надежда" are female Russian names, i.e., this is a pun.

каких счастливых му́ках он говорит? 14) Что обозначает последняя строка? 15) С каким ощущением связана эта песня?

Комментарии к тексту песни

•встреча́ться || повстреча́ться + с + instr. (to run into, encounter)
встреча́юсь, –ешься, –ются
•проживать (to reside) прожива́ю, –ешь, –ют
•такой + же... какой [и] / как [и] (the same [kind] [as]; as... as)
Наш кот — такой же большой, как ваш. (Our cat is as big as yours.)
Наш пёс — такой же, как ваш: лентяй.
(Our dog is the same as yours: a loafer.)
N.B. If the second part of this construction is followed by a verb, "какой" is used, e.g., У нас такой же попугай, какого я видел у соседей (We have the same kind [breed] of parrot as the one that I saw at our neighbors' place). If no verb is involved, then "как" is used, e.g. У нас такой же попугай, как у соседей (We have the same kind of parrot as the one at our neighbor's place).
N.B. Clearly distinguish between "такой же" and "тот же" (below).
•тот + же [са́мый]... что [и] (the same [**one**] [as])
"Он живёт всё в той же [самой] хижине?" "Да, в той же".
("Does he still live in the same cabin [самой: for emphasis]?" "Yes, in the same one.")
Он пользуется тем же словарём, что и я.
(He uses the same dictionary as I do.)
•так + же... как [и] ([in] the same way [as], in the same manner [as], as... as)
Я так же пишу, как [и] раньше. (I write the same way as before).
Я так же вспыльчив, как Полина. (I am as ill-tempered as Paulina.)
N.B. For the use of "такой" and "так" **SEE** "Старый пиджак."
•там + же + где [и] (in the same place [as])
Я жила там же, где [и] он. (I lived in the same place as he [did].)
••туда + же + куда [и] (to the same place [as])
Я поехал туда же, куда [и] вы. (I went to the same place as you [did].)
••тогда + же + когда [и] (at the same time [as])
Я пела тогда же, когда [и] она. (I sang at the same time as she did.)
•тот + кто/который (the [person] who / that; the one who / that)
N.B. If "тот/та/те" refers to **a)** a specific known person or **b)** an inanimate object, "который" is used, e.g., Та, которая здесь жила, уехала из страны (She / the one who used to live here has left the country) or Режь тем, который поострее (Cut with the one that is sharper).
If a **non-specific** person is involved, "кто" is used, e.g., Та, кто за него выйдет замуж, будет счастлива (She / the one who will marry him is sure to be happy).
If a noun is used instead of "тот/та/те" in the first part of this construction, "который" is used in the second, e.g., Художник, который здесь жил, переехал (The artist who used to live here has moved).
•счастливый (happy, lucky; рад: glad [**SEE** "Бумажный солдат"])
•так (thus, so, this way [такой→ such, so; **SEE** "Старый пиджак"])
•на + prep. + clothing/footwear (to wear [**SEE** "Старый пиджак"])
•из + name of material (made of (**SEE** "Я пишу исторический роман"])

•горящ (burning [full-form participle: горящий/ая; **SEE** "горе́ть || сгоре́ть" in "Чёрный кот"])

•устремлённый (directed)

••устремля́ть || устреми́ть + на/в (to direct)

устремля́ю, –ешь, –ют || устремлю́, устреми́шь, устремя́т

Генерал устремил войска на врага.

(The general directed / sent his troops against the enemy.)

•век (century, life-time, age [time period])

•разве (**SEE** "Он, наконец, явился в дом")

•обеща́ть || пообеща́ть (to promise) обеща́ю, –ешь, –ют

•ве́рить || пове́рить (**SEE** "Солнышко сияет")

•молодой (young [**SEE** "Песенка о Моцарте"])

•сам/а́/са́ми + себя/себе/собой (something done by someone to him/herself [**SEE** "Я пишу исторический роман"])

•рисова́ть || нарисова́ть (to draw, paint [with words or colors])

рису́ю, –ешь, –ют

•сочиня́ть || сочини́ть (to make up / compose [**SEE** "Ещё раз о дураках"])

•го́ре + dat. (someone will be sorry)

Горе тебе если ты не приготовишь уроки!

(You'll be sorry if you don't do your homework!)

•одёргивать || одёрнуть (to set straight [to stop someone's bad behavior])

одёргиваю, –ешь, –ют || одёрну, –ешь, –ут

•во́время (in / on time, at the right moment [не во́время: at the wrong time])

•тороплив́ый (hasty, hurried)

•судья́ (judge [this is a 2nd declension masculine noun]

•dat. + выпада́ть || вы́пасть + счастье + inf. (to have [the] good fortune / luck [to])

выпада́ет || вы́падет

Мне выпало счастье познакомиться с Хрущёвым.

(I had the good fortune to meet Khrushchev.)

•скрыва́ться || скры́ться (to vanish, flee, run away, hide)

скрыва́юсь, –ешься, –ются || скро́юсь, –ешься, –ются

•свя́зывать || связа́ть (to tie up / together; to connect / link)

свя́зываю, –ешь, –ют || свяжу́, свя́жешь, свя́жут

•возника́ть || возни́кнуть (to appear)

возника́ю, –ешь, –ют || возни́кну, –ешь, –ут (возни́к/возни́кла)

•му́ка (suffering, anguish [often in the plural; cf. мука́: flour])

•миновать (to go by / past, to pass, to be over, to spare)

N.B. Same form for imperf. and perf.: мину́ю, –ешь, –ют.

Меня миновала эта му́ка. (I was spared this suffering [lit.: it spared me].)

Поезд миновал деревню (The train went by / past the village.)

Зима миновала. (The winter was over [lit.: went by].)

•напра́сный (pointless, [in] vain)

•гляде́ть || взгляну́ть (to look at [**SEE** "Простите пехоте"])

•когда бы + inf. (if only one could)

Когда бы любовь и надежду связать воедино!

(If only one could bind love and hope into one!)

•past tense form + бы (would, would have [**SEE** "Бумажный солдат"])

Какая бы возникла картина! (What a sight it would be!)

••если бы + past tense form + [то] + past tense form + бы (if... then)

Если бы ты был художником, [то] жил бы ты впроголодь.

(If you were a painter, you'd live from hand to mouth.)

N.B. This construction has to do with contrary-to-fact scenarios.

•картина (picture [not a photograph], painting, sight, view)
•какой/какая (which [one], what a, what [**SEE** "Ещё раз о дураках"])
•долго (for a long time [**SEE** "Шёл троллейбус по улице")
•быть в разлуке (to be apart [**SEE** "О Володе Высоцком"])
•сводить || свести (to bring together)
свожу́, сво́дишь, сво́дят || сведу́, –ёшь, –у́т

Переведите на русский язык, пользуясь песней и комментариями

1. **You have the good fortune to** work on the most sensational criminal case of the year. You are a **young** lawyer, and **youth** should respect **old age**. Therefore, listen to my advice. **Look** at the **silent** little man—at **the one who** is sitting (over) there. You will never **believe** (it), but he is a very strict **judge** in court. This **judge** always **sets straight** excessively **hasty** or aggressive lawyers. And his wrath will not **spare** you, if you speak **at the wrong time**. That might affect the outcome of the trial. Remember: **silence** is **gold**. **You'll be sorry** if you ignore this warning.

2. "Why is Piotr's brother so **silent** today?" "He is **composing** a new song in (his) head."

3. The leader's **burning gaze** is **directed** into the **happy** future. His **brow** is wrinkled. He is **looking** at the **fate** of his people. **What a beautiful** statue!

4. **Centuries passed** and the emperor's **palace** crumbled. It was not a **pleasant picture**. And our **short life** begins and ends[1] **in the same manner**. Death doesn't **spare** anyone.[2]

5. "You say that her **brother** and **sister** have been **residing** in this building **for a long time** (now), but I don't **believe** that they ever **resided** here." "Are we talking about **the same brother** and **sister**?"

6. **He who** thinks that **youth** is eternal and forgets that **life** is **short** and **old age** is just around the corner **will be sorry**![3]

7. "(It) is **difficult** to **believe** that your **sister was wearing** the **same beautiful poplin dress** when I **ran into** her after[4] **we had been apart for such a long time**. Does she always **wear** this **dress**?" "Oh no, it's not **the same dress**; it's **the same kind** (of) **dress as the one that she wore a long time ago**.

8. If **you have the good fortune** to find **love again**, guard it even if it brings you **suffering**. I give **the same kind** (of) advice to others.

---

[1]**SEE** "Часовые любви."
[2]**SEE** "Шёл троллейбус по улице."
[3]Word order: "will be sorry" shold be in first place, i.e., just before "he who."
[4]Before / after + verb = перед тем / после того + как + verb.

9. When Misha talked about the future, he always **painted** such a **happy picture** that he did not even **believe himself**.

10. **Love** (had) **brought** these **young** people (together), but there was no **happiness** in their **brief** marriage. They got married[1] **at the same time as** my wife and I (did).

11. "Does anyone **really link love** with **happiness** in our enlightened **age**?" "Very few people, and **those who** do are very naive."

12. I **promise** you that these fighter jets are so fast that they will **appear** and **vanish** almost simultaneously before the **eyes** of the **surprised** spectators.

13. When the storm **was over**, I went outside and **ran into Liubov** Ivanovna Manilova. It was a very **pleasant encounter**. She was going **to the same place as I** (was).

14. The **judge**, **who was wearing** a robe **of** silk and velvet, came to court **on time**.

15. I **passed** a park and saw a **burning** building in **which** someone was screaming: "(We are) **burning**!" I am sure that **the** (person) **who set fire** to this building **will be sorry**. He will not **hide** from justice!

16. When she teaches,[2] **Nadezhda** Iakovlevna Kovaliova always **directs** all her attention **to** her students, and her **sister** teaches **the same way**.

17. When my **young brother** was alone last night, he was afraid of the dark.[3] Therefore, he told stories **to himself, drew pictures** and even sang songs. Otherwise, he **would have** cried all night.

18. Liova **made up** the story about the lottery money in order to[4] give his **sister** (some) **hope**, but she is **as** sad **as** she was before the good news.

19. All my **brothers** and **sisters hope** that our sick grandfather's **suffering** will end[5] tomorrow, but I think that their **hope is in vain** and tomorrow his **suffering** will be **as** terrible **as** (it is) today.

20. I am **so happy** that (they) will deliver my **beautiful** new **dress** and **the gold** earrings **at the same time as** the new shoes.

21. **What a picture**! Who **painted** this **picture**? It's the masterpiece of the **century**! I **would** buy it **if** I had the money.

22. "**Which judge** sentenced your **brother** to death?" "**The one who resides in the same** building as I (do)." "Oh, **what a pleasant** coincidence!"

23. His **suffering** stopped **at the same time as when** mine began.

24. The **view** was breathtaking! **If** I had a camera, **I would have** taken a **picture**.

---

[1]**SEE** "Старый король."
[2]**SEE** "Ещё раз о дураках."
[3]**SEE** "Ваше величество, женщина."
[4]**SEE** "Примета."
[5]**SEE** "Часовые любви."